CRIMES OF THE POWERFUL AND THE CONTEMPORARY CONDITION

The Democratic Republic of Capitalism

Adam Lynes, James Treadwell
and Kyla Bavin

First published in Great Britain in 2024 by

Bristol University Press
University of Bristol
1–9 Old Park Hill
Bristol
BS2 8BB
UK
t: +44 (0)117 374 6645
e: bup-info@bristol.ac.uk

Details of international sales and distribution partners are available at bristoluniversitypress.co.uk

© Bristol University Press 2024

British Library Cataloguing in Publication Data
A catalogue record for this book is available from the British Library

ISBN 978-1-5292-2828-1 hardcover
ISBN 978-1-5292-2829-8 paperback
ISBN 978-1-5292-2830-4 ePub
ISBN 978-1-5292-2831-1 ePdf

The right of Adam Lynes, James Treadwell and Kyla Bavin to be identified as authors of this work
has been asserted by them in accordance with the Copyright, Designs and Patents Act 1988.

All rights reserved: no part of this publication may be reproduced, stored in a retrieval system or
transmitted in any form or by any means, electronic, mechanical, photocopying, recording or
otherwise, without the prior permission of Bristol University Press.

Every reasonable effort has been made to obtain permission to reproduce copyrighted material.
If, however, anyone knows of an oversight, please contact the publisher.

The statements and opinions contained within this publication are solely those of the authors and
not of the University of Bristol or Bristol University Press. The University of Bristol and Bristol
University Press disclaim responsibility for any injury to persons or property
resulting from any material published in this publication.

Bristol University Press works to counter discrimination on grounds of gender, race, disability, age
and sexuality.

Cover design: Nicky Borowiec
Front cover image: alamy/Danny Spencer

Contents

About the Authors		iv
Prologue		v
1	The Philosophy of Power: A Critical Overview	1
2	Sleepwalk Through the Fires: Harm, Violence and Dangerous Subjectivities	30
3	The Era of Corporate Giants	53
4	Follow the Money: The Global Finance Industry	76
5	The Price of the Gun: The Arms Industry	97
6	Making a (Corporate) Killing	114
7	The Remote Control Over the Masses: The Media	136
8	Knowledge, Education and Power	162
Epilogue		183
References		186
Index		230

About the Authors

Adam Lynes is Associate Professor in Criminology at Birmingham City University, where he has taught since 2012, covering topics from criminological theory to organised and violent crime. He has published research focusing on violent crimes, from serial murder to family annihilation, and recently was a co-author on a new edited collection on dark tourism, published with Policy Press.

James Treadwell is Professor of Criminology at Staffordshire University and has also worked at the University of Birmingham and the University of Leicester. Previously, he worked for the crime reduction charity NACRO and as a probation officer in the West Midlands. He undertakes ethnographic and qualitative research for crime and criminal justice-related projects, including studies of the English Defence League and the August 2011 England riots.

Kyla Bavin has been Lecturer of Criminology at Birmingham City University since April 2022 and has worked as a visiting lecturer at a variety of institutions, such as Staffordshire University. She is currently in the final year of her doctoral studies that focus on the harms of social media.

Prologue

The song remains the same

At the time that we started putting pen to paper, the world had gone through a series of hardships. It could seem the horsemen are upon us. We endured COVID-19, though for many in the developed world, the impacts were far less than first feared, with the 6,953,743 deaths suggested by the World Health Organization at the time of writing being felt more by the poor and vulnerable. War returned to the edges of Eastern Europe (in Ukraine) with Russia's invasion, while ongoing conflicts in Africa, Syria and Yemen gained less attention. The 2008 financial crisis in Europe and the West gave way to inflation and a cost of living crisis. Death has stalked them all. Yet stories such as the deaths of five billionaires in the cold depths of the Atlantic Ocean as they went to view the wreckage of the Titanic often receive vastly more attention in Western media, far more than the 60,000 people who have died premature deaths in the European heatwave in 2023, with more than 400,000 people globally from extreme heat in just the last decade, according to the International Federation of Red Cross and Red Crescent Societies World Disasters Report (2020).

With the rising threat of climate change, we may be witnessing the death of optimism. In the UK, optimistic people can keep a roof over their heads, with Bank of England interest rate rises brought about to attempt to halt inflation and rising costs of goods, which are creating frustrations. Yet the last decade has been one of much political frustration in the West. Political leaders like Donald Trump and Boris Johnson were seen by many to embody vapid self-interest and all the worst traits of power, and certainly, both faced allegations of criminal misuse of power that none before them had. Indeed, the West has witnessed increasing political polarisation between those who identify politically as 'right' and 'left', although the validity of such descriptors becomes less clear (Winlow et al, 2017; Winlow and Hall, 2022). Globally, there is a sinking of optimism that we can undo the ecological genocide that consumer culture has inflicted on future generations. In the summer of 2023, *The Guardian* newspaper reported that the 'super' rich were warned to expect pitchforks and torches. The summer of discontent saw strike action across the UK, riots in France and reports of attempted coups in Russia.

Like the snake in the talons of the eagle, the Western precariat (Standing, 2011) may have started to stir from slumber. However, unrest and revolt are often short-lived. However, the situation remains the same. The now precariat (Standing, 2011) that exists both within nation states and globally still exists within an oppressive capitalist society created by the rich for the rich. While some may complain about the authoritarian and oppressive neoliberal state and demand an end to national borders, the same neoliberal states have been wholly lax in controlling the super elite and super wealthy, who already exist in a world without physical borders, buying citizenship where and as they select.

While the world looks on at the injustices of the free-market economy, the ravages of unjust wars and global inequality, the few still control the destinies of the many. Throughout history, there has been resistance to this 'parasitic' free-market ideology, yet it remains dominant. However, whether or not the United States (US) and its allies hold hegemonic power remains to be seen. Russia and China have deepened economic ties. In the West, acts of civil unrest have often led merely to the tightening grip of neoliberal forces. Rather than providing any real opposition, each riot, failed revolution and placard-waving march through major cities has given the often unseen and unnamed elites more impetus to remove even more civil liberties and rights under the guise of keeping us safe or maintaining the market. Each tenet of society reinforces the grip of the powerful elite over its global populace. Like a capitalist unholy alliance of education, politics, law and media, each facet forms force-related bonds around us like shackles consisting of debt, fear and good intentions. They set the narratives that we live by and fight for. As we struggle to free ourselves like a Chinese finger trap, our chains become stronger and more reinforced. The manipulation of nationalised resistance has helped to fully galvanise corporate dominance through the marketisation of struggle and the privatisation of egalitarian ideologies. Levi Jeans feature rioters in their adverts, while Shell and other energy giants indulge in greenwashing agendas, despite being some of the worst polluters, hurtling us further and further towards environmental devastation. There is no cause that is not a way to market products, though in much of the wider world, such corporate 'pride' is not exhibited in authoritarian and repressive places where such sentiments might be bad for business. As Hopgood has argued, human rights are the product of a particular worldview, geography, religiosity and time period, and as a global brand, may be in their twilight period (Hopgood, 2013), even if consumer capitalism is far from over. Globally, the precariat is exploited by corporations as they sell us a slice of social justice with our latest must-haves. In the game of global and neoliberal economics, the dice are stacked in favour of the corporate elite and against the entire rest of the precariat population, which have far more in common than the global privileged elite. Alternatives and futures have already been stolen by the de-regulated finance industry and unfettered capitalism that has rewarded a tiny number of people with more money than they could ever make by their own efforts, and vastly more money than they could ever spend. We have clearly arrived at an obscene inequity where the few can accumulate more wealth in 10 seconds than most readers will make in a year. This is not even factoring in that globally, one billion people still live on less than a dollar a day. Each generation is witnessing the corporate boot pressing more firmly down on the unsustainable gas as we hurtle toward catastrophe. Meanwhile, a mere 2,640 billionaires worldwide remain fixated on minimising taxes, as the pursuit of high growth extends its reach globally and limits the Western agenda, disregarding the enduring consequences.

When British Prime Minister Margret Thatcher said in the 1980s that there's no such thing as society, she may well have been right. This notion and its legacy persist. In the wasteland of neoliberal politics, landlords and the gig economy have generations of the precariat (Standing, 2011) failing to thrive yet grateful for the chance to be exploited and passively toiling and judging anyone as a Marxist stooge who attempts to stand up in the face of billionaire-inflicted adversity. The prevailing political narrative is 'if we tax them, we lose them'. Fearful of the fiscal hole that their tax avoidance creates, politicians hold financial elites in awe and reverence. In the UK, women the likes of Denise Coates (CBE) of gambling company Bet365 (352 on Forbes' rich list of billionaires) or Baroness Michelle Moane (who doesn't even make the list of billionaires being worth only a mere estimated £20 million) are treated like royalty for providing the patronage of employment for the masses in their business empires. Conversely, women facing despair, grappling with gambling addictions or resorting to shoplifting to sustain drug habits find themselves and their children stigmatised as societal blemishes, often subjected to imprisonment. Billions are given over to corporations and their shareholders to deliver good and vital services, while, in reality, this is nothing more than an elaborate heist. From ineffective personal protective equipment to track and trace contracts, the COVID-19 pandemic held a spotlight on the blatant chumocracy that has been a driving force of 40 years of asset stripping in the United Kingdom (UK) and hundreds of years of colonial plunder. We might now recognise the damage and advantages that historical asset stripping did to the rest of the world in past times, but we are often blind to its continuation as a contemporary practice.

It persists.

Through an intricate game of smoke and mirrors, the richest and the 1 per cent of financial elites at the top of the social strata hide their wealth and presence. Many people could name but a fraction of the 2,640 billionaires in the world today. They might get Elon Musk, Jeff Bezos, Warren Buffet, Bill Gates or Michael Bloomberg, but then struggle.

Instead, we point our fingers in any direction but theirs. Their crimes are diminished or vindicated via proxy. Tyranny is the preserve of the least powerful, yet it is they who are often held to account for the masters' crimes. An ideological Cold War rages across the globe, with the only victors being the nameless elites who can hide away on their yachts and underground bunkers. While the poorest struggle to survive, multi-billionaires can take advantage of a panoply of tax deductions in order to offset their reported or suggested income and employ armies of well-educated and status people to aid them in such an end. They frequently pay no tax on any income in any place, while the poorest and those at the bottom of the social strata lose most to taxes.

This book is an attempt to reconsider what we mean by power and, associated with that, how we consider crime. Once we realise the most nefarious crime of the powerful is how they cling to absolute power with impunity, how power obfuscates the worst harms and creates and stratifies this and all other 'crimes', we can reconsider issues of morality, ethics, regulation and justice. Through monopolies and cartels that transcend local governance, the powerful can subjugate entire states, rendering the democratic process to a set of erroneous techniques that ensure power to governments that are sympathetic to the financial oligarchy under the guise of popular consent.

If the financial elites truly possess a panoramic power, power that sweeps across the whole vista of contemporary lived life, then we may need to reconsider and re-conceptualise how we consider crime, and what may constitute 'crimes of the powerful' – a term that has only existed in criminology since it was coined by Frank Pearce in 1976. In this book, we seek to reconsider the 'crimes of the powerful', shifting a focus from the past to the contemporary and away from the usual to the 'unusual subjects'. We will focus on a two-tiered Western-dominated education system that ensures the 'right sort' enters the global establishment, while the rest of the precariat stays firmly on the periphery. We will also shine a spotlight on the mainstream media, which guarantees that all are given the right knowledge and know their place, and the currently Western-dominated financial institutions that allow the billionaire class liberty few can imagine. Attention will also be given to the arms industry and state-corporate nexus that allows a tiny minority great liberty, a liberty which they not infrequently misuse. Drafting this book during a period marked by Donald Trump's potential indictment in the US, amid swirling allegations regarding Biden and his son's behaviour and corruption and, simultaneously, the International Criminal Court issuing arrest warrants for Vladimir Putin and scandals like the demise of Jeffrey Epstein coming to light, it appeared sensible to reassess the implications of the powerful committing crimes. After all, if we really wish to consider who the truly powerful are, could not 'criminal' perhaps feature alongside the descriptors of business magnate, investor and philanthropist that the elite tend to like to cultivate? Perhaps too much academic criminology, and academia generally, has been the unwitting tool of the elites, who, through academic convention, continue to gatekeep knowledge as a privilege of the power elites by using language that acts as an impenetrable wall around the truth it attempts to convey.

To write this book, we have drawn on extensive notes and reading, research and scholarship that has spanned the teaching of numerous modules at several universities. We have also brought to bear our own unique biographies and the access that we have as criminologists who have taught cohorts of students who are now practitioners in all manner of associated industries. We have drawn on our extensive contact in criminal justice circles and agencies, our alertness to cases and examples not always at the fore in such discussions. However, while we have the benefit of such engaged and applied academia, the text presented here is predominantly based on documentary and theoretical engagement rather than original empirical engagement in the field under discussion. That is not to say we have not had the benefit of having access to some people very much in the know who have been able to aid us in formulating our arguments here. Over the course of this book, we will seek to provide some new considerations of the contours of the contemporary practices of capitalism and political, state and corporate wrongdoing that are often seemingly inexorably meshed together, and consider how the current 'elite' manage to 'keep getting away with it' not simply as a means to begin to consider the functionalism of crime as a means of holding offenders to account, but as a conceptual vehicle to understand not only 'who done it' but also how we got into this mess we are currently in, and how we might get out of it.

1

The Philosophy of Power:
A Critical Overview

This book is about the crimes of the powerful. It is, therefore, about power, harm and crime. It is intended to provide a broad philosophical examination of these interrelated concepts of interest to social scientists, including criminologists like us. Social scientists should care about power, and we would argue that we should overtly study it far more than they currently do. That may be a controversial point at which to start, for we suspect that many in academia would baulk at the suggestion that they do not consider power. Many would claim that they are making powerful and practical contributions to improving cities, regions or countries – improving economic opportunity, driving meaningful changes and improving the economic growth, services and quality of life for people and businesses in places across the globe in both more observable and obvious and complex ways. While various disciplines differ in their focus and methods, the centrality of power is core. Power creates an asymmetrical experience of lived life for everyone, albeit very differently and experienced very differently by different individuals and groups of individuals. However, despite this, it is important to consider that power is often both the core and the antithesis of the thinking in contemporary social science.

If you stop and think about it, power is an all-pervading feature of our social reality. Power happens, for example, if you think about it and visualise it when a parent is getting a child to tidy up her room or when a professor in a university is encouraging their students to read the works of a core thinker or a core text on their syllabus. Yet these are instances of power and maybe enthused with all manner of additional factors related to power and how it is exercised. Think again about the parent and child, and the professor just mentioned. Do they have the power? What do they look like?

Now, be honest, who envisaged the parent trying to task the child as residing in a basic home as a father? How many pictured the setting as being one that is familiar to them, mentally selecting a city they know well and a setting that is familiar? What of the professor? Was it a white male? What if she is a young black associate lecturer on a temporary contract whose student group includes both students who regard themselves as gender nonbinary and trans allies? What if the text is by a female author and criticises gender-affirming psychiatric support and sex reassignment surgery? What other issues or factors may be at play?

In these examples, power is exercised by the individual rather than a group over some other person (or persons). However, exercising power is often more complex than being something that one person exercises directly over another with no wider consequences. The examples also suggest the deliberate exercise of power, but can there be a situation in which a person exercises power over another person without necessarily intending to do so? In other words, can we exercise power over others without knowing it ourselves that we are doing this? Is there a subconscious element to power? Is power something we can see and affect? Do people have equal power, or is there an array of factors that impact how an individual has power or lacks it?

The literature surrounding power is vast. Power is often theorised within political contexts and focused on power as a form of domination. However, there is a need to grasp the impact of power within different settings, particularly in relation to the power granted to different social roles and positions.

One significant condition that distinguishes early and late modernity or postmodernity is the transformed nature of how power manifests itself. In the current epoch, often described now as the 'late modern' era, power is not so much regarded as merely the visible, obvious or overtly coercive forms of domination or suppression that are at play in social interactions, but rather as found in the normalised structures and discourses of exclusion. Power, in this sense, is located in the discourses and processes that are often taken for granted and more subtly reproduced. When power is seen merely as a form of domination (assuming that there is a binary divide and there are the dominators and dominated parties), strategies to resist its impact seem more tangible and observable. The question arises: When power structures become less apparent, how can we identify them? How can we resist such elusive forms of power? Furthermore, what are the circumstances and potential for change within these normalised exclusionary systems, considering that we are all, to some extent, involved in perpetuating them?

The examples mentioned earlier of the parent and professor were selected at least in part in the hope that they would lead readers to construct more obvious examples of power in their own minds. How many people made the parent the male father? How many cast the professor as female? Gender may well be a significant actor in framing power. The collection of societal expectations, behaviours and attitudes ascribed to women and men (referred to as 'gender') can, of course, serve as both the source and outcome of power dynamics, operating at all levels of influence, ranging from the private realm of households to the pinnacle of political decision-making, just as other facets of identity such as age, sexuality, race and religion no doubt must and do play a role. Specifically, the operation of gender tends to create power dynamics that benefit men, where, as Weedon has put it:

> In patriarchal discourse the nature and social role of women are defined in relation to a norm which is male. This finds its clearest expression in the generic use of the terms 'man' and 'he' to encompass all of humankind. ... To say that patriarchal relations are structural is to suggest that they exist in the institutions and social practices of our society and cannot be explained by the intentions, good or bad, of individual women or men. (Weedon, 1987, pp 2–3)

In understanding power relations such as this, then, we very much move power beyond the individual considerations of what would or can constitute and influence a form of structured power relationship that has a significant implication for power in society. In fact, an often cited reason for both the negative acts and omissions in police practice (or police malpractice) is its structuring of patriarchal 'culture', which is (in terms of policing) still largely dominated by the male-centric nature of the political system in which men hold power and women are largely excluded.

An appropriate analysis of power relations clearly requires more than an individual explanation of power, and to be able to articulate why people and institutions oppress each other, a theory of subjectivity, of conscious and unconscious thoughts and emotions, which can account for the relationship between the individual, the collective and the social, is needed. Such a theory of power goes beyond the actual or putative intentions and experiences of participants of power relations and aims, instead, to explain the very power relations involved in the formation of these. If we return to the police, individual police personnel are individually responsible for ensuring the use of their powers is lawful, proportionate and necessary, but individuals and collectives of these can be regarded as a source of the misuse of power. Yet so too, the notion that powers are created or exist in a structural and collective manner that reflects a dominant ethos and ethic is not necessarily as simple as it might first seem.

When the vigil for Sarah Everard culminated in controversy, even if arguably police powers were never just about what police officers do, for many people, the vigil was ultimately largely about the horrendous crime that one individual committed, far more than it was about the collective police response. So too, was it the patriarchy responsible for the Everard vigil or the later sacking of Cressida Dick, or was it ultimately acts and omissions that were in the hands of individuals? Yes, of course, those actions of individuals are influenced by a broader socio-economic, political and cultural climate. But we might ask, to what extent are failings or acts ever about systems when they are decisions and judgements enacted by individuals? When does the system start and individual accountability begin?

Traditionally, criminology has used the term 'crimes of the powerful' to describe criminal offences committed by those of (relatively) high status or those who hold relatively high levels of trust or positions of influence, often where the offence is made possible by, say, their status or occupation. Among myriad forms of crime that developed in the 20th century, one pertinent recent example is the efflorescence of high-tech, particularly internet, crime, which has raised awareness of crimes where individual status is core. However, criminology has also helped us to see that 'crimes' are committed by those working on behalf of corporations, governments, dictators and states. Certainly, certain academics with a critical perspective have initiated efforts to analyse the negative aspects of the Western concept of the 'rule of law'. They aim to examine how this notion has been wielded as a potent political tool by Western nations, legitimising acts of exploitation and violent extraction by stronger political entities against weaker ones through imperialism and colonialism (as seen in the work of Mattei and Nader, 2008). If the value is in rebalancing the recognition of the darker side of recent European history against the backdrop of modern mercantile capitalism, then much is well in a better historical understanding. However, such a historical framing of power is necessarily selective. Yes, we should perhaps recognise the crimes of the East India Company and, say, Britain's complicity in the transatlantic slave trade and the Opium Wars, but so too it is important to acknowledge that throughout history, the powerful existed across empires, where, often, power resided at the top and brutality flew downward. For instance, what of the Islamic Caliphates and the Trans-Saharan slave trade, where an estimated 80 million Africans were killed, men were castrated and subjects were forcefully converted to Islam by 'accepting the word of Allah'? The Islamic Caliphates massacred and destroyed the pre-existing cultures of Mena and Iran by forcefully converting the population to Islam and making them adapt to Arab culture. Or the Mongol empire of Genghis Khan? A 2003 study found evidence that Genghis Khan's DNA may have been present in about 16 million men around the globe who are alive today (Zerjal et al, 2003). Do they not benefit from his cruel acts? What have we to say of China under Chiang Kai Shek, who killed an estimated 10 million of his people? Today, it is accepted in the West that China is involved in the arbitrary detention of Uyghurs in state-sponsored internment camps. The forced labour and suppression of their religious practices, along with forced sterilisation, forced contraception and forced abortion that these people are subject to, are both a state act of genocide and a massive exercise of power. Nevertheless, this topic has attracted almost no criminological attention or mention whatsoever.

Why not consider the Roman Empire or the Assyrian Empire? How far must we trace back the historical shaping of the contemporary? Between the 14th and 7th century BC, the Assyrians implemented flaying and amputations and permitted mass deportations of people proud of the mass executions. They loved to impale their victims on large stakes. Such sights instilled terror and fear into the rest of the population. For the Assyrian kings, it was a showcase of their power. The holding of significant social, economic, military, religious or cultural power is, after all, hardly new, though it is characterised and represented in a massively selective manner. In its attempt to better understand contemporary power, criminology faces charges that it must decolonise and look anew at the world made in the modern era, but why has this shaped the world so much more than, say, the Roman empire or antiquity or the emergence of Abrahamic faiths? Such a call to decolonise does not consider the nuances and complexities of fluctuating power over time and place, but rather makes power a static fact of the contemporary West focused on its past exploitations rather than its ongoing present practice and looking at the historically afar rather than the present here and now.

An example of this is Phillip Green. The fashion retailer Arcadia came to be widely condemned when he sold the BHS company and its pension liabilities for just a single £1. In the wake of his actions in 2015, politicians lined up to condemn him, mooted stripping him of his knighthood. For many, while his actions may have been technically legal, they were immoral and roundly condemned by politicians and public alike. Yet in 2022, when British high street retailer Wilkinsons went bankrupt, a similar story played out. It was revealed that owners took £150 million out of the business, leaving the pension fund some £50 million in deficit and taxpayers with a £42 million bill to cover. Yet no action had been taken to close loopholes or make such practices criminal. Western politicians point instead to the lawlessness and criminality of other regimes. Many social scientists in the West today see power as the preserve of the US global order, but even that may be changing and this is, in historical terms, a very short-lived phenomenon at this moment. It also may be undone as new power allegiances form between state actors such as China and Russia, suggesting they creating alternative systems to liberal western capitalism.

In a speech at Davos, Russian President Vladimir Putin suggested, "Society has a question to ask to what extent business monopoly corresponds to the public interest", noting that many corporations now "are no longer just economic giants". In some areas, they are already "de facto competing with the state" (Foy et al, 2021). Of course, Putin's Russian state is concerned with corporations and corporate interests, but are his observations useful to social scientists? While Putin may have become a vocal critic of the state-corporate nexus in the West, Russia is hardly immune from such a nexus. It is not necessarily a great respecter of international rules and laws. On the 24 February 2022, despite having been a member of the United Nations (UN) since December 1991, Russia invaded its sovereign neighbour Ukraine, describing it as a "special military operation" (BBC News, 2022). The 1945 UN Charter, which sets out the conditions under which UN member states may legally resort to war or the use of armed force in general (a concept referred to as *jus ad bellum*), was violated. The 2022 Russian invasion of Ukraine can be grasped as illegal precisely as it broke and undermined the Charter, arguably one of the most significant international law documents. The power to disregard international law is a high power indeed.

Of course, the separation of state and corporate interests, notionally at least, seems more apparent in a liberal democratic, capitalist society in the West, across North America, Europe and Australasia. While such countries are not perfect, they are more transparent. Denmark, New Zealand and Finland topped the list of Transparency International's corruption perception index as the least corrupt countries (in 2021, the UK was 11th the US 27th to Russia's 136th place) (Transparency International, 2021). Do we really believe that the ethnocentric configuration of belief systems producing a powerful Euro-American using notions such as democratic governance, human rights and the rule of law is ever and always beholden to the problematic exercise of power? Undoubtedly, Western liberal democratic regimes and their position within the global order of consumer capitalism have experienced significant prominence since World War II. However, history reminds us that all world orders, including our own, are impermanent. They undergo periods of ascent and decline, and the institutions they establish, the guiding beliefs and 'norms', and the economic systems they sustain also witness fluctuations over time.

Following the Napoleonic Wars in the early 19th century, the British domination of the seas and the equilibrium among the major powers on the European continent contributed to a period of relative security and prosperity. The world was connected more closely together by revolutions in commerce and communication. The disintegration of the British and European orders in the 20th century did not lead to a new dark age. However, had Nazi Germany and imperial Japan emerged victorious, the outcome could have been drastically different. Considering this historical context, one might wonder if the termination of the current American-dominated order would have less severe repercussions. A surprising number of intellectuals, politicians and policy makers greet the prospect with equanimity, just as they see only the problematic nature of the current global order and how power currently operates. For that reason, much of the discussion on the crimes of the powerful locates them in the global, developed West with the rise of modern industrialism and modern industrial capitalism in the 17th and 18th centuries. Is this a reasonable and fair representation of history? Certainly, modern capitalism was built on power, and not all of it was exercised kindly. The epoch and the empires that characterised it could be ruthless and exploitative. If we return to it, there is an abundance of examples of crime and harm benefitting the social elites of the time, from the crimes of the East India Company and then the British Raj, to the practices of Leopold II as absolute ruler of the Congo Free State and the transatlantic slave trade. At the third World Conference against Racism, Racial Discrimination, Xenophobia and Related Intolerance, held in Durban in 2001, Europe acknowledged its role in slavery and colonialism in Africa as a crime against humanity (Sundberg, 2002). This represented a huge victory for Africans and African Americans and was a historical recognition of the criminal element of slavery, even though the former colonial powers stopped short of formally apologising in the final declaration. However, slavery had a part in making all manner of empires. Slavery occurred in civilisations as in almost every ancient civilisation, including ancient Egypt, ancient China, the Akkadian Empire, Persia, ancient Greece, ancient India, the Roman Empire, the Arab Islamic Caliphate and the pre-Columbian civilisations of the Americas. It was not until 1981 that slavery was outlawed in Mauritania in Northwest Africa and only in 2007 that the country passed a law that criminalises the act of owning another person (Sutter, 2012). So far, only one case has been successfully prosecuted there, and it is estimated that some 10 per cent of the population still, in effect, live in a form of slavery.

What is meant, then, by the phrase (and framing) 'crimes of the powerful'?

A person unfamiliar with the literature in criminology might be forgiven for regarding the term as somewhat amorphous and nebulous. Of course, a counterpoint is that such a term is not as ambiguous as many wordy academics may suggest and conveys the connection between political and economic power and crime. But the problem here is that crime is a contested term. What constitutes a crime? Simply put, crime is often defined by the politically powerful rather than simply being in the eyes of the beholder. Crime, even if it is the result and outcome of a certain social negotiation process, is not the result of an outcome process where all have the same power to define because what is 'crime' and who is 'criminal' are arbitrarily constructed by powerful actors – indeed, those among the social elite who hold political and economic power. While this may have resulted in some notional universals, the trafficking of drugs, for example, is widely held to be criminal according to the principles of international law. Yet, the demand for these illicit drugs aptly illustrates that there is no universal view of taking such substances as wrong. So too, what might be considered immoral but not criminal, say the withholding of medicines from the seriously ill or poor or withholding food from the starving, are not necessarily defined as 'crimes' and have no explicit recognition as such in international law, even if common morality and humanity would likely see them as inherently immoral and wicked. This may be one reason for the move from traditional criminology into new and additional concerns with 'harm' or harms and socially unjust and injurious behaviours in fields such as zemiology (the social scientific study of harm) or social justice scholarship. However, there is then a near infinite possible extension of the word 'crime' when one uses the word in the sense of something that ought to be illegal rather than something that is presently illegal. Harm clarifies this little. Moreover, often, the paradoxical situation where those that are said to commit 'crimes of power' are only held as doing so if legislation creates such prohibitions does not happen as the powerful do not legislate against their interest. This means such crimes go unnoticed, becoming 'invisible crimes' as Davies et al (1999) have termed them. Indeed, these above concerns can easily be connected, giving us 'invisible crimes and social harms' (Davies et al, 1999). Since the publication of texts such as Hillyard et al's (2004) *Beyond Criminology*, there have been calls to decriminalise, and criminology has shifted towards understanding harm and broader processes. There is clearly a difficulty with power, and often, we find that when you read through criminology books, it is either ill-defined or conceptualised; hence, how we approached the definitions of power when writing this book is important. Alongside this, though, we also considered the problematic nature of notions of harm. Power is at once a straightforward concept in that it is just someone's ability to control someone else or to influence someone else, and indeed, it can be that simple. But to see the crimes of the powerful, as core texts do, as some ill-defined individual or group exercise of power dynamics or played out at a miso, micro and macro level against an unresponsive, less powerful group, says little on the power of, say, the state or the transnational corporation. We certainly agree that the topics criminologists neglect to study are telling, and it is commonly acknowledged that criminology has a power problem. It has been suggested that only 3 per cent of criminological publications deal with crimes of the powerful at all, and these are typically critical criminologists writing at criminology's margins. Conventionally, criminology has little to say about the crimes of the powerful and tends to reinforce the dominant and statutory tendency to look down on the social strata for examples of wrongdoing. However, we contend that in such a narrative, while there is a degree of truth, there is also a great deal of simplicity. Even though crimes perpetrated by states and corporations have substantial economic, physical and social consequences, they remain relatively understudied in research. Despite most of criminology acknowledging the existence of crimes committed by organisations against their employees, which encompass violations of health and safety regulations leading to workplace injuries, illnesses, accidents and occasionally even fatalities, these instances, too, arise from human behaviours.

Environmental crimes may extend across international boundaries fuelled by the erosion of geographic and trade barriers between countries and raise important issues regarding enforcement, regulation and control at the start of the 21st century, but even if guided by an often invisible hand, there is always and ever a human hand in such behaviour. Such crimes are not yet guided primarily by artificial intelligence (AI), although, in the not-too-distant future, they could well be.

Criminology is indeed an increasingly diverse discipline. This phenomenon can be attributed to more than just a more diverse and representative group of scholars entering academia and pursuing their independent research agendas. It is also more than merely a reflection of the subject's rapid growth in new regions like Asia and the Global South.

What is striking is criminology's inclination to identify specific niche areas of study that could better mirror the diversity of the postmodern population, encompassing their intersectional relationships, structural contexts and cultural norms. We are not the first to note that these days, criminologists are often little concerned with 'crime', the one thing that once, at least, gave the field the notional object of inquiry. The decline in the emphasis on crime in criminology is commonly viewed as a positive advancement, indicating the discipline's increasing confidence and significance, which suggests that the subject is thriving and in good condition. In becoming an ever more diverse and broader subject, though, criminology has arguably too often neglected what should be its core concern related to political and economic power, how the law is passed and enacted, and how and why some people feel unattached to the broader social good. Criminologists have strayed a long way from crime and power, suggesting that the latter is everywhere and omnipresent, an amorphous thing to be found almost universally in every social setting and social interaction. Criminology has arguably lost its concern with the economic and political elites, the functioning of law toward social good and the notions of justice.

As a result of these developments, we are witnessing the initial signs of climate change, resource conflicts, state-sponsored terrorism and large-scale migration into the chaotic, crowded and unequal urban settings of emerging megacities. In 1950, there were only three such cities, but by the second half of the 21st century, they are projected to accommodate approximately 70 per cent of the global population (United Nations, 2018). The Anthropocene may prove apocalyptic for many, but the wealthiest 10 per cent of the global population currently takes 52 per cent of global income, compared with an 8 per cent share for the poorest half, and financial globalisation makes it increasingly hard to measure wealth at the top strata among the new global oligarchy who enjoy free citizenship and movement.

However, social science has little to say on this. Indeed, identity politics and contemporary social theory have paved the way for elites' struggles to capture and dominate the discourse, shielding the very real issues of the corruption of real democratic politics and economics and making these invisible. Arguably, the crimes of the powerful are not crimes at all but the routine practices of advanced capitalist business practice. Contemporary Western public life is dominated by the neuroses of the more privileged, who are keen to deny they really hold that. The petty concerns of the self-pitying well-offs and social elites have colonised politics, culture, the news and mainstream media. Newspapers overflow with sob stories from private school-educated intellectuals who come from wealth and status but talk at length about the harms of being misgendered. Netflix is a hotbed of dramas about privileged individuals as hard-done-by victims. Multi-millionaire royalty, politicians and celebrities tell all about their struggles with mental illness and their hardships. However, almost nobody in intellectual circles notes that this political, sexual, and cultural fixation with privilege has become vogue to the point that it eclipses all else. In amongst it all, power is omnipresent, yet the true power of political connections and material wealth is unmentioned. If there is an alternative to this democratic capitalism rising in the East, it is less democratic and transparent and more authoritarian.

Added to this contemporary condition and closely linked is that while we are aware of corruption, which is still increasing worldwide, few people see this process for what it is – one of political and economic power enabling corruption on a massive, global scale. Certainly, numerous influential figures, often engaged in virtue signalling, purportedly concur that corruption is a moral issue that demands global ethics as a solution. However, despite various endeavours to enhance ethical standards, transparency and accountability, the impact of these measures remains limited, and we routinely do not ask why that is. The saying that power can corrupt is well known. However, it is seldom acknowledged in discussions that corruption is rooted in a criminogenic moral culture, particularly within late capitalism. Moreover, corruption, power and elite social positioning are intricately interconnected. Elite actors have financial power and with that comes the power to purchase goods and services to ensure confidentiality, legal processes and media to manage reputation and risk. Kuldova et al. (2024, forthcoming) have recently shed some light on the thin practices of what they term regulatory elite compliance industries that help the rich and powerful appear as ethical or shield and hide away their unethical practices. Fundamentally, such behaviours are underpinned by the criminogenic and immoral culture of late capitalism, where this defiance industry the elite employ are the ones who give shape to regulatory agencies that are supposed to combat the ills of corruption.

Crimes of the powerful are indeed more often not crimes at all because the rich can afford for their behaviour, even when wicked, immoral, unscrupulous or harmful, to be anything but a crime. On the rare occasion that their worst acts are considered crimes, they are explained away as oversights, omissions and benign neglects. They are anything but deliberate acts hard-wired into contemporary culture. For example, the work of Atkinson (2020) explored how the super-rich encroached on London and subsequently resulted in a city characterised by extreme inequality, socially corrosive and geographical demarcations that separate and perpetuate the divide between the 'haves' and 'have-nots', and a means for the elite to hide their wealth. One of the ways such wealth is concealed is via money laundering. Atkinson notes how this has happened on a massive scale and how 'the laundering of illicit wealth underpins much of the excess of the alpha housing market' (p 84) as a normal part of market practice. Not only is such laundering of wealth tightly embedded and interwoven with the housing market and construction of property catered to the elite, but there are also clear signs of deliberate neglect from the point of view of the state in which there has been 'the sense of disconnection between sections of the political class and the imperatives to act on questions of inequality, corporate fraud, offshore evasion and laundering' (p 235).

As academics aligned with new manifestations of criminological realism, we share the sentiment that academic criminology has largely lost its initial intellectual vigour and dynamism. The constant expansion into diverse areas of interest does not significantly contribute to the development of fresh approaches to security or a comprehensive theoretical framework capable of explaining the prevailing challenges we encounter. A scarcity of novel ideas and concepts currently exists, and these are urgently required to confront the contemporary reality of 21st-century capitalism and its numerous and rapidly evolving issues concerning crime and harm. Similar deficiencies in generating new ideas are observed in certain social science fields, which have not adapted adequately to the tumultuous times characterised by staggering economic inequality and injustice. These fields have yet to grapple with the systemic fraud and misconduct prevalent in corporate finance and the banking industry. Moreover, they lack persuasive and theoretically nuanced explanations for the decline in crime in Western societies, and their understanding of the transformation of criminal markets due to the internet's emergence as a platform for illegal entrepreneurship is both limited and unconvincing (Hall and Winlow, 2015). Little has been said about the criminogenic effects of consumer and household debt and what appears to be a significant rise in corrosive forms of socio-symbolic violence. Moreover, while liberal criminology notes an ever-growing myriad of obvious harms at home, the narrowness and unwillingness of the liberal left still cannot bring itself to admit that the vast majority of Western electorates are depoliticised, absorbed in the corporate media spectacle and more enthusiastic about competing against one another for positional consumer goods than they are about seeking solidarity and organising opposition to the capitalist system's excesses (see Treadwell et al, 2013).

This is only mirrored by the narrow willingness to see excessive harm as almost wholly the preserve of some of the world's most transparent, democratic and accountable nations. Amid the devastating impact of a lethal pandemic, economic and physical insecurity, and violent conflicts, advocates of democracy have suffered significant setbacks in their fight against authoritarian adversaries. It is noteworthy that many authoritarian regimes in the world hardly raise a murmur of concern within the liberal commentariat. The Taliban's injunction on education for females might cause the occasional stir of indignation; however, the fact that 23 per cent of the world's entire population lives under repressive regimes that give them few basic rights, as in places such as Syria, Eritrea, Uzbekistan, Turkmenistan and Sudan, often receives little attention.

The consequences of the prolonged decline of democracy have transcended national boundaries, extending globally and affecting even those enduring the harshest dictatorships. The decline of democracy has led to assertions about its inherent inferiority. Advocates of this notion include official commentators from China and Russia, aiming to bolster their global influence while evading accountability for their wrongdoings. Additionally, within democratic nations, antidemocratic actors view this as a chance to consolidate power. In both contexts, powerful elites cheer the breakdown of democracy and are exacerbating it.

In 2020, the malign influence of the Chinese regime, the world's most populous dictatorship, was particularly significant. Beijing intensified its global disinformation campaign and censorship to counter the consequences of its initial coronavirus outbreak cover-up, which significantly impeded a swift global response during the early stages of the pandemic. Moreover, China's efforts included increased interference in the domestic political discourse of foreign democracies, extending its rights abuses beyond its borders and severely undermining Hong Kong's freedoms and legal autonomy. Surprisingly, these actions have been largely overlooked by criminologists and remained unaddressed in numerous publications on crimes of the powerful in recent years. Perhaps this leads to the obvious point that we have tended to conceive power as residing at the higher echelons of the social strata rather than looking down. However, we have shown an alarming tendency to see power as something that resides exclusively in the West. Political and economic power is clearly much more global and much more panoramic.

Power and the power to harm

The term 'power' may appear, at least at first glance, a rather simple concept. From our own experiences as academic criminologists who teach on a range of topics, it is not uncommon for students to often not consider power when it comes to the issue of criminality and too often take the legally defined criminal offences at face value and universal in nature. It is also fair to suggest that in the course of study, such perspectives often give way to a challenging form of social constructionism where everything is contested. Crime as a social construction is, of course, a powerful message and something of a universal in all criminological texts, and yet, there also has to be some engagement with the nature of legal systems and the operation of these and the constructed nature of laws, rules and systems. Functionalists in the social sciences have long charted that laws, rules and regulations, be it in the form of those telling us what to do or keeping us from doing what we want, serve to create parameters around acceptability and functioning social order. To live in a civil society, we must have some rules to follow. Paradoxically, however, the dark side of the rule of law and how it has been used as a powerful political weapon by Western countries in order to legitimise plunder – the practice of violent extraction by stronger political actors victimising weaker and the less powerful – often in the service of Western cultural and economic domination, remain marginal concerns even in critical scholarship (Mattei and Nader, 2008). It is reasonable to propose that the notion of the rule of law is a fundamental principle of governance, wherein all individuals, institutions and entities, both public and private, including the state itself, are answerable to publicly declared laws. These laws are to be administered impartially and adjudicated independently while adhering to international human rights norms and standards and are commonly perceived as a mere social construct. However, the actual state of affairs may be quite distant from this ideal.

While notionally, at least, most people may see the rule of law as fundamental to international peace and security, political stability, and achievement of economic and social progress and development, as well as it being at the core of protecting rights and fundamental freedoms, it would seem fairly uncontroversial to say most people believe the most effective exercise of power occurs when it is wielded responsibly by individuals who are sensitive to, and actively involved in, addressing the needs and interests of others, and in praxis globally this is far less often the case than perhaps we would like.

Power, then, is a complex concept that includes the ability or capacity to do or not do something. It also includes exercising influence, control or force through various means. Power, or lack of power, can have an important impact on people's circumstances and, therefore, on their lives, and clearly when it comes to moral and ethical arena and debates around crime, justice and regulation, right and wrong, good and bad, power is ever-present. Inequalities in wealth or capital and the distribution of power lead to the better off in any society being able to take advantage of their circumstances to a greater extent. One consequence of this advantage is that they persistently enjoy better cultural and social conditions that then again influence this advantage and affect access to these resources and opportunities shaped by social, economic and political processes. How the discourse of power is used in many contexts may impact lives. Understandings of conceptions and categorisations of power carry different implications, not merely for understanding its relationship to inequalities but in the practice, mechanisms and routes to address and redress power imbalances.

In contemporary social science, power is frequently and closely related to ideas of domination, coercion and oppression, understood as 'power over'. Such an exercise of power is not necessarily overt or involving force, violence or threat. Coercive power can be covert through dominant or advantaged groups shaping legislative rules (laws), public debate or political decisions, or otherwise influencing the perceptions or options of more disadvantaged groups. As such, power is routinely vested in major political, economic or cultural institutions. It has been described as 'structural oppression', an idea and a conception of power with much purchase in social sciences today. This conception of how power operates to favour and privilege some groups over others creates injustice and disadvantage. Structural oppression influences the life experiences and subsequent inequalities in outcomes of those who are less advantaged.

Regarding conceiving how power operates concerning crime, it is common to see crime and harm increasingly connected. Are there common characteristics of acts that are labelled as crimes? How do we define a crime? The easy answer is that a crime is whatever the law declares to be a criminal offence and punishes with a penalty. Of course, the other long-standing notion is that criminal law primarily protects the interests of society rather than arbitrates on individual civil matters. In this, there is an implicit recognition that the wrong of the conduct prohibited in law is not merely to an individual but to the collective society more broadly and that harm transcends individuals. While harm is, of course, a central component of many legally recognised and sanctioned criminal offences, students – along with the general public at large – often struggle to recognise how harm can manifest beyond such actions. This struggle to disentangle and differentiate between legally constructed criminality and harm is difficult for many reasons (see Raymen, 2022). From our own experiences as academics, the primary reasons include difficulty in critically questioning the motivations and ideological underpinnings of the state in the formation of codified criminal conduct, along with a rather rigid perception of how crime and violence can only seem to manifest via the actions of an individual or recognised group. It is important to stress that the latter reason is predominantly informed and sustained by the former, along with mainstream media accounts and depictions of criminality as simply acts of physical violence.

Academic work that seeks to push the boundaries of conventional criminology outward into new substantive areas of research, towards interdisciplinarity, and towards making broader theoretical contributions that transcend the empirical concern with crime and criminal justice, have become a part of critical criminology. For many, this is regarded as a positive development, but what happens when critical criminology loses an economic and political focus and becomes increasingly mired in a politics of identity that fails to see the actions of the individual and is too focused on the structural? As zemiology grows and critical criminology shifts a greater proportion of its attention beyond the category of crime and the criminal justice system and towards systemic, legal and normalised forms of social harm (see Hillyard et al, 2004; White, 2013; Hall and Winlow, 2015; Pemberton, 2016; Cooper and Whyte, 2017; Hall and Winlow, 2018; White, 2018; Raymen, 2019; Raymen and Smith, 2019a; Briggs et al, 2021; Raymen, 2022), then there is a need to think again about the use of the term 'power' and what it is being suggested it is.

This text is our attempt to reconnect criminology with concern with power and move in a manner quite different to that set out in some alternative texts. In doing so, we will consider a range of crimes that challenge the perception that violence only stems from within the individual agent. However, at the core is a hope and a desire to see crimes of the powerful again connect with the individual, to rebalance debates on agency and structure, and to once again centre on the vital importance of political economy. We will first situate such discussions within the current theoretical landscape, including considerations towards what exactly constitutes 'power', along with the limitations of criminological approaches and the importance of adopting a zemiological and social harms framework. So too, an in-depth overview of what constitutes violence will be provided that will draw primarily from the works of the principal founder of the discipline of peace and conflict studies, Johan Galtung (1969), and the Slovenian philosopher Slavoj Žižek (2008). This overview of the study of harm, along with a discussion of the philosophy of violence, is crucial, as it will serve to provide the foundation to frame the subsequent chapters. We will then draw upon the contemporary theoretical paradigm of ultra-realism. Specifically, it offers a unique perspective on contemporary subjectivity in its socio-economic context (see Hall and Winlow, 2015; Smith and Raymen, 2016; Wakeman, 2016; Ellis, 2017). Ultra-realism states that criminology must return to its fundamental question: Why do some individuals and groups risk harm to others as they pursue their instrumental and expressive interests rather than seek solidarity with one another? In providing an overview of this critical criminological position, it will become apparent that it provides a holistic account of violence and harm across social and economic strata, thus demonstrating there is little that separates the motivations and desires between the 'haves' and 'have-nots'.

It is important to stress from the outset that the notion of 'power' is malleable. Instead, this sub-section will provide a conceptual overview and discussion, which will highlight how, outside of some rudimentary thematic connections, power has the potential to be recognised within a multitude of dimensions and contexts, including but not limited to knowledge, economics, culture and politics. Power, within a context beyond the natural sciences and, in particular, physics, is not fixed or specific to a certain domain. As such, this introduction to the concept of power introduces some of the key thematic connections of what constitutes power within the milieu of human interactions and, more generally, society at large. However, while power is hard to pin down, it is important that we recognise the true nature of economic and political power for what it is, along with other vital components, within the discourse of crime.

So too, we will provide a brief overview of how these prescribed core components of power can manifest in various settings ranging from, for instance, those with state-sanctioned positions of authority to the economic elite. It is also important to note that this book is not intended to provide a comprehensive historical overview of the philosophical debates of attempting to define power, nor does it aim to capture and list every possible conceptualisation, definition or example of power within the contemporary landscape. Instead, this book – via the lens of critical criminological theory – serves as an introduction and guide to how the actions and behaviours of those operating within the upper strata of society can cause a multitude of harms that generally receive little attention when compared with more orthodox accounts of deviancy and state-centric acts of criminality that, for so long, have been at the centre of criminological inquiry – though more on that later in the chapter.

The concept of power is as 'ancient and ubiquitous as any that social theory can boast' (Dahl, 1957, p 201). Notions of what exactly constitutes power have been at the centre of many great and highly regarded philosophers, including Plato, Aristotle, Machiavelli, Hobbes, Pareto and Weber. With such a list of great thinkers, it is evident that many seminal social theorists have dedicated a significant amount of attention to power and the phenomena connected with it. Power, similar to notions of harm, may appear relatively straightforward and easy to define initially and upon first inspection. However, similar to the aforementioned and brief introduction to harm in the previous sub-section, there are many diverging and, at times, conflicting accounts of what exactly constitutes power. This, as we will come to see, is based primarily on disciplinary contexts such as the natural sciences and social sciences, in which divergences on the term can begin at the very ontological basis of the term.

For example, in the field of physics, power is fundamentally conceptualised and defined as the measure of energy transferred or converted per unit of time. In the International System of Units, the watt is used as the unit of power, equivalent to one joule per second (Basu, 2018). Within the domain of physics, there are various types of power, including average power, mechanical power, electrical power, peak power and radiant power (Breithaupt, 2001). When we begin to move away from the natural sciences, however, the ability to define power becomes more complicated. Power as a noun, in its most basic form, is the ability to do or act, or the capability of doing or accomplishing something (Zimmerling, 2005). This standard dictionary definition of the term is, by its nature, ambiguous and not necessarily negative or harmful. For instance, we can all relate to key moments in our lives when we overcome a perceived challenge, such as passing a school exam or being successful in a job interview. Here, it is important to reiterate that power does not necessarily require the use of or the threat of force, otherwise referred to as coercion. Indeed, much of the recent sociological discussion regarding the nature of power revolves around the subject of its means to enable it. Specifically, such discussions pertain to how power has the means to make social actions possible. So too, it is important to acknowledge that within the context of the social, having power can also be generated when an individual or group has significant amounts of influence, again further demonstrating that force is not the exclusive factor behind what constitutes power. For example, within the realm of business, Bacon (2011) notes that positive forms of influence in order to improve productivity include logical persuading, legitimising, exchanging, stating, socialising, appealing to relationships, consulting, alliance building, appealing to values and modelling.

Philosophies of power

Almost every political philosopher, social theorist and intellectual grasps with the issue of power. Philosophical discussion of various forms by which the social body can be governed often draws lineage back to Greek works, including but not limited to Plato and the discussion of aristocracy, timocracy, oligarchy, democracy and tyranny in descending order of goodness. From early on, philosophers distinguished between moral powers (authority, right to order something), which correspond to *potestas* in Latin, and physical power (ability to do something or to operate a constraint on somebody else), corresponding to *potentia* in Latin. Of course, these debates and discussions often separated power from force. The use of power need not involve force or the threat of force (or coercion). Added to power are a range of moral and ethical standpoints concerning the use of power, both without oppression (or a form of softer or more legitimate power) compared with authoritarian hard power.

Thomas Hobbes (1588–1679) was a prominent thinker of the 17th century who endeavoured to apply the emerging scientific methods and the rigorous logic of ancient Greece to the field of sociology. In his renowned work *Leviathan* (1651), he expounds on the concept of power and advocates for the establishment of a commonwealth as a means to create a well-functioning society.

Hobbes divided motivation into appetites and aversions, predating Freud and his pleasure-pain principle by a couple of centuries. Hobbes defined power as the ability to secure well-being or personal advantage 'to obtain some future apparent good' (Hobbes, 1651: 58). He saw people as having 'natural power' that comes from internal qualities such as intellectual eloquence, physical strength and prudence.

Hobbes noted that power is relative only to the power of others. If I have less power than you, then I am effectively powerless in your presence. This leads us to a perpetual power struggle with other people, each vying for ever greater power and each seeking to acquire the power of others. He also noticed that there are some people who can never get enough power and who seek to use others rather than cooperate and live in harmony with them. This he considered a dysfunction.

Max Weber is not primarily remembered for his work being concerned with power. However, he suggested that power is 'the probability that one actor within a social relationship will be able to carry out his will despite resistances' (Weber, 1978, p 53).

Weber's contribution to the discourse on power lies in acknowledging that power is inherently tied to a relationship. The nature of that relationship can be diverse, leading to different manifestations of power. For instance, the power dynamics between a learner and an educator are distinct from those between individuals encountering each other at a supermarket. This aspect highlights a limitation in Hobbes' definition. However, Weber's definition may imply that resistance is invariably negative, but is that always the case?

For Hannah Arendt (1970), power is 'the ability not just to act, but to act in concert' (p 44). Arendt, a German Jewish political philosopher, authored numerous influential works on the Nazi war crime tribunals. One of her notable ideas was the juxtaposition of violence with power. Violence was portrayed as a means to forcefully obtain what one desires from others, as exemplified by the Nazis. On the other hand, power was seen as the capacity to unite as a collective to achieve shared objectives. However, this conceptualisation of power is limited as it primarily focuses on the individual, causing the loss of the notion of social relationships, as seen in Weber's perspective. Nevertheless, Arendt's *On Violence* and other works are very much framed by experiences of the Holocaust as a crime 'against mankind, committed on the body of the Jewish people' and a way of considering the impacts and harms of power as executed, whereas power needs to be distinguished from strength, force and violence. Differing from mere physical strength, power is not inherent to an individual but emerges from a collective of actors uniting for a shared political objective.

Unlike force, it is not an inherent natural phenomenon but rather a human construct resulting from collective participation. Moreover, unlike violence, power is not built on coercion but thrives through consent and rational persuasion.

According to Arendt, power is a unique phenomenon because it results from action and is wholly based on persuasion. It is regarded as a product of action since it emerges from the collective efforts of multiple actors, and its foundation lies in persuasion, as it involves securing the consent of others through unrestrained discussions and debates.

Talcott Parsons' (1967) view of power was that of a 'mechanism operating to bring about changes ... in the process of social interaction' (p 299). Parsons, a functionalist sociologist from the US, explored the role of the family during the 1950s and 1960s. His work led to a distinct conceptualisation of power, wherein the notion of the family emerged in response to societal changes. According to his perspective, power is not an attribute possessed by specific individuals but rather a characteristic inherent in society as a whole. It is possible that in our emphasis on recognising the significance of structure, we may have overlooked the role of agency. This raises questions about the place of the individual in this analysis. Is there room for the individual to be powerful within this framework?

Of course, the most common and highly cited social theorist on power is now undeniably the French philosopher Michel Foucault, who has arguably been most eminently notable and influential in shaping social scientific conceptions of power. He led the discipline away from merely analysing actors who wield power as a tool of coercion or focusing solely on the specific structures in which these actors operate. Instead, Foucault has introduced the notion that 'power is everywhere', diffused and ingrained within discourse, knowledge and 'regimes of truth' (Foucault, 1991; Rabinow, 1991). For Foucault, power is what makes us what we are, operating on a quite different level from other theories. His work marks a radical departure from conceptions of power and cannot be easily integrated with previous ideas, as power is diffuse rather than concentrated, is embodied and enacted rather than possessed, is discursive rather than purely coercive, and constitutes agents rather than being simply deployed from on high.

Foucault contests the notion that power is centrally located in a 'leviathan-like' state and accessed by those in high positions of authority. Instead, Foucault argues, 'power is everywhere' and 'comes from everywhere' (Foucault, 1998, p 63). Foucault elaborates on this perspective on power, stating that power is recognised and comes into fruition through reciprocally approved forms of knowledge and scientific understanding – among other disciplines and domains of knowledge – to construct the 'truth' and thus reality. On this matter, Foucault states:

The important thing here, I believe, is that truth isn't outside power or lacking in power: contrary to a myth whose history and functions would repay further study, truth isn't the reward of free spirits, the child of protracted solitude, nor the privilege of those who have succeeded in liberating themselves. Truth is a thing of this world: it is produced only by virtue of multiple forms of constraint. And it induces regular effects of power. Each society has its regime of truth, its "general politics" of truth—that is, the types of discourse it accepts and makes function as true; the mechanisms and instances that enable one to distinguish true and false statements; the means by which each is sanctioned; the techniques and procedures accorded value in the acquisition of truth; the status of those who are charged with saying what counts as true. (Foucault, 1977, p 131)

Such 'truths' are reinforced via institutions and formal systems we, as individuals, traverse and become encapsulated within, such as the education system, the media (now, of course, including the growing presence of social media), and the ebbs and flows of political and economic beliefs. With this in mind, Foucault brought attention to the notion of 'disciplinary power' that can be detected in the organisational systems and state-run services such as the courts, prisons and education systems (to name a few). Their systems of surveillance, first envisioned by Bentham (1995) in the form of the panopticon (a social control mechanism), no longer required physical violence, as individuals developed to discipline and 'correct' themselves and conform to the standards, norms and rules of society. Further still, Foucault's interest in relation to power resulted in him examining how the human body is also susceptible to such disciplines and ultimately is controlled to act in certain ways in which the regulation of customs, habits, health and reproductive practices are made to reflect the 'truth' of a given society (considered as 'biopower'). Such forms of power fundamentally, via discourse, create and embed norms of what is acceptable and, conversely, what is not. However, it is important to reiterate that such 'truths' that maintain ideology, norms and values are constantly adapting and changing. Foucault's contributions have unveiled the profound influence of entrenched norms, which can operate outside our conscious awareness. Consequently, individuals may unconsciously adopt and conform to these norms, shaping their attitudes, values and actions without explicit signs of authority or exercise of power from traditional sources of authority or conventional notions of power.

Yet, contrary to some interpretations, Foucault believed in possibilities for action and resistance. He was an active social and political commentator who saw a role for the 'intellectual'. His ideas about action were, like Hayward (2000), concerned with our capacity to recognise and question socialised norms and constraints. Challenging power does not involve pursuing some unassailable 'absolute truth' since even truth is a construct of social power. Instead, the challenge lies in disentangling the power of truth from the prevailing forms of hegemony in the social, economic and cultural realms. Discourse can serve as a domain for both power and resistance, offering opportunities to elude, undermine or contest strategies of power:

> Discourses are not once and for all subservient to power or raised up against it. ... We must make allowances for the complex and unstable process whereby a discourse can be both an instrument and an effect of power, but also a hindrance, a stumbling point of resistance and a starting point for an opposing strategy. Discourse transmits and produces power; it reinforces it, but also undermines and exposes it, renders it fragile and makes it possible to thwart. (Foucault, 1998, pp 100–101)

However, there is also a great deal to criticise Foucault on, beyond his very evident flaws as a character and accusations about his conduct (it is now widely thought he may have sexually abused young men in North Africa). Foucault departs from the conventional perspective that portrays power as a dynamic where the strong oppress the weak or the wealthy oppress the poor. Instead, he posits that power is dispersed throughout society in the contemporary world. This argument contends that genuine and inherent forms of power become obscured, rendering power seemingly meaningless. Foucault insists that disciplinary power cannot be possessed, acquired, seized or shared but has purely structural origins. However, power can, factually speaking, only be said to exist when materially manifested. Nor should we wholly reject the notion that theoretical investigations into a specific state of practice – the discourse of state in the publication of reports of official inquiries into law, order and justice issues, such as that found in commissions, tribunals and committees of inquiry – highlight the malfeasance of power involving issues from the likes of wrongful imprisonment, police corruption and state violence (Burton and Carlen, 1979). Yet, such material can highlight structural manifestations of effect, but so too they shed light on acts and omissions of people as individuals as well as the prevailing ideology. They do not stand merely as agency-based ideology, where the behaviour of people wielding power is removed and where power is ever contested; they reveal realities of political and economic power. However, if we move into constructionism and playful contestation, such meanings become merely part truths competing against many alternative interpretations. It is perhaps unsurprising, given the oft way postmodernity played fast and loose with such facts, that it is often now said postmodernist philosophy, pioneered by Foucault, 'put societal power structures and labels ahead of individuals and their endeavours' (Truss, 2020). Indeed, Foucault is best known today as the theorist of discourse: symbolic expressions of institutional power that are neither true nor false but serve as practical channels for organising society.

Marxism, for example, is discourse, as is race, and so too economics and politics. However, 'science' is also a discourse, to the extent that this term is used politically to assert authority and issue certain claims. Nevertheless, linked with others in postmodernist and post-structuralist movements, Foucault is now critiqued. As a man, Foucault was "enraptured by the beauty of the Ayatollah Khomeini's Neanderthal regime" (Wheen, 2004) and quoted as saying:

> 'They don't have the same regime of truth as ours, which, it has to be said, is very special, even if it has become almost universal. ... And in Iran it is largely modelled on a religion that has an exoteric form and an esoteric Content. ... Everything that is said under the explicit form of the law also refers to another meaning. So not only is saying one thing that means another not a condemnable ambiguity, it is on the contrary, a necessary and highly prized additional level of meaning. It's often the case that people say something that, at the factual level, isn't true, but which refers to another, deeper meaning, which cannot be assimilated in terms of precision and observation.' (see Wheen, 2004)

Power indeed. It ought to be remembered that a core thrust of Foucault's work was how the post-Enlightenment power oversaw the expansion of bureaucratic structures, coldly manufacturing entirely new categories of populations and behaviours purely to use them administratively. Undeniably, for arch post-structuralists and those using Foucault today, there is often an ability to present his ideas as rather more fixed than they were. However, we should note that his final series of lectures at the Collège de France was called 'The Courage of the Truth' (Foucault, 2011). On the last page of the manuscript of his last lecture, Foucault noted that 'only by deciphering the truth of self in this world, deciphering oneself with mistrust of oneself and the world, and in fear and trembling before God, will enable us to have access to the true life' (p 338). It may well be that Foucault was returning to reality and a different understanding of truth and perhaps power itself. Yet, returning to the more harmful aspects of power, the Iranian regime puts gay men like Foucault to death after an administered authoritarian Judicial process. It often executes them by hanging them by the neck, having raised them off the ground by a crane, but only after flogging their backs bloody. This is no contested truth. Power and understanding of truth and what is right, moral, ethical and good might matter more than post-structuralists sometimes let on.

What constitutes good and evil, right and wrong? When terms like power and authority are used, they are differently understood and conceived of.

While some commentators are keen to separate the collective and the individual or to delineate the lines between power, force and authority, there is a great deal of complexity. In definitions, force is often integral to power and is inexorably interwoven in praxis and reality.

Power is not a violent force, but the ability to rely on a latent well of violence might be a vital component of power. While force is more generally defined as a strength or energy that is an attribute to movement or physical action, in the social sciences, this takes a more violent manifestation consisting of coercion or compulsion with the threat of the use of violence. So too, while power and force are not one and the same in the social sciences, they may more frequently overlap than is now credited. Nor is power about violence and the willingness to use it, although, again, it can be. In conventional (and criminological) terms, most violence involves an overt act or an explicit and aggressive encounter between offender(s) and victim(s). In contrast, there are covert violent and harmful acts in terms of the offenders' efforts to avoid detection and contact with victims, and this may be one reason there is a logic in keeping power and violence (or force) separate. Indeed, some relatively powerless people may still use force or violence. The defining characteristic of some covert criminal actors is power, but rather, it is a lack or absence of power, though the context of any individual actor's powerlessness varies, which better illustrates their behaviour. Take, for example, a disgruntled Amazon employee who surreptitiously damages company property after having been fired. Is this an act of a powerful actor? If it is, then all crime can be seen as about power. Yet, clearly, the disgruntled employee does not have the power of, say, a finance manager or national director. Indeed, some perpetrators of crime clearly lack the physical ability to overpower their targets, while others are hampered by economic, political or personal weakness. However, they all can turn to force or, indeed, violence. In the US, the very expression 'going postal' to describe the spree shooting of former colleagues and employers by employees aptly captures such an example. However, if we make the individual who acts in such a manner 'powerful' or describe their actions as about 'power and control', are we doing something of a disservice to the realities of power?

Returning to the work of Bacon (2011), the concept of influence can also manifest in potentially harmful forms, including such actions as avoiding, manipulating, intimidating and threatening others. As noted by Bacon, these are negative because they take away the other's legitimate right to challenge the will of another or others, and bullies, dictators and autocrats usually adopt such negative forms of influence. Of course, at a micro level, power can be witnessed in almost all interactions between people. For instance, Dahl (1957) states: 'My intuitive idea of power then, is something like this: A has power over B to the extent that he can get B to do something that B would not otherwise do' (p 203). Dahl continues, noting that there is far more to this account of power in that factors include (a) the source or domain of power, (b) the means or instruments of power, (c) the amount or extent of power and (d) the range and scope of power. In social science, power is the capability of an individual, dependent on a variety of factors previously outlined, to impact the actions, opinions or behaviour of others. This formation and use of power at an individual level, which can include physical manifestations of violence but a range of other factors that could impact other people, will be examined in some detail across the book. However, as Dahl states:

> Power is a relation, and that it is a relation among people. Although in common speech the term encompasses relations among people and other animate or inanimate objects, we shall have our hands full if we confine the relationship to human beings. ... Let us call the objects in the relationship of power, actors. Actors may be individuals, groups, roles, offices, governments, nation-states, or other human aggregates. (Dahl, 1957, p 203)

With this in mind, while we will indeed be examining the actions of people, we will also be examining the concept of the 'objects in the relationship of power' beyond the individual subject and include more abstract examples consisting of groups, organisations and state agencies and political and economic power. Continuing this focus on actors of power beyond just the actions of individuals, there are definitions of power that reside within a more political context, stating that power is defined as political or national strength (Zakaria, 1998). This brings us to the discipline of political science.

Political science studies how power is dispersed in diverse political contexts. For example, in the UK, the political system is divided into three distinct branches: legislative, executive and judicial. Scholars may investigate how public opinion influences political parties, elections and the overall political process. Keeping within the context of politics, however, social scientists are inclined to be more concerned with the capabilities and influences of governmental control on society and how public conflicts stem from the dispersal of power. Social scientists are also interested in examining how the use of power, stemming from such sources as the government, impacts local, state, national and international schemas, which in turn affect people and groups differently due to variables including identity and socio-economic position. The predominant focus and attention towards the role of government in the attempt to define power appear, at first glance, to make sense. This is perhaps due to how many academics and social scientists generated understandings of power from work developed by Weber, who stated that power is the ability to exercise one's will over others, perhaps involving force, despite the opposition of others (Weber, 1978). Stemming from this, academics, including political scientists and those within the social sciences, recognised that power can have an impact beyond personal relationships or dynamics between individuals. In particular, power has the capacity to shape and influence larger dynamics like social groups, professional organisations and, of course, governments. We can perhaps illustrate this point with obvious examples, including dictatorships, in which a ruler with total power controls a country, typically one who has obtained control by force (Schmitt, 2013). So too, within the globalised context in which we now exist (Hopkins, 2002), it is important to note that powerful states have the capacity to greatly influence other nations within this global stage. For instance, while there were perhaps positive examples of this during World War II, in which North America used its significant economic might and influence to bring together an alliance to face the threat of Nazi invasion, more contemporary examples exhibit the harms caused by such state interferences. For instance, while North America's efforts in the 1940s were predominantly centred on preventing the rise of fascism, recent international actions are indicative of an ambition to maintain the country's position as the leading superpower. As Noam Chomsky (2003) explains, the war on terror was not the full picture and instead was a platform for the socio-economic elite who controlled the US to pursue an 'imperial grand strategy' to maintain global hegemony through military, political and economic means. He argues that in doing so, they have repeatedly displayed an indifference for democracy and human rights, in stark contrast to the US government's declared support and upholding of such values and what they supposedly fought against during World War II. Here we can perhaps witness how power, and harm that is produced from such sources, such as government, does not necessarily have to be readily apparent or stem from overtly oppressive systems such as Nazi Germany or other forms of authoritarian regimes.

So far, we have examined what is arguably the most visible form of power in the form of the nation state and governments, which is often considered to be a form of legitimate or state power. There is perhaps some comfort in conceptualising and defining power within the context of the state and/ or sovereign.

Indeed, this is something we have already covered in part, considering the work of Hobbes and his view that the essence of power is state sovereignty. Specifically, he argued that the purest form of power would be implemented from the position of sovereignty – a form of power he called 'the leviathan' (1651). While the importance of such centralised, or 'legitimate', forms of power is important, such a myopic conceptualisation within the contemporary landscape will prevent us from recognising how other types of power can also result in harm. Returning to Foucault (1991), he argued that there were many forms of force and, therefore, power that transcend notions of state violence. For instance, there is also corporate violence due to enormous concentrations of capital, gender-based violence in the form of patriarchy, the subtle racist violence of real-estate redlining (Rothstein, 2017) and, most recently, mass incarceration (Pfaff, 2017).

Let us continue this discussion with Foucault in mind as we briefly enter the domain of criminology. Edwin Sutherland (1949), upon examining the crimes committed by those working within 'white-collar' professions, defined such individuals as those with high social status and respectability. Rothe and Kauzlarich (2016) provide an important addition to this discussion, noting how crimes committed by such individuals are violations of either implied or delegated trust – a trust which is entwined within the privileged position in which they reside. As echoed earlier, Rothe and Kauzlarich (2016) stress that, within the domains of criminological enquiry, power is 'not an identifiable object; rather, it is produced and reproduced within social structures: power subjugates. Power is exercised, obtained, legitimated, and maintained through capital accumulation of varying types from the economic, military, and political, to social status, discourse, and knowledge' (Rothe and Kauzlarich, 2016, p 4).

Rothe and Kauzlarich (2016) develop this further, stating that crimes of the powerful involve an intense and symbiotic relationship between actors within state, corporate and international financial institutions (p 8). So too, the authors acknowledge the need to include actors operating within the context of organised crime, noting that intense levels of power are required in order to operate, compete against potential rivals and evade detection. While this is acknowledged, this particular book intends to primarily focus on legitimated forms of power that, for the most part, are tightly embedded within the fabric of 'normal' or 'civil' society. The authors also conceptualise crimes of the powerful within the broader political-economic model of neoliberalism (a concept that we will routinely return to throughout this book) in order to demonstrate how such harmful acts stemming from state crime, state-corporate crime, international financial institutions' crime, corporate crime, organised crime, and militia and some transnational crime are enabled and continue to exist almost unabated within a globalised context (p 9). Neoliberalism is characterised by specific attributes, including economic liberalisation measures like privatisation, austerity measures, deregulation, free trade and cuts in government spending. These policies aim to augment the involvement of the private sector in both the economy and society. According to Rothe and Kauzlarich (2016), recognising the seemingly disparate forms of power would neglect to consider the 'symbiotic nature and relationship they have with each other, leading to the systemic, routine production and reproduction of crime and harm' (p 8). This theme of interconnectedness and symbiotic relations will be routinely identified throughout this book as we examine economic, political, cultural and judicial forms of power and authority. With that being said, this book hopes to provide some useful additions to the work of Rothe and Kauzlarich by, as previously stated, presenting the under-acknowledged forms of harm stemming from other sources of power, including the fast-fashion industry, big pharma and big-tech companies. In examining these manifestations of power, we can begin to identify how some of the most significant harms are deeply embedded into the very fabric of normality, which is sustained not by conventional notions of traditional authority or force but by our complicity to consumer ideology that underpins many people's way of life – something that will be explored in greater detail in Chapters 6 and 7.

To summarise this brief conceptual overview of the term 'power', it is evident that this is far from a simple essence that can be neatly understood, recognised or defined. Rather, it is arguable that identifying power is not so dissimilar from the analogy of an iceberg. Similar to an actual iceberg, in which only 10 per cent is visible above the water, resulting in the false assessment of the potential threat to sailors, the remaining 90 per cent is hidden from view and potentially poses the real threat. Despite these conceptual hurdles, though, we have identified that power is, fundamentally, an ability to influence change via a multitude of means and instruments. So too, this does not necessarily mean that power is exclusively within the sole remit of the privileged few, nor is it solely used for negative or harmful purposes. For instance, most recently, the Black Lives Matter movement has assisted in transforming the statistics of police shootings by naming the victims of police brutality and putting in motion more media outlets to take it upon themselves to look into the issue of how certain police officers are misusing their discretionary powers (King, 2018). Power then, in many ways, is an instrument that is neither simply good nor evil, and its potential to produce harm very much lies within the hands that wield it. Perhaps an important addition here, given that we are examining harms generated by those who wield forms of power, is to consider the term 'elite' in conjunction with power.

In sociological theory, the term 'elite' is a small group of dominant, authoritative and influential people who hold a disproportionate amount of capital, privilege, political clout or skill in society. Defined by the Cambridge Dictionary, the 'elite' are 'those people or organisations that are considered the best or most powerful compared to others of a similar type' (Cambridge Dictionary, ND). According to American sociologist C. Wright Mills, there are three branches of the 'power elite'. These are the Political Leadership, the Military Circle, and the Corporate Elite (Mills, 1956). Mills continues, stating that the governing elite in the US predominantly pulls its members from political leaders, as well as close advisers, owners of large corporations, and high-ranking military officers (Mills, 1956). It is important to stress that these groups overlap, and members of such elite circles are inclined to circulate from one sector to another, thus consolidating power in the process. This group of influential individuals with substantial power comprises bureaucratic, corporate, intellectual, military, media and government elites. They wield control over key institutions, and their attitudes, motivations, and actions significantly impact the decision-making of policy makers (Mills, 1956). A study conducted by Dye (2002) further expanded on this, determining that this elite group's characteristics were largely influenced by factors including age (for instance, most corporate leaders were approximately around the age of 60), gender (as of October 2017, only 32 [6.4 per cent] of the Fortune 500 chief executive officers [CEOs] are women), ethnicity (as of October 2017, only 4 [0.8 per cent] of the Fortune 500 CEOs are African American), education (further or advanced degrees often from prestigious institutions where donations are common) and membership to prestigious social clubs (see Zarya, 2017). In essence, such individuals operate and exist within a social strata to which very few have access, and they appear to be characterised by significant economic, political, cultural, educational and social forms of capital. As previously alluded to, such forms of capital are not mutually exclusive, and one form of capital appears to feed into and nourish other forms, such as the economic rewards that tend to be received for those who have tremendous cultural capital (Hollywood stars and fast-fashion businesses, for instance). Suppose we were to imagine that the essence of power is the capacity to influence and change things. In that case, such individuals and groups that fall within this 'elite' status have far more of this essence than those who do not exist within such strata. While we may all have limited capacities to influence and change things at an individual or micro level, what truly separates the elite is their capacity to influence and change things at a far grander, or meso, level. As such, this book is about the harm global social elites of various types can cause with the significant amounts of power they have access to. With this brief conceptual overview now presented, attention will now shift to providing a more nuanced and critical account of violence and the subsequent harm caused. Specifically, we will need to challenge some prevailing mainstream assumptions and perceptions of crime, harm and violence in order to first identify and then address such issues.

The main purpose of this overview was to provide an outline of the scale and nature of the phenomenon of power and that providing a single definition could be counterproductive and myopic in nature and scope. For instance, we have explored how notions of power are, in themselves, neither innately positive nor negative, with a plethora of examples illustrating the social good and harms caused depending on those who yield and use power in its various manifestations, including but not limited to economic, cultural, political, military, legitimatised and non-legitimised manifestations. While we have observed and discussed clearly visible forms of power (perhaps most explicitly in the form of state or legitimated forms of power), we have also witnessed how power can be given by the unwitting consent of the powerless. In essence, the powerless predicate their own feelings of social exclusion by investing meaning into particular narratives or 'truths', thus further legitimising the perceived higher position of the elite class in society. Power, then, is malleable and can manifest in different forms and contexts but, as previously stated, is generally understood as the ability to influence others. While we may all have limited forms of power depending on one's societal position, it was determined that the elite were those who operate and exist within the upper echelons of society and have access to far greater 'reserves' of power than the average person. In social science today, we see power in the end result, the social production, as it were, of the effect. Power determines the capacities, actions, beliefs or conduct of actors. But not all are alike in their ability to possess or wield power. While we might say power is everywhere, it really is not. It is mostly there when people have money, material influence and political influence. The two are often symbiotic and inseparable. Today's power elite are global, and they may not share much beyond vast wealth and influence. Nevertheless, every one of the 2,640 billionaires is inexorably tied to corporate interests.

At this point, it is prudent to critically define what we mean by both 'violence' and 'harm' in order to demonstrate how damage can be caused by those who reside within the elite class before presenting an overview of ultra-realist theory.

2

Sleepwalk Through the Fires: Harm, Violence and Dangerous Subjectivities

So far, we have critically explored notions of power, paying particular attention to the significant amounts often residing with society's elite and upper echelons. While we acknowledge that power can be beneficial and provide the means to promote social good and development, this book is concerned with how such power can, and often is, behind some of the greatest challenges and harms we currently face. In order to articulate, identify and measure the scale of such harms, we must first challenge orthodox perspectives of what we constitute as 'crime'.

It is important to stress that this book is by no means minimising or ignoring the lived realities of those who experience physical or direct forms of violence, crime and harm, but that in order to fully conceptualise the crimes (and non-crimes) of the elite, we must first recognise that such physical manifestations are but one example of 'violence' and criminal harm. Recognising the various forms that violence and crime can take, we will then critically explore the concept of 'harm'. Similar to direct forms of violence, there is perhaps a similar fallacy that harm can also be caused by the actions of a clear and identifiable agent, along with misconceptions as to what actually constitutes harm in itself. With a more critical understanding of both these concepts, attention will then move to how the current political-economic system formulates and generates harmful and dangerous subjectivities that are not afraid of causing and inflicting harm in pursuing their instrumental and expressive interests. With a critical understanding of the core motivational factors behind the actions of certain members of the elite class, along with what constitutes power, violence and harm, we will then be able to move on to more illustrative case examples found within subsequent chapters.

The tapestry of violence

This book focuses on identifying harms caused by those holding tremendous amounts of power due to their position within the elite strata of society. To accomplish this, we need to move beyond orthodox and myopic understandings of the nature of violence and how harm can stem from beyond the actions of clear and readily identifiable agents. For instance, when asked what images spring to mind when asked about violence, most people will often recall examples of extreme physical violence, including assaults, armed robbery, serial murderers, terrorism and, most recently in the UK, knife crime. Such responses are of no great shock or surprise, given that such examples saturate our mainstream media and, to a degree, criminology-related courses. There is perhaps some comfort in conceptualising and recognising violence within such a context. For instance, we can rest easy when we consider society's greatest threat to peace, civility and normality can be pointed out, categorised and punished by the state's criminal justice system. Such forms of violence do not ask too much of us with regard to pondering the nature or philosophy of evil and violent acts, and we can continue to live our lives when we know there are others who prevent, detect and punish such individuals who commit such acts. This is made easier when we consider how the criminal justice system is almost entirely centred upon the criminalisation of physically violent acts. So too, it is important to acknowledge and keep in mind that the criminal justice system is oriented around the individual offender who, equipped with *mens rea*, chooses to engage in criminal behaviour.

Under such stipulations, the individual, depending on the severity of their actions, is then sentenced to a range of punishments for the 'scales of justice' to be brought back into balance. While this book is by no means diminishing the severity of such physically violent acts, it is essential to highlight that many of the harms we will be examining are simply not perceived as harmful by those in the elite strata or, as previously discussed, the general public. Due to this lack of acknowledgement, understanding or disavow (depending on one's position) of such harms, it is no surprise that such harms are also not recognised by the criminal justice system. To begin to identify such harmful acts, we will first need to critically define what we mean by 'violence'.

Violence is often considered to be an essential component of most acts of crime. Violence is often referred to as behaviour involving physical force intended to hurt, damage or kill someone or something. With this in mind, most conceptualisations of violence consist of an identifiable agent inflicting harm on another individual or group. For instance, a husband killing their wife, acts of terrorism and someone paid to kill another individual. One of the central issues with the aforementioned terminology is that it alludes to a common tendency among academics to disregard the philosophy of violence. According to Bufacchi (2005), there are two ways of conceptualising violence. First, there is a 'minimalist conception' that emphasises bodily harm through physical force (Glasser, 1998). There is also the work of Stanko, who states that violence comprises 'any form of behaviour by an individual that intentionally threatens to or does cause physical, sexual, or psychological harm to others or themselves' (Stanko, 2001, p 316). This form of violence is often referred to as being indicative of 'direct violence'. Its foremost distinguishing trait is the fact that most of its outcomes are visible, for example, the bodily results of violent conflicts. Due to its visibility and subsequent media attention, it is frequently assumed that direct violence is the most severe of all conceptualisations, which, according to the Norwegian sociologist Johan Galtung (1969), is not true for it is 'precisely this visibility that makes it easier to identify' (Lynes et al, 2021, p 17). In order to identify harm that is a result of other forms of violence beyond the physical, we need to broaden – at an ontological level – what we mean by 'violence'.

To identify and articulate violence beyond the realms of the individual agent, we need a more wide-ranging conceptualisation that can recognise different types of violence and subsequent harms not recognised by the aforementioned definitions. This latter approach, as noted by Felson (2009), attempts to capture those behaviours that result in harm, though they are 'not necessarily physical' (cited in Ray, 2011, p 9) in nature. Such an approach appeals to Galtung's (1969) concept of 'structural violence', whereby factors such as job insecurity, unemployment, cuts in public spending and dismantling of social welfare (to name but a few) cause social harm and can be considered violent in nature. As noted by Galtung (1969), structural violence is a means to define social arrangements that place individuals and groups in the way of harm. These arrangements are structural since they are ingrained in the political and economic organisation of our social world; 'they are violent because they cause injury to people' (Lynes et al, 2021, p 18). Cooper and Whyte (2022) attempt to 'zoom in' to more specific instances of such forms of systemic violence, arguing that structural violence is too broad to explain specific events, such as the role certain organisations and bodies played prior to the Grenfell tragedy in which 72 people lost their lives. In their analysis of this tragic event, the authors note that the fire was a result of:

[a] form of collective decision-making that we describe as institutional violence; it reflects the routine order and detached administration of a form of violence that is intimately connected to a more insidious targeting of subject groups and populations in ways that produce and increase the likelihood of other, ongoing, violent circumstances occurring. (Cooper and Whyte, 2022, p 207)

With this in mind, we will occasionally oscillate between both structural and institutional forms of violence where relevant, with the latter having utility when examining specific organisations or institutions throughout the latter chapters.

Returning to broader, or structural, forms of violence, Žižek (2008) takes the principles of structural violence but provides a figurative face for its existence: capitalism. Žižek dialectically inverts our orthodox perception of violence as being something that disrupts our sense of 'normality' (consider acts of terror or gang violence, for instance) and instead, the violence that sustains this very sense of 'normality' in the first place. This form of violence is often described as 'something like the notorious "dark matter" of physics, the counterpart to an all-too-visible subjective [direct] violence' (Žižek, 2008, p 2). Specifically, he argues that we need to shine a light on the violence that is 'inherent to the system itself: the violent consequences of the smooth functioning of the capitalist economic and political system' (cited in Oksala, 2011, p 475). This form of violence manifests in the forms of 'exploitation, hunger and poverty, ecological decay, human misery, inadequate welfare systems and systemic inequality' that are needed for the 'machinery' of global capitalism to continue unabated (Oksala, 2011; see also Zizek, 2008). Such violence produced by intrinsic economic structures denotes the harm experienced by individuals and groups who endure structural inequalities in the form of wages (for instance, around one billion people in the world live with less than US$1 per day), income, resources or opportunities. One of the central arguments of Žižek, and perhaps most pertinent to the topics covered in this book, is that we are simply focusing on the wrong issues if we wish to create a more equal and peaceful society. This violence inherent 'to the system itself' is defined by Žižek as 'objective violence'. To surmise, mainstream media, criminal justice systems and consequently the general public are fixated on the violence that disrupts 'normality', forever failing to recognise and even articulate the violence embedded into this very state of normalcy. While many would struggle to identify or choose to recognise such violence, this is only further compounded by those who are marginalised or socially excluded, as they are, due to the very nature of their marginalisation, unable to truly articulate and determine the structural forces that harm them (Treadwell et al, 2013). This is an important conceptual hurdle to overcome, as not taking such a perspective on violence would severely limit our capacity to recognise the various ways harm can manifest.

A pertinent example of this violence embedded in 'normality' is the ever-increasing concern of climate change, largely exacerbated and fuelled by our way of life (Soron, 2007). While the severe impacts of climate change have been well known over several decades (Bonds, 2015), we are now observing abrupt economic impacts and climate disasters (such as the UK's new record-high temperature of 40.3°C in 2022 and serious and severe rainfall deficiencies in Australia). Bonds (2016) notes that 'the bulk of these [climate-related] deaths will be experienced in the Global South, among groups who contributed least to global warming but are also most vulnerable to its effects' (p 10; see also Parr, 2014). While there is indeed a much-needed call for action in the Global North (as of writing, there are also growing occurrences of the Just Stop Oil protests across the UK and Europe), there is a general sense of apathy that will likely not change until such deaths are felt within the more developed nations. Such sentiments were echoed by Gabon's environment minister, who stated that "the world will only take meaningful action on the climate crisis once people in rich countries start dying in greater numbers from its effects" (cited in Greenfield, 2022). Soron (2007) emphasises that the systemic violence of climate change is shaped and energised by the machinery of global capitalism, in which corporate profits, state interest and economic growth have been given a privileged position at the expense of environmental sustainability, equality and justice (see also Klein, 2014).

Alongside these more physical and structural forms of violence, there is also another component to this 'tapestry of violence' (Lynes et al, 2021). Understanding the importance of this third concept of violence, symbolic violence, is critical to understanding how we, as a society, struggle to conceptualise violence beyond physical manifestations. Žižek, building upon the work of Lacan and psychoanalysis, expands upon this notion of symbolic violence, stating that:

> Subjective violence is just the most visible portion of a triumvirate that also includes two objective kinds of violence. First, there is a 'symbolic' violence embodied in language and its forms, what Heidegger would call 'our house of being'. As we shall see later, this violence is not only at work in the obvious – and extensively studied – cases of incitement and of the relations of social domination reproduced in our habitual speech forms: there is a more fundamental form of violence still that pertains to language as such, to its imposition of a certain universe of meaning. (Žižek, 2008, p 1)

For Lacan, the symbolic is the unconscious order of laws, principles, internalised forms of domination and the subsequent absorption into language (Lacan, 1997). Žižek utilises Lacan's definition of the symbolic to demonstrate an unexpressed yet engrained order of power and subjugation. Recuero (2015) states that while objective violence is easily perceived against a background of 'normality', 'it is precisely in this background that symbolic violence stands, sustaining, through language, the current status quo' (p 1). As such, the power of symbolic violence is in its ability to naturalise and legitimise configurations of domination and subsequent inequalities and harms. Within the context of power, symbolic violence denotes the influence and ability that persons and groups exercise due to their elevated status in a particular society's social structure and configuration. As such, this form of violence does not necessitate physical violence to be sustained, and those subjected to it accept this as if it were innate and unavoidable.

Within such discussions of violence, it is important to consider Galtung's (1990) conceptualisation of cultural violence. Cultural violence also serves to provide the pre-context for physically violent acts, along with the reasons for persons or groups to 'destroy each other and to be rewarded for doing so' (Lynes et al, 2021, p 21). As an example of such form of violence, we could consider the use of radios and the dissemination of propaganda that subsequently incited and provoked members of the Hutu population to take part in the massacres of their Tutsi neighbours during the Rwandan genocide of 1993. Alongside this, such forms of cultural violence shape and inform our understanding of violence and influence our responses to such acts. For instance, while we may respond a certain way towards the thought of gang violence or the acts of a lone gunman in a shopping mall, we may respond very differently, if at all, to the threat of thousands of people at risk of freezing to death in their homes due to not being able to pay energy bills in a time companies are recording historic profits (Weaver, 2022), or factory workers committing suicide in China due to work conditions (Merchant, 2017). According to Galtung:

> Cultural violence makes direct and structural violence look, even feel, right – at least not wrong. … One way cultural violence works is by changing the moral colour of an act from red/wrong to green/right or at least to yellow/acceptable; an example being 'murder on behalf of the country as right, on behalf of oneself wrong'. Another way is by making reality opaque, so that we do not see the violent act or fact, or at least not as violent. (Galtung, 1990, pp 291–92)

Taking the above quote into consideration, cultural violence is the dominant narrative that validate, rationalise and legitimise both structural violence and various forms of direct violence, such as state-authorised use of violence, including acts of war, making it seem acceptable or inevitable. For instance, members of society are continually harmed by the results of structural violence and are routinely victims of 'perceived righteous or morally permissible forms of direct physical and psychological violence at the hands of others' (Lynes et al, 2021, p 22) who are often in positions of power.

As you progress through the following chapters, remember the various other forms of violence that may not be readily visible and may be hidden from view. Consider how the multitude of structural and cultural factors may have created vulnerabilities with regard to the victims of harmful practices carried out by the most powerful people and groups in society. In bringing this concise overview of structural and, to a degree, cultural violence to a close, it is important to reiterate that the inequalities and injustices caused by structural violence create the space in which direct (or interpersonal) violence can manifest. As stated by Ray (2011), 'conditions of hunger, sickness and destitution are then "violence", and it is often from such structurally induced conditions that further violence emanates' (p 9). So too, it is now evident that we can experience harm far beyond the direct and physical actions of another, and that many such forms of violence are hidden from view. This book intends to shine a light on such examples of non-physical violence, but to do so, we also need to explore critically what we mean by 'harm'.

Transcending legal definitions

When we discuss notions of 'harm', it is important to briefly underpin such discussions with the understanding of the limitations of criminology and why zemiology is key in filling these conceptual deficiencies. By no means is this suggesting that criminology is redundant, and, as noted by Lacey and Zedner (2012), 'criminology has the vital role to play in ensuring that the normative questions are neither framed nor answered as purely normative or legal issues' (p 177). Instead, it is important to stress the significant contributions both criminology and zemiology can provide when working in unison and towards a common goal. Nevertheless, the following statement by Muncie (2013) encapsulates the need for criminology to look beyond the category of 'crime' if it is ever to truly address and provide meaningful solutions to some of the most significant contemporary issues that we face:

> A social harm perspective is based on the premise that notions of 'crime' offer a particularly narrow version of the range of misfortunes, dangers, harms, risks and injuries that are part of everyday life. A concept of social harm enables criminology to move beyond legal definitions of 'crime' and to acknowledge a wide range of immoral, wrongful and injurious acts that may or may not be deemed illegal but are arguably more profoundly damaging. In doing so, a social harm perspective may require an abandonment of criminology (as it has been conceived). (Muncie, 2013, p 430)

This notion that we must 'abandon' criminology as it currently stands is not unique to contemporary times. At its core, criminologists must continually challenge long-standing assumptions and perspectives as new challenges, conflicts, crises, technologies and inequalities emerge. For instance, Sutherland's (1949) pioneering work on white-collar criminality displayed the limitations of the discipline and stated that criminology was poorly suited to assessing the harms caused by white-collar criminality. This was mainly because such forms of behaviour and activity did not correlate with pre-existing notions of criminality, which were predominantly occupied with examining the actions of those living within the lower economic strata of society. Sutherland's work signified one of the key historical moments in which the discipline's foundations and assumptions of criminality and its corresponding human actors were brought into question. No longer were socially harmful actions relegated to society's poorest, and the discipline was faced with the quagmire of taking the state's definition and codification of criminal behaviour at face value. Schwendinger and Schwendinger (1970), prompted by US foreign policy disasters and the damning legacy of the Vietnam War, continued with this critical perspective by arguing that state institutions that tolerated, maintained or failed to prevent and stop human rights violations, including racism, sexism or poverty, were not only negligent in their civic duty but co-conspirators in crimes against humanity.

Fast forward 26 years and Henry and Milovanovic (1996) developed constitutive criminology, which 'redefines crime as the harm resulting from investing energy in relations of power that involves pain, conflict and injury'. At its essence, such an approach suggests that some people (whom we would conventionally label as criminals) invest much of their time and effort in activities (recognised and codified in law as criminal) that predominantly physically and/or psychologically harm others. Via such a perspective, Henry and Milovanovic define such individuals as 'excessive investors' who have the power to harm others. According to the authors, the way to reduce their extreme investment in such actions is to empower their victims. Thus, rather than seeing punishment in traditional terms, including examples such as incarceration that provides minimal support for the victim, we should see it in terms of 'redistributive justice'. This form of justice reconfigures the primary purpose of justice away from hurting the offender, which propagates the 'cycle of harm' observed in England and Wales' high recidivism rates (Ministry of Justice, 2021). Instead of current criminal justice practices that compound and perpetuate harm, this approach puts forth the notion to 'redress the offence' by 'compensating the victim'. This form of peace-making criminology emphasises reconnecting offenders and their victims in ways that actively seek to redress the balance of harm. At its crux, such a perspective facilitated the discussion that the social world enables a host of hidden harms that deserve criminological consideration. Further still, it facilitated the capacity of criminologists to acknowledge that social and legal institutions often facilitate or embed such harms and thus are not recognised by services working within and as a part of the criminal justice system. Not long after the pioneering work of Henry and Milovanovic, Tifft (1995) drew attention to those crimes and harms that, due to a mixture of lack of legal status or cultural norms and a range of activities, including sexual harassment and racial violence (to name but a few), received very little consideration or attention from agencies of criminal justice. According to Tifft, these omissions are even more egregious, given that they fundamentally threaten human dignity.

This growing body of work provides a fascinating snapshot throughout the recent history of criminology. It demonstrates the continual need to reflect and revise long-standing assumptions and positions related to criminality and harm. Perhaps the most extensive critique of criminology comes from Hillyard and Tombs (2017), who expertly outline the nine key limitations of criminology. First, they argue that crime has no ontological reality and is a social construct. Second, criminology is claimed to perpetuate the myth of 'crime'. In primarily recognising only the harmful actions of the powerless as crime, criminology fails to address the harmful actions of the powerful. We can, of course, witness this preoccupation with relatively powerless actors by simply examining the general demographic characteristics of prisons:

> The Surveying Prisoner Crime Reduction (SPCR) study, a longitudinal cohort study which tracks the progress of newly sentenced adult (18+ years) prisoners in England and Wales, found 24% of prisoners to have lived with foster parents or in an institution (Williams et al, 2012). In terms of living circumstances, SPCR found 16% of prisoners reported having been homeless (either sleeping rough or in temporary accommodation) immediately prior to their incarceration. (Newburn, 2016, p 340)

Third, crime consists of many petty events. For instance, much of what we call crime is petty, for example, shoplifting. These 'crimes' are not as harmful as other events but take up the majority of the time and expenditure of the criminal justice system. Fourth, crime excludes many serious harms. Socially harmful issues facilitated by the powerful, for example economic inequality, the ecological crisis of climate change, and the disregard for the health and safety of employees, have far-reaching consequences than most conventional forms of crime but are routinely ignored. Next is the problematic nature of the construction of crime, in that the law individualises culpability and responsibility; thus, anything that challenges these beliefs, for instance corporations, is not held to account for socially harmful actions. The sixth critique is the harms caused by criminalisation and punishment. Specifically, despite its proclamation to work towards creating a more peaceful and lawful society, the criminal justice system is self-defeating and perpetuates social harm. This is followed by the next critique, which is the ineffectiveness of crime control. In particular, the aims of criminal justice perpetually fail in the mission to reduce reoffending rates, which can be observed in failed rehabilitative initiatives and high recidivism rates. According to Hillyard and Tombs (2017), the next limitation is how crime as a concept legitimises crime control initiatives. The focus on 'crime' perpetuates investment and expansion of crime control, which is heavily inspired and influenced by the right-realist school of thought, perpetuating crime and more 'crime' being recorded. Lastly, and perhaps most pertinently, given the focus of this book, the final critique is how crime as a concept serves to maintain power relations. Social, political and economic discourse deeply harms largely socially excluded, economically marginalised and politically disenfranchised communities. So too, most of the 'crimes' individuals from such communities commit due to these aforementioned points are the primary focus of criminal justice systems, consequently perpetuating unequal power relations. In synthesising these key criticisms towards criminology, it is important to acknowledge that crime is a social construct. By recognising only the harmful actions of the powerless as crime, criminology fails to address the harmful actions of the powerful.

While we have drawn attention to the conceptual deficiencies within criminology, it is important to note that zemiology is not absent of critique. For instance, it is vital that we critically define what we mean by harm and, more importantly, 'social harm'. This is further compounded when we consider the words of Yar (2012), who stated, 'this lack of specificity leaves the concept of harm lacking the very same ontological reality that is postulated as grounds for rejecting the concept of crime' (p 59). It is important to stress here that the notion of 'harm' has been an important and integral component in the formation and delivery of criminal justice systems (Zedner, 2011), 'with the focus typically on identifying the causation of harm to others as a basis for restricting individual conduct, and for protecting individual rights vis-à-vis the state' (Copson, 2018, p 17). Zemiology instead works towards identifying and addressing 'the social determinants of [as opposed to individual culpability for] harms' (Copson, 2018, p 17). In particular, zemiology transcends beyond the actions of the individual as the source of harm and, instead, situates discussions pertaining to social harms that impact human needs. It is important that we make this conceptual differentiation between criminology and zemiology. As Pemberton (2015) states, if we fail to move beyond the rigid identification of harm as the product of individual actions, we will continue not to recognise some of the most significant challenges of our time: 'If the social harm debate remained within the confines of criminology, it would be stuck within a conceptual cul-de-sac, whereby the individualising tendencies of the criminal law would constrain the possibility of producing systematic and holistic analyses of harm' (Pemberton, 2015, p 6).

Further to this point, Pemberton has provided one of the most conceptually in-depth accounts of what constitutes social harm and has proposed an 'ontological' definition composed of three dimensions. First, there are physical harms, which include, but are not limited to, the following:

> Premature death or serious injury through medical treatment; violence such as car 'accidents'; some activities at work (whether paid or unpaid); exposures to various environmental pollutants; domestic violence; child abuse; racist attacks; assaults; illness and disease; lack of adequate food; lack of shelter; or death, torture, and brutality by state officials. (Hillyard and Tombs, 2008, p 15)

Perhaps the most striking example of the importance of acknowledging such harms is that 'between 28,000 and 36,000 deaths a year [are] attributed to long-term exposure' to air pollution (Public Health England, 2019). Another poignant example is research conducted at University College London on the impact of austerity, which reported that an estimated 120,000 deaths could be linked to health and social care cuts (Watkins et al, 2017). These two examples are in stark contrast to the recorded rate of homicide: 'The incidence rate for homicide remains very low, with 9.9 homicides recorded per million population during the year ending March 2021' (Office for National Statistics, 2022).

The second type of harm is autonomy harm, which, at its crux, are those obstacles and challenges that present only limited or no opportunities for self-actualisation. Within such a conceptualisation, poverty may be understood as harmful because of the significant number of requirements or needs that those living within the upper echelons of society (including the elite) take for granted or as a given. For instance, within such economically marginalised groups, 'food, shelter, sanitation, healthcare, [and] education' (Pemberton, 2008, p 86) are severely limited or non-existent (depending on the level of economic exclusion). Drawing upon the work of Doyal and Gough's (1991) theory of human need, Pemberton states that we can witness how such forms of harm can severely limit one's ability to achieve autonomy and reach their fullest potential.

Third is defined by Pemberton as relational harms, which consist of the harms caused by the damaging effects of social exclusion and stigma. Specifically, Pemberton (2015) states that 'relational harms result from either enforced social exclusion from social networks, or the injurious nature of misrecognition' (p 105). In its most extreme manifestations, social isolation can result in tremendous harm with regard to the lack of informal and formal support networks and the disintegration of community values, and assists to enable and conceal other harms. As noted by Pemberton (2015), 'autonomy and relational harms are less obviously injurious than physical harms' (p 105). However, similar to Galtung's concept of structural violence, it is precisely this lack of visibility that makes them so dangerous.

With regard to the 'social' component of harm, it is important to acknowledge again the work of Pemberton, who notes that such harms are 'socially mediated' and, as such, are perceived as 'preventable harm' in that these are entirely foreseeable and preventable in a more ethical and moral society. This brings us nicely to the emerging deviant leisure perspective outlined by Raymen and Smith (2019b), who note that socially accepted and normalised forms of leisure, such as the night-time economy, legalised gambling, tourism and lifestyle drugs, cause a range of harm. Firstly, there are subjective forms of harm that 'involve an easily identifiable perpetrator visiting harm upon a clearly identifiable victim in action related to a clearly defined leisure activity' (Smith, 2016, p 7). Second, there are environmental harms that consist of those ecological damages caused in the pursuit of leisure activities, including, for instance, the rising levels of waste on beaches. Third, socially corrosive harms fundamentally dissolve notions of community and actively promote exclusion as an important demarcation of the 'haves' and 'have-nots'. An example of this, according to Smith (2016), is 'the creation of artificial scarcity, the privation of that which would otherwise be plentiful and free to the public' (p 9). Lastly, there are embedded harms, which are 'embedded within legitimate consumer markets and while imbued with potential for the creation of malleable identities based on the notion of cool, are deserving of closer criminological scrutiny' (p 9). Again, the gambling industry, now at the fingertips of everyone with a smartphone and routinely advertised online, including in the form of YouTube advertisements, are at the heart of a myriad of individual and social harms. Including such a wide range of harms provides the means to adequately identify how the elite and most powerful can cause injuries far beyond just physical manifestations. It is important to stress that, returning to the domain of criminology, the zemiological focus on harm is by no means designed to omit or neglect the significance of accountability for individual acts that result in various forms of harm, but instead build upon and enhance the social sciences to recognise, identify and subsequently address harms that stem beyond the actions of an individual. Instead, as noted by Hillyard et al (2004):

> To utilise the social as a departure for explanation and theorising need not, and for us does not, entail a rejection of the need to account for human agency. But it is to accept a view of the world that sees human agency as highly delimited by structures, structures which must be known and of which we must provide accurate accounts. (Hillyard et al, 2004, p 271)

Again, zemiology and the 'social harm perspective is not necessarily an abolition of crime nor the criminal justice system' (Copson, 2018, p 19), but instead carefully identifies and examines various inequalities, social injustices and economic ideologies that generally underpin and fuel traditional forms of state-recognised acts of criminality. As stated by Copson (2018), only in this reduction of social harms can we truly begin to 'punish individuals for their culpable acts' (p 19) and be properly informed of the significant social harms that are routinely ignored or, due to the lack of such understanding, are unable to be articulated. It is also worth recognising that criminology and zemiology, despite seemingly shared general goals, have routinely come into 'conflict' about what the approach to tackling such prevailing issues should be. For instance, both are indeed critical of the role and practices of the state and criminal justice system (with particular reference to critical strands of criminology). However, discrepancies appear to be most apparent in what should be done to improve current state approaches to both crime and social harms. Despite these apparent issues, it is perhaps advantageous to take the words of Copson (2018) into consideration as we travel through the various chapters and case examples of this book:

> Rather than denying this debate through the collapsing of one perspective into the other, or polarising them into hostile camps of mutual antipathy, it is, perhaps, incumbent upon all critical scholars to act as 'democratic under-labourers' (Locke, [1690] 1975 cited in Loader and Sparks, 2011: 124), recognising our sites of divergence, and fostering dialogue between them if we are to achieve our shared goals and effect meaningful change. (Copson, 2018, pp 20–21)

Such 'fostering' of dialogue between the two fields of study to push beyond this antipathy referred to by Copson and an attempt to result in meaningful developments that assist both disciplines' shared goals can be seen in the work of Raymen (2022). Raymen, in *The Enigma of Social Harm*, provides arguably the most sophisticated and critical examination of zemiology's attempt to provide a philosophically robust ontology of harm. Raymen demonstrates that all previous attempts, including the aforementioned points by Pemberton (2015) and Canning and Tombs (2021), are fundamentally influenced and shaped by liberalism. While we cannot provide the sheer breadth of Raymen's thesis here, the crux of the argument is that as a society, we have been strongly influenced by liberal principles, emphasising individual choice and pluralism over shared objectives, and due to this, we are currently missing a crucial aspect when it comes to social harm. We lack a unified vision of the human and social good, a coherent and rational framework for defining this common standpoint, and a solid ethical foundation beyond mere rights-based ethics (in his work, Raymen refers to Neo-Aristotelian ethics with a focus on the telos or shared good as one possible solution). Consequently, various parties relativise harms, while others assert them authoritatively using an emotivist approach (Raymen, 2022). All the various definitions and typologies place emotivism and the individual's subjective experiences and perceptions at the forefront. While such an approach may seem intuitive given the context of many such discussions, it ultimately results in extreme emotive and subjective relativism full of inherent antagonisms and contradictions.

We recognise that some of our discussions in this book are not currently criminalised. Yet, the manifestation of extreme power for nefarious purposes that does untold damage to others who lack their material wealth, influence and control could, in any instance, be a crime. Indeed, if crime has any use or function, it should be as a form of collective moral enterprise that keeps such behaviours in check. That this only happens sometimes shows the limitations of (Western) nation states, not in the excessive authority they wield, but the permissiveness they show when it comes to the most powerful actors within and without when they have the wealth and status. In the West today, the concern remains the excessive and arbitrary state, not state permissiveness, but this permissiveness damages. We hope to reconfigure the debate and consider how crime can be functional. We need crime to keep power in check.

This brief introduction to harm and social harm consists of a configuration of social, environmental, economic and psychological damage imposed on society, either intentionally or unintentionally. So too, it is a concept that assists criminology in transcending outside legal descriptions of 'crime' to include those harms that are not necessarily recognised by the state or orthodox and administrative forms of criminology. With an overview of the core components of power and how violence can manifest in ways far beyond physical acts, we can now observe the range and types of social harm such forms of violence can generate. Specifically, it was determined how physical acts of violence and subsequent harm are but one 'colour' on a tapestry that includes 'colours' far beyond the normative understandings of such issues. While it is understandable that people tend to focus on those extreme acts of violence that disrupt normality (such as serial killers, knife crime and acts of terrorism) due to the perceived news value, we should also consider those acts of violence and subsequent harm that fail to make the headlines and, for some, that are inherent within normality itself. Despite this need to re-orientate this discussion, we continually fail to properly identify, articulate and critically discuss these under-acknowledged forms of violence. With this in mind, this book will attempt to draw much-needed attention to such harms often stemming from the upper echelons of society and pull such damaging activities out of the backdrop of normality it so comfortably hides and nestles within.

A criminology fit for purpose: ultra-realism

To critically examine and frame the subsequent discussions, it is important to provide a contemporary theoretical framework that transcends normative accounts of human actions and behaviours within a 'civilised' society. So too, it is imperative that we avoid falling into the trap of many branches of critical criminology, which generally follow the 'cliché that the crimes of the powerful cause more harm than the crimes of the powerless' (Hall and Winlow, 2018, p 48). For instance, as noted by Hall and Winlow (2015), critical criminology's notion of how the demonisation of the poor at the hands of the economic, cultural and political elite resulted in a 'divide and conquer' of societies most vulnerable is an important if rather narrow position. This, they argue, obscures the deeper, more sophisticated and important analysis of ideology that explains why people experiencing poverty collude in their own alienation and do not stand up to the ruling class in a more organised and effective way (p 39). So too, other branches of critical criminology, including cultural Marxism, have tended to assume that 'power' is universally associated with domination (Hall and Winlow, 2015). Alongside this, structural critical criminology's primary focus is on how existing laws provide far too much attention to the activities of the poor rather than the careful scrutiny of enforcement or regulations towards the more powerful, which also raises important issues. For instance, such an approach runs the risk of severely neglecting the very serious harms that the poor and powerless can commit (for instance, murder and assault) and disregarding the lived reality and injuries caused to victims of such acts (Lea and Young, 1984). As such, this book does not necessarily attempt to 'point the finger' at individuals who fall within the elite class, as to do so would be 'simply to lobby for a political reorganisation of the socio-economic culture' (Hall and Winlow, 2015, p 41). Further to this, and in line with the ultra-realist perspective, it would be pertinent to 'hold to account not just those who dominate in the current social structure but the whole liberal-capitalist way of life and its core drives, dreams, desires, subjectivities and culture' (p 41). At its crux, the ultra-realist perspective will provide the nuanced and holistic account of modern-day harmful subjectivities that exist in a system that promotes individualism and intense competition. Such a system provides the means for few to achieve tremendous wealth and power and fundamentally prevents those less fortunate from forming meaningful opposition. By adopting such a position, we can begin to see the 'cultural scripts' and the key features that connect those willing to inflict harm on others in the pursuit of their own interests in all strata of society, while also not disregarding the very real harms caused by those who lack the same levels of resources and power found within the elite class. We can, in simple terms, look up and look down.

In commencing this brief overview of ultra-realism, it is important to critically examine some long-standing views about modern and, more specifically, 'civilised' society. Specifically, there is a general acceptance of the idea that homicide and rates of physical violence have declined as societies have developed and evolved. From the 1300s, beginning in England and appearing later in Europe, interpersonal violence in public places consistently declined until the mid-1950s, and a similar thing happened in other capitalist nations. Some argue that this was an indicator of society becoming more civilised. No longer were we in a situation akin to philosopher Thomas Hobbes' theoretical 'state of nature' in which it was every person for themselves, living in constant threat of violence from others in our attempts to secure the resources we needed to live. As nations began to organise themselves around the principles of centralised government, more precise rules and codes around behaviour began to take root and were formalised through criminal law (Pinker, 2011). The state emerged as a protector of the people, and citizens agreed to give up some of their freedoms by deferring to the authority of the state. The state would protect people through mechanisms such as the criminal justice system; in return, they would behave civilised. Indeed, Elias (1994) described the civilising process – where the state became the only social actor who could legitimately use violence through punishment and war – to keep all citizens safe. The state, therefore, had a monopoly on violence, which, Elias argued, led to greater self-control and fewer violent altercations. As such, when people know what the rules are, know what is expected of them and know what will happen if they disobey them, they will be considerably less likely to engage in physically violent acts. According to ultra-realists, one of the central limitations is that Elias' approach to conceptualising the civilising process is 'the presence of some sort of suprahuman teleological orientation' (Hall, 2007, p 85) underpinning its arguments. One of the fundamental issues with this approach is that, according to Hall (2007), it would appear that Elias has either 'unhelpfully naturalised the relationship between pacification and civilisation or conflated the terms themselves' (p 85). Hall continues, stating that:

> This rests on a weak notion of a natural, universal psychological aversion to violence and a natural, universal empathy expressed in the guilt felt by knowledge of the pain and fear it creates in others. This is a dangerous assumption: it allows us to take our eye off the maintenance of the socio-economic environment required for the establishment and reproduction of the sensibilities required to make these psychic conditions and social interactions possible. (Hall, 2007, p 85)

This brings us to transcendental materialism, which argues that human subjects are hard-wired for plasticity (Johnston, 2008). We are extremely malleable and, as a result, can situate into drastically diverse societal, cultural and economic environments. According to Raymen and Kuldova (2020), 'drives, desires, and the anxieties at the core of the subject are always in tension with one another, and always accessible to the symbolism of the external world' (p 249). Particular drives can become prominent while others remain latent as they are stirred in diverse ways by the pre-existing symbolic order. Hall and Winlow (2015) develop this further, stating that these symbolic orders can be conservative, hierarchical and regressive, or they can be 'reflexive, progressive and egalitarian if they leave sufficient space in which the subject can freely move' (cited in Raymen and Kuldova, 2020, p 249). The crux of this approach is that for the subject driven to avoid a traumatic encounter with the Lacanian Real, any symbolic order is better than no symbolic order at all. Consequently, this explanation of subjectivity does not follow the philosophical ideal that suggests a natural essence of inherent goodness or intrinsic selfishness acting as a driving life force at the core of subjectivity, 'one which is entirely separate from and pre-exists the subject's entry into the social world' (Raymen and Kuldova, 2020, p 248). In essence, be it pro-social or violent behaviour, there is no embedded propensity towards such actions, but instead, amorphous libidinal energy in which complex, conflicting drives, desires and symbols can be reconfigured, depending on one's environment.

This brings us to the central criticism of the civilising process, with the decline in crime being questioned by many. Some scholars argued that while there may have been an overall decline in violence, this was not evenly distributed across the social class spectrum or throughout all localities within nations. Indeed, there were significant spikes in violence and homicide rates in particular spaces and places, which went against the overall trend of decline (Leyton, 1986; see also Mares, 2009). In order to understand such statistical observations, along with a more nuanced account of violence consisting of more symbolic manifestations, Hall (2012a) proposes an alternative interpretation to the civilising process, which he terms 'pseudo-pacification'. This concept centres on the idea that harm in the form of fatal violence may have declined, but in other forms, it continues to exist. The values and beliefs that underpinned people's decisions to physically harm or kill have not gone away – they have simply been repositioned and repurposed. Hall claimed that the decline in fatal violence was not attributable to civility or progress but out of necessity to create favourable conditions for a market economy (Hall, 2012a). Trade could not prosper if people felt the constant threat of physical violence from others. In order to do business, a non-violent environment was required. Legal frameworks that outlawed physical violence emerged, paving the way for trade and exchange in the early days of capitalist, market economies. However, the individualistic pursuit of profit also meant that people could not simply act in kind, altruistic ways in their dealings – if so, their businesses would not survive. Therefore, people retained elements of aggression, but this did not manifest as physical violence. It emerged as competition cloaked in performances of politeness, 'good manners' and etiquette – a much more civilised form of conflict. According to this process, the increasing competitive individualism and pursuit of wealth and material security in the economic and socio-cultural spheres was a conversion, 'but one of amorphous libidinal energy in which complex, conflicting drives, desires and symbols were reconfigured as they faced a future in the new and uncertain context of a burgeoning urban market economy' (Raymen and Kuldova, 2020, pp 250–251). While we retain our harmful libidinal drives, its enactment shifts. Indeed, while homicide rates steadily declined throughout modernity, property crimes and unethical behaviour increased (Ellis, 2019). In Hall's terms, we have not been 'civilised' or 'pacified'; we have been 'pseudo-pacified'.

Hall's thesis draws attention to the nature of political economy in understanding individual subjectivity – something altogether neglected by Elias and Pinker. Hall and Wilson (2014) argue that neoliberal capitalism contains inherently harmful elements. As such, those who harm and kill cannot be understood as aberrant deviations from 'the rest of us' but as the extreme embodiment of and conformity to contemporary life's ideologies and values. More recently, Ellis (2019) has applied the pseudo-pacification thesis to an understanding of the increase in homicide rates in England and Wales from 2014 to 2018. Ellis argues that government austerity policies in the aftermath of the 2008 financial crash have fundamentally changed the relationship between the individual and the state, whereby older universalistic and collectivist approaches to governance have been replaced with a much more individualistic and atomised perspective. As such, the already marginalised and disconnected became increasingly likely to act on violent impulses: 'The latest increases in lethal and serious violence do not represent subcultural deviations amongst "outsiders" from a "civilising" value system that restrains primal violent urges and maintains civilising sensibilities. Rather, they appear as unrestrained and often quite extreme manifestations of liberal capitalisms' disavowed dark heart, (Ellis, 2019, p 874).

Consequently, eruptions of physical violence can be seen as a breakdown of the pseudo-pacification process – a condition in which the 'stimulation of these violent desires and energies come to the surface, breaking through the "electrical wire" which provides the ethico-legal restraints which harness and direct such energies' (Raymen, 2018, p 437). This is echoed by Hall (2012a), who states:

> The historical evidence does not point to a general 'civilising process' … but a complex psychosocial process in which direct and unashamed violence and intimidation were gradually sublimated into a multitude of criminalised and legalised forms of exploitation, deception, and appropriation, which ran alongside and in tension with what can only be described as a sort of insulating sleeve of ethico-legal restraints, like

the thick but flexible insulation around an electrical wire carrying a powerful current. (Hall, 2012a, p 32)

Fundamentally, the transition into deregulated and neoliberal capitalist realism (Fisher, 2009) has repurposed these violent libidinal drives while, at a macro level, dissolved notions of community values, welfare and support provisions, and intensified privatisation of traditionally state-owned agencies proliferate. In the absence of stable economies and pro-social systems, the space for physical violent outbursts will continue to proliferate. Here, we turn to the work of Heidegger (Wrathall, 2005), who argues that the essence of violence has nothing to do with ontic violence, suffering, war, destruction, and so on. Essential violence, according to Heidegger, is something that grounds or at least opens up the space for the explosions of ontic or physical violence itself. As noted by Hall and Winlow (2018), 'anxious populations are supporting governments that promise state hardening, privatism, securitisation, militarisation, and strict border controls' (p 54). This, they argue, is the creation of cultural hardening, established and repeated by deepened exclusionary sentimentalities and subjective toughening as people become progressively competitive and self-interested (Crank and Jacoby, 2014). These cultural currents are beginning to break down the pseudo-pacification process, which means that more individuals are likely to express anger and hostile competitive urges in physical rather than sublimated symbolic forms (Hall, 2014). This breakdown in the pacification process is subsequently tied to the decline in community values, and the 'most selfish, predatory, reactionary and short-term elements ascended to the top and glorified by the media, beg to influence the general cultures in the USA and Britain' (Hall, 2007, p 83). Through this personal 'emancipation' to strive towards individual success and increased encouragement of consumption, the civilising process was, Hall argues, no longer necessary in an age of 'globalised flexible accumulation and competition between permanently uprooted individuals' (Hall, 2007).

In attempting to explain this rise in interpersonal violence and the proliferation of harm in contemporary society, it is important to consider the significance of special liberty – a consequence of capitalism that has, according to Hall and Wilson (2014), stripped away many of the pre-capitalist, collectivist ideals and in its stead created an environment in which the right to express one's motivations and yearnings freely is continually exerted. This breakdown in the pacification process has created the 'dark side' of liberal individualism, a sociopathic 'anti-ethos that consists of a sense of entitlement felt by an individual who will risk harm to others to further his own instrumental or expressive interests' (Hall and Winlow, 2015; see also Hall, 2012a). Writing in this tradition, Winlow (2014) has also suggested that 'the individual is therefore as free as the external control system allows him to be to act with impunity, free to rob, plunder and destroy without ever acknowledging the harms their activities visit upon others' (Winlow, 2014, p 175).

As stressed by Hall (2015), this form of special liberty is not limited to the structural elite class, and this breakdown in the pseudo-pacification process and the rise of the neoliberal political economy has resulted in this form of liberty existing within the 'general cultural current' (p 129). Specifically, individuals from all echelons of society have the permission and the inclination to inflict harm on others, 'to simply get things done so that the competitive logic of business can be served' (Hall, 2015). This mindset – shaped and encouraged by the contemporary political economy – vertebrates throughout the entire social structure, from corporate boardrooms to ghettos to the privacy of one's home. Hall states that:

> To the subject of special liberty, who regards himself as a miniaturised sovereign state, the everyday 'other' individual is a sublimated variant of *homo sacer*, a worthless unit not necessarily to be killed – although in extreme cases this does happen – but to be exploited with impunity in order to serve the logic of the market and the enrichment of the master. (Hall, 2015, p 129).

Such an understanding assists in recognising how economic transformations have generated the ideal environment where people are fundamentally willing to inflict or allow harm to be caused in the pursuit of their enrichment. Fundamentally, the logic of such a system that pits individuals against each other produces 'winners' who 'ascend into an exclusive metropolitan cloud' (Atkinson, 2020). At the same time, 'the intensification of the socioeconomic competition between atomised and largely apolitical individuals creates an increasing supply of losers amongst the working class' (Hall and Winlow, 2015, p 120). According to the authors, such spaces are defined as the 'shadow economy' – spaces comprised of relatively unregulated parafunctional socio-economic spaces in which individuals either engage in depressive hedonistic activities, fantasied nationalism or illegal entrepreneurship in illicit markets. Hall and Winlow continue, stating that:

> These unregulated spaces of the cloud and the grounded shadow-economy are conducive to the operation of special liberty, the sentiment that one is entitled to do whatever it takes to participate in profitable market activity and achieve economic security and social status, even if it risks the infliction of harm on others and their social and physical environments. (Hall, 2012a cited in Hall and Winlow, 2015, p 120)

In essence, we need to acknowledge that there is little difference with regard to the motivations behind individuals – rich or poor – who are willing to either inflict or allow harm to be felt by others in the selfish and individualist pursuit of instrumental or expressive interests. This is indicative of the social dispersal and transmission of the 'dark side of the bourgeois competitive-individualistic mentality, constantly practised by big business and professionally hidden from view by politicians and mass media' (Hall and Winlow, 2015). Consequently, the harms of the elite and the motivational forces behind them are becoming the model of 'crimes of everyone', though at vastly different scales and contexts given the sheer disparity between those in the 'clouds' and those living precariously in the realm of the 'shadow economy' (Hall and Winlow, 2015). When we consider the sheer impact of consumer ideology in which feelings of anxiety, perpetual desires and detrimental individualism are cultivated to serve the logic of the market, these conditions 'combine to create dangerous subjectivities fixated on the achievement of material and symbolic survival within a brutally competitive landscape' (Tudor, 2018, p 13). Further to this and illustrative of such conditions, Tudor's (2018) study on fraud demonstrates how such offenders justify their actions based on notions of 'toxic sovereignty'. Specifically, one of the key features of neoliberalism (and arguably an attractive one to entrepreneurs) is the emphasis on individual liberties, and as such, they are 'considered to be a sovereign entity whose freedoms must be protected from excessive regulation or arbitrary interference' from the state (Tudor, 2018, p 8). Unfortunately, when we consider the previous discussions pertaining to the detrimental effects of consumer ideology and the central drivers of competition at the core of late capitalism, there are those who use such notions of individual freedoms to justify their harmful activities. Tudor continues, stating that:

> Both business and consumption were central to the way in which the fraudsters defined themselves (Tudor forthcoming) and both arenas represented areas of life in which they expected to be granted freedom to 'realise their potential'. As a result of the primacy accorded to their quest for profit, distinction and pleasure in their narratives, the respondents found it inconceivable that their efforts might be tempered by any considerations which might limit their efficacy in allowing them to reach their goals. Consequently, they were unwilling to accept the limitations necessitated by compliance with legal and moral frameworks. (Tudor, 2018, p 14)

Tudor's findings run congruent and support the ultra-realist position, in which the participants of this study point towards the ruthless and competitive economy and business environment in which they operated. In essence, such individuals do not necessarily see their actions as anomalies but, instead, as conforming actions that were necessary to survive and not generate 'disadvantage[s] in business' (p 15). Tudor's findings further echo the importance of consumerism for such individuals, with participants repeatedly attempting to demonstrate the lifestyles and consumer goods their activities bought them. Tudor elaborates further, stating that such emphasis on consumption 'was underpinned by a much deeper sense of anxiety owing to the fact that they felt their access to these goods was essential to their existence; their symbolic survival was dependent upon it' (p 18). Perhaps one of the most important findings of Tudor's study was that such forms of criminality was an expression of special liberty characterised by 'this excessive form of sovereignty', which was 'symbolised by the renunciation of limitation of their business pursuits' (p 19). While the participants of Tudor's study were convicted of fraud, such findings can be extrapolated to make sense of how those who operate within the 'metropolitan cloud' not only reached such lofty heights, but also why and how a plethora of harms originate from such lords of the new kleptocracy who hide in the shadows to the lowly operator on the streets willing to get their hands dirty for just a few dollar bills of vast and inconceivable sums of sullied money that is now conquering the globe (Burgis, 2020).

To summarise this theoretical overview, ultra-realism provides a much-needed contemporary account of late capitalist society. In particular, it fundamentally brings into doubt the supposed 'civility' of Western culture and how socio-economic and political forces have created an anxious and ontologically insecure populace that struggles to relate and see each other as equals as the logic of the market re-orientates and redefines such relations to rivalries and as a basis for competition. So too, the classic liberal emphasis on individual sovereignty has been polluted by excessive consumption and the right to pursue instrumental and expressive interests at any cost. As such, ultra-realism provides a holistic theoretical position in which to ensure that we do not examine the crimes and harms of the elite within a 'vacuum' but instead as a result of 'the whole liberal-capitalist way of life and its core drives, dreams, desires, subjectivities and culture' in which we are all immersed and live within (Hall and Winlow: 2015, p 41).

Providing the theoretical 'Rosetta Stone' for the critical understanding of violence and subsequent harm is essential. Moreover, in taking a more holistic approach to the nature of violence, in which physical manifestations represent only the tip of the iceberg, it is only then we can begin to make sense of more structural and cultural forms of violence that are not only difficult to identify but also deeply embedded into the very fabric of 'normality' – spaces in which we normally seek solace and escape from the crimes that dominate news headlines and television screens. With a more complex interpretation of violence in place, we can now recognise how harms, particularly social harms, can also be experienced without the need for a readily identifiable subject. With the inclusion of zemiology, we can also begin to identify some of the limitations of orthodox and some critical strands of criminology and that including a social harms approach is integral to overcoming some of these discipline deficiencies. With just a few illustrative examples presented in this chapter so far, it is evident that we need to fundamentally re-orientate our prevailing assumptions about what actually generates the most harm in society and consider that perhaps current state approaches to criminality are both potentially harmful in itself but also ill-equipped to address some of the most systemic and pertinent dangers we currently face. Lastly, we explored the significance of ultra-realist theory in making sense of how current political and socio-economic arrangements provide the ideal environment for generating and propagating potentially harmful subjectivities within all strata of society. In particular, we have witnessed how long-standing assumptions of the supposed 'civility' of contemporary Western capitalism are flawed and that the notion of individual liberty has provided the justifications and rationales to inflict or allow harm to occur in the pursuit of individualistic and selfish interests.

We will now embark on our exploration of the realm of corporate giants armed with a deeper comprehension of power dynamics, as well as a critical and up-to-date perspective on violence, harm and dangerous subjectivities.

3

The Era of Corporate Giants

If you stop to think about it, corporations are deeply embedded in almost every facet of our lives. While there are obvious examples associated with consumerism with our food, water, clothing, entertainment, fuel, tourism and technological devices, corporations have also encroached in other areas where the state, typically, has a vested interest. Let us take, for instance, criminal justice. Most are aware that private prisons owned by corporations play an integral role in incarceration in North America, with 27 states and the federal government incarcerating 96,370 people in such prisons in 2021 (Kristen and Monazzam, 2023). Perhaps less well known is that there are similar privatised prisons in the UK, with 14 currently operating (Damji, 2022). Naturally, issues of such privatisation have raised questions pertaining to the primary motivation of profit, which in turn incentivises incarceration, the quality of service provided due to cost-cutting measures and the risk of corruption due to potential influence over policy makers to ensure continued business (Taylor and Cooper, 2008; Daems and Beken, 2018). Companies are also profiting from producing a range of prison equipment; for instance, the Pakistan-based company Fine Cotton Textiles produces prison jumpsuits. One of the company's owners, Ahmad Afzal, noted in 2016 that 'because crime is crazy and there are lots of inmates. … We are happy, the number [of customers] is increasing every day' (cited in Neate, 2016). There is so much money to be made in the production of prison equipment that there are now even conventions for companies to promote their products to eager law enforcement and corrections staff, with one such conference in 2015 being noted for exhibiting 'a $580,000 prison bus with bullet-resistant windows and high-technology onboard surveillance systems to restraint chairs and work-out equipment' (Webster, 2019).

We also have to consider the incredibly powerful and influential corporations behind the medicines prescribed by doctors, with companies such as Pfizer, Merck and Co., AbbVie, Johnson & Johnson, Roche and AstraZeneca often listed as some of the wealthiest pharmaceutical companies in the world.

In the book *Bad Pharma: How Drug Companies Mislead Doctors and Harm Patients* (Goldacre, 2012), the British physician and academic Ben Goldacre suggests the pharmaceutical industry is harmful and, in particular, that its relationship with the medical profession and the extent to which it controls academic research into its own products should be the subject of more scrutiny. Goldacre notes that the whole edifice of medicine was broken because the pharmaceutical industry systematically distorted the evidence on which it is based. He criticised the industry, which he said finances most clinical trials into its own products and much of doctors continuing education. He suggests that clinical trials are often badly managed and based on poor research, clinical trials are conducted on small groups of unrepresentative subjects and negative data is routinely withheld, and independent academic papers may be planned and even ghost-written by pharmaceutical companies or their contractors without proper disclosure.

Certainly, there are numerous examples of harmful practices in the medical and pharmaceutical industries, the harms of which often only become fully apparent many years later. One example was in the late 1950s and early 1960s, where the use of the drug thalidomide by women who were pregnant or who subsequently became pregnant resulted in the 'biggest man–made medical disaster ever', with more than 10,000 children born with a range of severe deformities, as well as thousands of miscarriages (Omoto and Lurquin, 2015). The drug was licensed in 1958 and withdrawn in 1961 in the UK. Nearly half of the roughly 2,000 babies born with defects passed away within a few months, leaving 466 survivors as of 2010. In 1968, following an extended advocacy campaign, the Distillers Company, which had distributed the drug in the UK (and is now part of the multinational alcoholic drinks group Diageo), eventually reached a compensation settlement for the UK victims and paid out approximately £28 million in compensation.

During the 1970s and 1980s, a total of 4,689 individuals with haemophilia and other bleeding disorders were exposed to human immunodeficiency virus (HIV) and hepatitis viruses through tainted clotting factors, leading to infections (The Haemophilia Society, ND). Several individuals unknowingly infected their partners, often due to being unaware of their own infection. Consequently, over 3,000 people have lost their lives; out of the 1,243 individuals who contracted HIV, less than 250 remain alive. We now know that 380 children with bleeding disorders were infected with HIV. Many people who did not have a bleeding disorder were infected with hepatitis C because of blood transfusions during that period. A large number were unaware of their infection for many years before diagnosis. It is not known how many people were infected.

Factor concentrate was manufactured by combining human blood plasma from as many as 40,000 donors and concentrating it to obtain the necessary clotting factor. Even a single contaminated sample had the potential to infect the entire batch. Since blood and blood products were acknowledged carriers of viruses like hepatitis, utilising pooled blood products significantly elevated the risk of infection. Moreover, when the UK encountered a scarcity of domestically produced factor concentrate, imports from the US were relied upon, which sourced blood from high-risk paid donors, including prisoners and drug addicts, further heightening the risk of contamination.

Despite the risks involved, prominent clinicians and governments overlooked them and neglected to implement suitable measures to discontinue using these products and switch to safer alternatives. Additionally, pharmaceutical companies and leading clinicians withheld essential information regarding these risks from patients and patient groups, failing to provide them with the necessary knowledge to make informed decisions about their health and treatments.

In 1975, the then health minister, Dr David Owen, declared that funds had been allocated to ensure the UK achieved 'self-sufficiency' in blood products. However, this objective was never realised. Subsequently, outbreaks of hepatitis started to emerge in haemophilia centres across the nation. In 1982, the first death of a man with haemophilia, infected by acquired immune deficiency syndrome (AIDS), was reported in the US. This marked the initial warning regarding the potential risk of contracting AIDS from contaminated blood products. Additional alerts were issued in the medical journal *The Lancet* and by the World Health Organization in 1983, emphasising the need to caution people with haemophilia about the dangers associated with these products.

Before 2022, individuals affected by the contaminated blood scandal in the UK received no financial compensation. In 2022, Sir Brian Langstaff, Chair of the Infected Blood Inquiry, proposed an interim compensation amount of £100,000 to all individuals currently registered on a UK infected blood support scheme. The government accepted this recommendation, and payments were disbursed in October 2022. However, certain groups, such as bereaved parents and children, were still not included in these compensation payments.

In 2004, the government established an additional fund to provide compensation to individuals who had contracted hepatitis C. Subsequently, in 2017, infected blood support schemes in England, Wales, Northern Ireland and Scotland replaced these funds and trusts. During the same year, Prime Minister Theresa May announced the launch of a statutory public inquiry into the contaminated blood scandal. The inquiry officially began in 2018 and continued with April 2019 to January 2023 hearings. Tragically, since the inquiry's announcement, it is estimated that more than 500 individuals affected by the scandal passed away, and further lives were lost before the inquiry concluded its investigations in autumn 2023. Of course, this is but one example; in the US, the Sackler family-owned Purdue Pharma, the company that sold OxyContin, a high-strength painkiller that arguably fuelled the US opioid epidemic, perhaps responsible for the deaths of more than half a million Americans over two decades, is another (National Institute on Drug Abuse, ND).

Pfizer is expected to generate substantial profits from its COVID-19 vaccine. However, the most significant long-term advantage for the company could be the positive public relations (PR) it has gained as a consequence. The PR was highly necessary as before COVID-19, Pfizer had a negative reputation compared with other pharmaceutical companies. Pfizer was compelled to recall an artificial heart valve from the market due to defects that were linked to several hundred fatalities. In 1986, the US Food and Drug Administration withdrew its approval for the product. After facing numerous lawsuits, Pfizer subsequently reached a settlement involving hundreds of millions of dollars in compensation (*The New York Times*, 1992). Over the past two decades, Pfizer has faced severe criticism for allegedly prioritising profits over the affordability of AIDS drugs. The company was compelled to compensate families of children who lost their lives during the contentious Trovan drug trial (Lenzer, 2006). Additionally, Pfizer paid approximately US$1 billion to resolve lawsuits, asserting that its Prempro drug was linked to breast cancer (Staton, 2012). Furthermore, the company paid US$273 million to settle US cases that accused Chantix, the smoking cessation drug, of inducing suicidal tendencies (McMillen, 2017).

It was perhaps most telling of their immense power and our reliance on such pharmaceutical companies during the COVID-19 pandemic, in which many of these companies produced vaccines while recording record profits. Specifically, Pfizer, BioNTech and Moderna generated US$1,000 of profit every second, while the world's poorest countries remained largely unvaccinated in 2021 (Oxfam International, 2021). Even prior to the pandemic, companies such as Purdue Pharma – owned by the billionaire Sackler family – were largely seen as responsible for the catastrophic opioid crisis in which a documented 17,029 people died due to prescription drug overdoses in 2017 alone (National Institute on Drug Abuse, ND). This is, of course, not even considering the predominantly privatised nature of healthcare in the US, with approximately 80 per cent of the general acute care hospitals in the US controlled by private non-profit or for-profit organisations (Crawford, 2023). A Stanford study determined that while such processes result in growth and increased revenue, patients covered by Medicaid – the nation's public insurance programme for low-income residents – were significantly impacted with regard to available beds and other levels of care (Duggan et al, 2023). This is perhaps not so surprising when we consider that this is a country plagued by reports of increasing hospital bills, with one notable case making the news when 70-year-old Michael Flor was greeted with a US$1.1 million bill after receiving treatment for

COVID-19 (Westneat, 2020). While those readers based in the UK may be shocked, even appalled, by healthcare in the US, it should be noted there has been a steady advance of privatisation regarding the National Health Service (NHS), with the Health and Care Act of 2012 taking away the government's ultimate responsibility to provide an NHS for all. This opened the way to changing how the NHS was managed and allowed NHS trusts to contract out services to private providers (Davis and Tallis, 2013). As a result of this Act, from 2013 to 2020, there was a continuous rise in the privatisation of the NHS in England, where services were outsourced to companies motivated primarily by profit. This outsourcing to the private sector was associated with notable increases in mortality rates for conditions that could have been treated, possibly due to a decrease in the standard of healthcare services (Goodair and Reeves, 2022). As noted by Meek (2014), this is a process that can be traced back over the last 30 years, in which there was a clear and 'consistent programme for the commercialising [of] the NHS that is independent of party-political platforms' (p 163).

These are just a few examples of how corporations have infiltrated almost every facet of our lives. However, they are emblematic of Žižek's notion of 'objective violence' outlined in Chapter 2. This form of violence, as he noted, constitutes the violence that takes place to maintain our sense of 'normality' rather than the more physical and visceral violence that otherwise disrupts this. In his book *Violence* (2008), Žižek discusses these more critical, systemic forms of violence and compares 'objective violence' to dark matter in physics in that it constitutes the majority of violence. However, it is almost impossible to locate due to its very nature.

How is it that there are corporations that now dwarf the economic worth of entire states? Why is it that despite what we are told regarding the regulation of businesses, crimes and harms are being continually committed with little to no response or punishment? Moreover, perhaps most pertinently, why have we generally settled into dull, zombie-like complicity whereby we have allowed these powerful corporations and billionaire owners to operate with impunity? The last question we will explore first by momentarily visiting a brief moment that took place in 2011 that, for the briefest of moments, appeared to finally seek redress for the economic inequalities and social injustices brought on by the overwhelming power of corporations.

A momentary dream of a brighter future

Something miraculous happened between 17 September and 15 November 2011. For these 59 days, it seemed that people came together to fight for a unified cause that finally sought to reveal the true enemy behind the catastrophic 2008 financial crash and the decades of growing inequality, corruption and greed that have come to define late-stage capitalism. This event refers to the now barely mentioned 'Occupy Wall Street' movement that, for the briefest of moments, attempted to reveal the poisonous manner in which corporations exerted influence over democratic institutions and sought palpable change. The proponents of this movement suggested a peaceful occupation of Wall Street as a means to draw attention to the absence of legal repercussions for those responsible for the worldwide financial crisis and the escalating wealth disparity, which affected not only the less fortunate but also the once prosperous and stable middle classes. The economic downturn of 2008 significantly worsened this situation. The movement's rallying cry, "We are the 99 per cent" addressed the income and wealth disparities in the US, specifically pointing out the contrast between the wealthiest 1 per cent and the rest of the population. This slogan highlighted the shortcomings of 'trickle-down' economics, which gained prominence in the 1980s. It is also interesting to note that the Hell's Angels motorcycle gang first coined and popularised this slogan, which the movement's founders borrowed. The movement's goals comprised a reduction in the influence of corporations on politics, a more balanced distribution of income, more stable and better-payed forms of employment, reforms to the banking industry, forgiveness of student loan debt and alleviation of the foreclosure situation, which left 10 million people losing their homes after the 2008 financial crisis (Lerner, 2018).

During the early days of the movement, there was an air of optimism that real change could occur, with one protester being recorded as stating: "Something has started, and nobody wants to give up. For the first time in history, we have that link now that unites us from one city and country to the other and makes that voice even louder" (cited in Perkel, 2011). People across the US and from all walks of life began to converge with a shared purpose and common enemy. It did not matter what age, gender or ethnicity you were – all were united by the fact that they were the '99 per cent'. Members of Adbusters, a Canadian publication opposing consumerism, led the organisation of the protest. The group, headed by founder Kalle Lasn and editor Micah White, managed the event's logistics, location and promotional activities. White played a crucial role by sharing the first #OccupyWallStreet tweet, which gained significant traction among online supporters. The utilisation of the occupy hashtag played a pivotal role in catapulting the movement to global attention, making it one of the most influential activist endeavours to spread rapidly through social media platforms worldwide. Initially, the organisers intended to gather at the Charging Bull statue on Wall Street and One Chase Manhattan Plaza. However, law enforcement authorities set up barriers at both public parks before the 17 September event. Fortunately, the nearby Zuccotti Park remained unaffected by these measures. As a result, thousands of individuals flocked to occupy Zuccotti Park over the following two months (Taylor and Smucker, 2021).

However, despite this early optimism, which resulted in separate protests across the US and other countries, by 2013, all associated protests had died out, and the protests on Wall Street ended after only 59 days. How did this happen? How did a movement that appeared to crystallise and articulate the frustrations and injustices so many faced fade into history? Unsurprisingly, the answer can largely be attributed to the punitive responses of law enforcement. Law enforcement has historically been employed when there may be perceived existential threats or attempts to undermine the smooth functioning of capital. Examples of such incidents encompass the Lattimer massacre of 1897, where 19 unarmed workers were fatally shot and dispersed during a peaceful march (Shackel, 2019). Another case occurred in 1927 during a coal strike in Colorado, when state police and mine guards employed pistols, rifles and a machine gun to open fire on a group of 500 striking miners and their wives, leading to what is now known as the Columbine Mine Massacre (Sam Lowry, 2006). The 2011 movement, though, was not just coordinated at the level of the local police but also the Department of Homeland Security and the Federal Bureau of Investigation (Taylor and Gessen, 2011).

The Occupy movement ostensibly ended after police (under the instruction of Mayor Bloomberg) raided the park encampment on 15 November 2011. While the original event made headlines, expanding into a wider international 'Occupy movement', the moral sentiments of the protest have faded or been hijacked by subsequent groups, many with radically different goals. These groups kept the mass 'social activism' model pioneered by Occupy, but less so anger for the corporate financial system it aimed to reform.

Occupy ended with coordinated action with major financial institutions, which entailed the utilisation of online monitoring, forceful detainment, disruption of gatherings, the use of projectiles and excessively tight handcuffing leading to injuries (see van Gelder, 2011; Wolf, 2012; Penney and Dadas, 2014). The mainstream media and those attempting to cover this movement, whether to support or critique it, were also blocked, especially when the police raids commenced (Weisenthal and Johnson, 2011). So too, a predominant theme in the mainstream media was that of depicting the protesters as responsible for much of the violence despite the documented accounts of the use of force by the police. As noted by Cissel (2012), all 12 members of *The New York Times*' board had affiliations with at least two other major corporations, businesses, banks, advertising companies, pharmaceuticals or government-influenced industries that were at the heart of the movement. Some notable examples include Merck Schering-Plough Corporation, the world's second largest pharmaceutical company; Flamel Tech, a drug delivery business; and the Carlyle Group, a defence equity firm known for its corruption and financial gains during times of war, which had direct ties to both Bush administrations. The board also comprises executives from Tropicana, Nabisco, Verizon, Telecom, Bell Atlantic, Hallmark, Lehman Brothers, Pepsi, Sara Lee and Staples (Cissel, 2012). Cissel, in their comparative content analysis that examined articles written by mass and alternative media sources, stresses that despite acknowledging the potential of bias from both positions (alternative media are traditionally opposed to the state and corporations), such economic interests between mainstream media and the corporations targeted by the movement cannot be overlooked.

By 15 November 2011, the Occupy movement had all but disappeared, and the engines of capital, along with its aforementioned destructive qualities, continued unabated. This once clear and shared understanding of the ills we face in modern society has since evaporated into the ether. While there is the occasional angry tweet or academic text (the irony is not lost here), this level of coordinated protest witnessed in 2011 has not been seen since. There have been other important social movements since then, but when we consider the wealthy and powerful elite, nothing has come close to the Occupy Wall Street movement. If you were to stop a random person in the street and ask them what the most pressing issues are that we currently face, they would likely list off some if not all of the usual suspects that are routinely fed to us by the mainstream media, including the threat of climate change, immigration, minorities and right-wing extremism (to name but a few). The wealthy power elites have clearly only learnt from this movement, aware that other enemies need to be created and presented before the people to keep attention away from them and their actions. As eloquently put forth by Hall and Winlow (2015), '"divide and rule" is a crude and ancient political tactic, but it still seems to work quite well, and even better if the ruled do the dividing themselves' (p 42).

Before going further, it is worth providing a brief overview of the symbiotic relationship between the state, corporations and law enforcement to provide some context to what transpired back in 2011 and set the stage for subsequent discussions.

The enforcers of the elite

Law enforcement agencies are ubiquitously empowered to uphold and protect state legislation in almost every geographical location across the globe. They are afforded a host of powers, such as the legitimised use of force to curtail civil disobedience and, in the case of the Occupy Wall Street movement, protests (Wood, 2015). Controlling a populous by way of law enforcement, however rudimentary, has always been part of the fabric of any society (Roth, 2014). However, today's global punitive systems can have their foundations traced back to colonialism, resulting in modernity's industrial expansion (Giuliani, 2015). Prisons were built across the New World, and penal colonies were established to control the indigenous populations of newly acquired territories and protect imperial acquisitions (Moore, 2015). Those charged with upholding colonial law and controlling the newly assimilated subjects often did so with extreme prejudice and brutality (Tun, 2018). Furthermore, during the years of the transatlantic slave trade (between the 15th and 19th centuries), it would also have been the jurisdiction of the law enforcers of the epoch to apprehend, contain and punish runaways. On these imperialistic underpinnings, the building blocks for contemporary policing have been laid, and although many of the practices have evolved, many remnants of colonial supremacist attitudes persist. Even after widespread decolonialisation (1947–1979) and the abolition of the American slave trade (1865), the colonial model of policing and incarceration was adopted throughout the territories. Moreover, the brutality and social control over minorities have often become sustained practices (Lynch, 2011; Embrick, 2015). Incidents of police brutality and shootings in the US regularly make headline news throughout the world's media. According to Embrick (2015), the shootings of unarmed black citizens and their mass incarceration can be perceived as state-sanctioned lynching in contemporary America. However, comparable global studies into the unequal treatment of black and minority ethnic citizens by law enforcement agents highlight that this problem is not isolated to the US but is a globally recognised phenomenon within law enforcement (Souhami, 2011).

Although statistics reflect that a disproportionate number of black and minority ethnic people are affected by unethical policing practices, heavy-handed policing techniques have often been used against the public regardless of ethnicity, particularly when exercising their right to protest. Worldwide, the increasing use of colonial-style militarised policing has been employed against protestors (Wood, 2015). Some of the most coercive policing methods are being waged against the public in the protection of corporate interests, such as police brutality documented at the Barton Moss anti-fracking camp in the UK and Standing Rock in the US (Wong and Levin, 2018). However, the latter has as much to do with imperialism and race as it does capitalism. When the Marxist view of crime and deviance is applied, academics, such as Pearce (1976) and Reiman (1984), describe the criminogenic nature of capitalism. The corporate class or ruling classes define what constitutes a crime and create the laws that will protect their position and their ability to control the means of production to generate capital. Thus, the working classes are suppressed and controlled (Marx and Engels, 1967). Furthermore, the ruling class dictates not only the parameters of a legal system that reinforces its dominance but also how that system is applied to the different sections of society (Pearce, 1976). This theoretical framework defines the state as the defender of the corporate class and suppressor of the majority for financial gain. The police, as the state's defenders, must, by default, be the enforcers of capitalist practices. Conversely, these practices are normally in direct conflict with the values that society has been hegemonically manipulated to believe that the police uphold (Gramsci et al, 1971).

Yet, criminology has perhaps been slower to consider how the economic imperative that underpins policing can be fused with racist assumptions and practices. Colonial policing, like Western policing in its recognisable and modern form, essentially developed as tied to capitalism. What was exported to the colonies was a model of policing developed in the metropolis that was ultimately not merely about crime but was concerned with the maintenance of social order. That social order was not just any social order but an order conducive to the interests of the propertied, wealthy and merchant capitalist classes. It was a social order that privileged private property and profit-making. An order that kept the mass of the population in their place and pacified. An order that disciplined labour. Of course, social order had been kept previously. However, in Britain, at least, a growing discomfort with militarism and the riot act after the death of chartist protesters took place at St Peter's Field, Manchester, England, on Monday, 16 August 1819, at what was to become known as the Peterloo Massacre, drove demands for change. However, it should be remembered that prior to statutory policing, many functions of policing did exist, but the existence of the Marine Police, including the Thames River Police, predates the establishment of the Metropolitan Police in 1826. Of course, while the Thames River Police were clearly tied to vast profits being made in slavery in the colonies, in London, the Gordon Riots dramatically exposed the weakness of having to rely on watch schemes that existed prior to the formation of standing police forces. During those riots in 1780, when large parts of London fell into the hands of the rioters for five days, the army could have been used to support the civil authorities, but this raised a number of problems. The distrust of powerful governments meant there was strong opposition to the existence of a large standing army and the use of troops against civilians.

Prior to the creation of state-backed police in England, there was an expansion in privately employed watchmen during the 18th century. In some prosperous areas, neighbours joined together to fund patrols, and by the mid-19th century, some 150 communities in London were using some form of private policing provision to provide guarding patrols to secure members' properties. Many warehouse owners, dockyard operators and turnpike trustees operated small forces of watchmen, some of whom were sworn as constables or enjoyed special statutory powers. The most famous of these private forces was the Thames River Police, established in 1797 by dock owners as part of a strategy to impose new working practices. However, we should be cautious not to view statutory control of the police as an inherent issue or problem. Any 'abolition' of policing would unlikely abolish private policing, a practice that remains today. An instance exemplifying private corporate policing is the British Post Office Horizon scandal, where numerous sub-postmasters were wrongfully subjected to civil and criminal prosecutions for theft, fraud and false accounting in criminal courts. This scandal, which some consider to be possibly the most extensive miscarriage of justice in British legal history, spans over 20 years and remains unresolved. It underscores the exercise of private corporate power in criminal justice.

Following legal action by convicted sub-postmasters against the Post Office, 555 convictions were deemed unsafe and unlawfully obtained. As of 2022, a total of 736 prosecutions had been identified, with 83 convictions overturned, and more were anticipated to be annulled in the future. The number of people impacted by other types of abuse by the Post Office may be far, far higher.

In 1999, the UK Post Office, part of Royal Mail, introduced a computer accounting system, Horizon, developed by the Japanese company Fujitsu. From February 2003 to 2010, Royal Mail was under the leadership of its CEO, Adam Crozier. On 1 April 2012, the Post Office attained independence from the Royal Mail Group and underwent reorganisation, becoming a subsidiary of Royal Mail Holdings, with a distinct management and board of directors. Effectively, it was sold off by the conservative and liberal democrat coalition government. By 2013, the Horizon system was employed by over 11,500 branches and handled approximately six million transactions daily, despite known concerns about its accuracy and effectiveness. Since 1999, some sub-postmasters have been reporting unexplained discrepancies, financial losses and issues with the system. The Post Office maintained that Horizon was 'robust' and that none of the discrepancies were due to Horizon. Some sub-postmasters unwilling or unable to make good the shortfalls were prosecuted by the Post Office for theft, fraud and false accounting. Between 1991 and 2015, there were 918 successful prosecutions.

The Post Office has a long history in the UK, with the institution in its present form as an arm of government dating back to the 17th century. From its initial focus on mail carriage, the Post Office expanded its operations to become the major point of contact between the state and citizens. Due to its role in providing banking and other financial services, such as foreign currency exchange and as a cash handler, the Post Office has always been susceptible to criminal conduct, especially fraud committed by staff members. Rather unusually, the Post Office maintains its own investigations unit, staffed largely by former members of the police service, and going to the heart of the present legal problems, the Post Office itself acted as prosecuting authority in cases where individuals were accused of fraud or dishonesty.

Most of these cases involved private prosecutions by the Post Office in the criminal courts, primarily relying on information technology evidence alone without establishing criminal intent. Public prosecutions also took place in Scotland and Northern Ireland. Their solicitors convinced some sub-postmasters to plead guilty to false accounting, as the Post Office indicated that it would drop theft charges. Once the Post Office obtained a criminal conviction, it pursued Proceeds of Crime Act orders against the convicted sub-postmasters, enabling it to seize their assets and force them into bankruptcy. According to press reports, these actions by the Post Office resulted in numerous job losses, bankruptcies, divorces, unwarranted prison sentences and, tragically, one suicide. The impacts on individuals were significant. This includes the case of Noel Thomas, a man who had worked for the Royal Mail for 42 years, who spent his 60th birthday in prison because of the errors, or Seema Misra, who was pregnant with her second child when she was convicted in 2010 of theft and sentenced to 15 months in jail. Local press reports at that time described her as the 'pregnant thief', and her husband was physically attacked in the aftermath of her conviction. Yet, in 2021, in court documents, Hudgell Solicitors have revealed that in 2010, senior Post Office management took a decision that Horizon would not be subjected to an independent review because:

> If one were commissioned – any investigation would need to be disclosed in court. Although we would be doing the review to comfort others, any perception that POL doubts its own systems would mean that all criminal prosecutions would have to be stayed. It would also beg a question for the Court of Appeal over past prosecutions and imprisonments. (Cited in Court of Appeal, 2021)

It has been widely recognised that the criminal process, as well as the law itself, is a double-edged sword. It serves not only as a tool for enforcing social policy, social control and social rights but can also be wielded by those with the motivation, power and economic resources to undermine them.

This problematic relationship between the agents of the state and corporations is also reflected in the neoliberal practices of the privatisation of policing (Spitzer and Scull, 1977; Forst and Manning, 1999; Paster, 2003), and yet, much policing pre-official and colonial policing was at heart a privatised system. From the bribery and lobbying of state officials for preferential legislation to unpaid taxes of these corporations, now contracted to provide for-profit security and policing, this adds another dimension and evolution to the entrenched inter-relationship and shared goals between the nation state, the corporation(s), and the police or agents of control. Ultimately, the neocolonial capitalist system of inequality and exploitation provides a framework that harbours a moral juxtaposition between the fortification of a society that global law enforcement has sworn to protect and serve the corporate oligarchs that decide the parameters of their jurisdiction. This relationship designed to maintain the status quo and the smooth functioning of capital has a detrimental effect on global society that transcends borders, cultures, gender and race.

The era of corporate giants

While there have been some often cited examples of the Occupy Wall Street movement's successes, including, for example, emphasis on income inequality in broad political discourse and, relatedly, inspiring the fight for a US$15 minimum wage (Rosenfeld, 2019), these corporate 'giants' have only seemed to grow much bigger. For instance, in 2011, when the movement took place, there were a recorded 1,210 billionaires with a combined wealth of US$4.5 trillion (Forbes, 2011). However, by 2022, there were approximately 2,640 with a combined wealth of US$12.2 trillion (Peterson-Withorn, 2023). Such an increase was likely inevitable, given the logic of neoliberal capitalism. However, this number was arguably significantly boosted during the COVID-19 pandemic, which saw one of modern history's most significant wealth transfers (Clifford, 2020). As small businesses crumbled under the weight of the pandemic (Roth, 2021) and nearly 7 million people lost their lives (World Health Organization, 2023), the world also witnessed the 'extreme concentration of economic power in the hands of a very small minority of the super-rich' (Chancel et al, 2022, p 3). We are now in an age where some corporations are in fact, economically speaking, bigger than some countries, with the likes of Apple, Amazon and Microsoft now holding market caps larger than some countries' entire gross domestic product (GDP). Apple, a company we will return to later, recorded a market cap of US$2.97 trillion as of 2023, while Amazon was recorded at US$1.3 trillion and Microsoft at US$2.47 trillion (CompaniesMarketCap, 2023). To put these numbers into perspective, Apple and Microsoft exceeded Australia's GDP, estimated at US$1.7 trillion, along with Italy's US$2.108 trillion and Brazil's US$1.609 trillion (Statista, 2023). If you were to add these three companies' market caps together, they would even dwarf the GDP of countries such as the UK, which was estimated at US$3.07 trillion in 2022 (Trading Economics, 2023).

Given the size of some corporations, serious questions need to be asked regarding where power resides when considering the state-corporate nexus. In attempting to define this era of tremendous corporate influence, Crouch (2004) introduced the concept of 'post-democracy' to illustrate how corporations exert excessive political influence in shaping governmental policies. Within this 'post-democracy', there exists a valid apprehension regarding the detrimental impact of wealth backed by business interests on the well-being of Western liberal democracies (Lessig, 2012). For a long time, businesses have attempted to curry favour with governments and ultimately influence policies that suit and serve their instrumental interests. For instance, during America's 'Gilded Age', which was characterised by the rise of industrialists, business moguls and oil tycoons, it was not uncommon for such businessmen to buy their way into politics, with former

President Rutherford B. Hayes writing in his diary in 1886 that 'this is a government of the people, by the people and for the people no longer … it is a government by the corporations, of the corporations and for the corporations' (cited in Lessig, 2018, p 73). The beginning of the 20th century marked the beginning of the Progressive Era, which brought an end to the corruption prevalent during the Gilded Age. As will be noted in Chapter 7, journalists played a significant role in uncovering political misconduct, thereby creating a pathway for President Theodore Roosevelt to implement a series of reforms. These reforms encompassed tax and election reform and measures to curb corporate influence and power. However, despite such reforms, there is growing apprehension that Western liberal democracies are heading in an unfavourable trajectory. The regulations concerning the utilisation of financial resources in American politics are antiquated, and the equilibrium within the system of governance is again disrupted by corporate influence. As Brown (2015) noted, a notable surge in corporate influence results in the incremental wearing down of democratic principles within numerous countries globally. As noted by Hillman, Keim and Schuler (2004), the primary aim of corporate political activity is to ensure the support of favourable policies and legislation while undermining those that may negatively impact the interests of business and profit-making. This tactic seems to be working, with Alzola (2013) stating that corporations are spending increasing amounts of money on activities intended to sway public policy in their favour. This was only exacerbated.

With the heralded arrival and implementation of the neoliberal agenda, the immense economic power of corporations is again echoing the themes of the Gilded Age as they move to gain a stranglehold on political power. This move is indeed startling, if not surprising, and provides insight into the hierarchies of power within the contemporary world as the influence and buying power of corporations and the wealthy elite threaten to diminish the influence of governments. Some US politicians have sounded the proverbial alarm and provided warnings similar to those of former President Rutherford B. Hayes over 100 years ago. In the book *Captured: The Corporate Infiltration of American Democracy* (Whitehouse, 2017), Senator Sheldon Whitehouse – a democrat who serves as the junior US senator from Rhode Island – argued that 'corporations of vast wealth and remorseless staying power have moved into our politics to seize for themselves advantages that can be seized only by control over government' (p 19). As opposed to the more overt examples depicted during the Gilded Age, such attempts to buy influence have now evolved to constitute the gradual and incremental chipping away of existing policies and regulations, akin to the well-known metaphor of slowly boiling a frog alive. This, as noted by Whitehouse, is not just the corporations themselves but also their billionaire owners who are actively pursuing this agenda, with lobby groups being the emblematic 'foot soldiers' serving their interests and so-called philanthropic foundations serving as 'proxies to billionaire families who want influence' (Whitehouse, 2017). Since 2010, the influence of such processes has only grown. Citizens United vs. Federal Election Commission was a pivotal US Supreme Court case decided in 2010. The case revolved around the documentary film *Hillary: The Movie* (2008), produced by the organisation Citizens United, which criticised Hillary Clinton, then a candidate for the Democratic presidential nomination. The Federal Election Commission argued that the film's distribution violated the Bipartisan Campaign Reform Act of 2002, which restricted corporate and union spending on electioneering communications. In a 5–4 ruling, the Supreme Court invalidated crucial components of the Bipartisan Campaign Reform Act. Justice Anthony Kennedy, in authoring the majority opinion, asserted that limitations on autonomous political spending by corporations and unions were in violation of the First Amendment's safeguarding of free speech. The decision affirmed that corporations and unions, functioning as legal entities, possess equivalent free speech rights to individuals, granting them the freedom to expend unrestricted funds on autonomous political endeavours, whether in support of or in opposition to candidates. Due to these incremental encroachments of corporate influence on politics, the corporate powers have been reciprocated with favours, resulting in fundamental alterations to the functioning mechanisms of the US democratic system. According to Whitehouse, these changes consistently grant greater influence to large corporate entities within governmental processes, effectively restructuring democracy to cater to corporate advantages at the expense of the people.

Clear examples of this are apparent in the UK and the US if we look at arguably the most important resource we depend on: water. In 2022, the environmental performance of England's water companies was so poor that the Environment Agency called for prison sentences for chief executives and board members whose firms are responsible for the worst pollution (see Laville, 2022). The annual report on England's nine water companies focuses on the treatment of domestic wastewater and sewage (see Environment Agency, 2023). It says the industry has not reduced the number of pollution incidents or increased compliance with conditions for discharging treated wastewater.

At the time of writing, one British water company, Thames Water, was fighting for survival, having run up £14 billion in debts (Cahill, 2023). Despite being privatised without any debt, water utilities operate as uneventful and foreseeable monopolies, possessing extensive land holdings and enjoying an assured income with virtually no risk of losing customers. The perplexing question arises: How could such a business face financial ruin? The underlying issues leading to this predicament were planted during the 1989 privatisation when the government sold water entities in England

and Wales for a mere £6.1 billion (Sikka, 2023). With the absence of parallel water and sewage pipes, competition becomes impracticable, resulting in companies having, in essence, lifelong customers.

The industry has embraced a private equity business model with elevated prices, minimal investment and financial manoeuvres to maximise returns for shareholders and executive salaries. Rather than shareholders making long-term equity investments, the model relies on debt since interest payments are eligible for tax relief, effectively resulting in a public subsidy.

An alarming 2.4 billion litres of water are lost daily due to leaks caused by inadequate infrastructure (Gill and Millard, 2022). Despite a population increase of nearly 10 million, no new reservoirs have been constructed. Water companies have the obligation to supply clean water; however, they have exacerbated contamination issues by discharging sewage into rivers. Neglecting to address leaks and sewage dumping has led to higher profits, increased dividends and enhanced performance-related executive compensation. A report from the House of Lords approximated that the industry requires £240 billion to £260 billion in new investments by 2050, a significant difference compared with the government's suggested figure of £56 billion (see Murphy, 2023).

The industry, however, has prioritised cash extraction. Since privatisation, it has distributed £72 billion in dividends, with an additional £15 billion expected by 2030 (Horton, 2022). Furthermore, the industry currently bears debts amounting to approximately £60 billion (Hiscott, 2023). The recent crisis at Thames Water has brought years of regulatory leniency into the spotlight. Thames Water loses approximately 630 million litres of water daily due to leaks and frequently discharges large quantities of raw sewage into rivers (Laville and Carrington, 2023). Since 2010, the company has faced sanctions on 92 occasions for its failures, resulting in fines totalling £163 million. In 2017, they were fined £20 million for a series of significant pollution incidents on the River Thames (Environment Agency, 2017). In 2023, they were fined a further £3 million for a series of illegal sewage discharges across the country (Laville and Horton, 2023). Despite this, the recently resigned chief executive saw their salary double over the past three years. After privatisation, Thames Water dispersed £7.2 billion in dividends and currently carries debts amounting to £14.3 billion, secured against assets valued at £17.9 billion. Surprisingly, auditors PricewaterhouseCoopers consistently provided the company with a clean financial assessment despite its evident lack of financial resilience (Thames Water, 2023). As the Bank of England increased interest rates in late 2022, Thames found that it could not make the minimum required investment and service its debt (Kollewe and Wearden, 2023).

Of course, similarly, the US has the Flint Water Crisis, one of American history's worst human-caused environmental disasters. It started in 2014 after the household water supply for the city of Flint, Michigan, was contaminated with lead and possibly lethal legionella bacteria (Michigan Civil Rights Commission, 2017). Amid a financial crisis in April 2014, Flint's water source was altered by a state-appointed emergency manager. Instead of being sourced from Lake Huron and the Detroit River, the city's water supply was switched to the Flint River. Flint, a former car manufacturing boom town that fell into economic decline, tried to save money by switching the water supply. Almost immediately, Residents complained about the water's taste, smell and appearance (Michigan Civil Rights Commission, 2017). It is also worth noting that demographically, the people of Flint were disproportionately poorer and a majority black city. The filmmaker Michael Moore suggested that the water crisis in Flint is a 'version of manslaughter' and described it as a racial crime and 'ethnic cleansing' (cited in CNN, 2016). While the language seemed extreme, exposure to harmful lead from ageing pipes filtering into the public water supply exposed around 100,000 residents to elevated lead levels. Several scientific studies confirmed that lead contamination was present in the water supply (see Pauli, 2020). The city switched back to the Detroit water system in mid-October 2015 and later signed a 30-year contract with the new Great Lakes Water Authority on 22 November 2017, but the damage was significant. Blood tests found that children had high levels of lead in their system. Reading scores in Flint have subsequently fallen by 50 per cent, according to the state education department (see Riley, 2018). Lead is a neurotoxin that causes irreversible brain damage, and the life course trajectory of an entire generation of Flint children may have been irreversibly impacted.

In January 2016, the Michigan governor proclaimed a state of emergency, and soon after, President Obama declared a federal state of emergency. This declaration facilitated additional support from the Federal Emergency Management Agency and the Department of Homeland Security. Approximately 6,000 to 12,000 children were subjected to drinking water containing elevated lead levels (Fahel, 2017). Children in particular face significant risks due to the long-term consequences of lead poisoning, which may include a decline in intellectual functioning (Fahel, 2017). The water supply change was strongly suspected to be a cause of an outbreak of Legionnaires' disease that killed 12 people and affected another 87. However, the original source of the bacteria was never traced, and so the link was not proven. In January 2021, nine officials, including former Michigan governor Rick Snyder, faced charges consisting of 34 felony counts and seven misdemeanours for their involvement in the crisis. Among them, two officials were charged with involuntary manslaughter. A total of 15 criminal cases were filed against local and state officials, but only one minor conviction has been secured, with all other charges being dismissed or dropped.

Climate crises are another important area in which the government-corporate nexus is apparent. For instance, politicians, despite potentially being well-intentioned when it comes to addressing the threats to the environment, generally need more knowledge. This is where the aforementioned lobbyists, the 'foot soldiers' of corporations, enter the picture. Corporations responsible for contributing to the climate crisis, including fossil fuel companies and banks, allocate significant resources to such lobbyists (Helm, 2017). Throughout the years, these corporations have exerted considerable effort to persuade politicians that they possess the necessary expertise to rectify the dire consequences of climate change despite their role in bringing the world to the brink of environmental disaster. The scale of this influence was uncovered by an online database generated by F Minus (2023), which determined that over 1,500 lobbyists in the US were employed by fossil fuel companies. Astonishingly, these lobbyists simultaneously represent numerous entities such as liberal-led cities, universities, technology firms and environmental organisations, all claiming to be actively addressing the climate crisis. While state lobbying regulations prevent multi-client lobbyists from advocating for opposing sides of specific legislation or governmental actions, there is currently no prohibition preventing a fossil fuel lobbyist from simultaneously working for a company or organisation that experiences adverse effects from the climate crisis. An example of this can be witnessed in Baltimore, a city that in 2021 legally pursued big oil companies for their contribution to climate-related harm, only to discover that it shared a lobbyist with ExxonMobil, one of the defendants named in the lawsuit. Similarly, Syracuse University, a trailblazer in the movement to divest from fossil fuels, shared a lobbyist who represented 14 clients in the oil and gas industry (Touchberry, 2023). In essence, these lobbyists work for both sides and ultimately ensure that the much larger and richer corporations within the fuel and energy businesses not only look more legitimate by working with lobbyists tied to respected institutions such as universities, but are also likely to leverage their wealth to receive information from such clients to further their goals and interests (Touchberry, 2023). Such corporations have also exerted their incredible influence on other governments, including the UK. Based on a freedom of information request obtained by Greenpeace UK's investigations unit, it was revealed that in 2020, executives from ExxonMobil, Shell, Chevron, Equinor and BP had a private dinner with the former UK trade minister in Texas. During the meeting, natural gas was advocated as essential in addressing climate change, emphasising its role as a 'crucial solution' (Kennedy, 2021). More recently, in 2023, a lobbying firm was paid over £200,000 by the gas industry to establish and operate a parliamentary group to persuade government ministers to endorse new fossil fuel projects. The All-Party Parliamentary Group on Hydrogen, consisting of 17 Members of Parliament and Lords, have consistently advocated for government support of 'blue hydrogen', derived from natural gas. These technologies have faced criticism from scientists who argue that they divert attention from proven low-carbon alternatives based on renewable energy (see Howarth and Jacobson, 2021). Interestingly, both current and former chairs of the All-Party Parliamentary Group on Hydrogen are Conservative MPs who have previously been associated with fossil fuel companies that could benefit from the group's lobbying efforts (Webster, 2023a).

Away from the environment, you also have other examples of corporations exercising their wealth to lobby for their interests, with the National Rifle Association (NRA) spending approximately US$140 million towards pro-gun election candidates since 2010 (BBC News, 2023). In 2022 alone, there were 646 mass shootings and a total of 44,357 deaths caused by firearms (Gun Violence Archive, 2023) in the US, and despite several attempts to address gun violence at a political level, very little progress has been made. While this is indeed an emotive topic for many and deeply politicised, the importance of the NRA in this matter cannot be overlooked. Following the tragic Sandy Hook mass shooting in 2013, where 20 children and six teachers lost their lives, then President Barack Obama tried to introduce comprehensive reforms. These reforms aimed to include a ban on military-style assault weapons, a reduction in ammunition magazine capacity and stricter background checks on gun buyers. However, the NRA quickly lobbied against such proposals in an effort to counter the Obama administration's efforts. While there were multiple potential reasons for these proposed measures failing at Congress, the organisation's role cannot be overlooked when we consider that they have supported a number of elected officials, including former senate leader and current minority leader Mitch McConnell, who received more than US$1.2 million in direct donations, independent expenditures and other patronages over his career (Brady Campaign to End Gun Violence, ND). This currying of favours within the context of arms extends to the wider weapons industry. Recent findings have exposed the American multinational aerospace and defence conglomerate Raytheon's involvement in undermining American democracy through political contributions. The company has donated a total of US$110,000 to 62 members of Congress who had voted against the certification of President Biden's electoral victory (Verma, 2022).

Moving away from industries that make products that kill to those that produce goods that are supposed to extend or improve quality of life, the pharmaceutical and wider health industries also spend tremendous amounts of money to influence government policy and legislation. According to recent federal disclosure filings analysed by OpenSecrets (Sayki, 2023), pharmaceutical and health product companies set a new record by investing more than US$372 million in lobbying Congress and federal agencies last year. This substantial amount surpassed expenditures from all other industries, constituting over half of the total lobbying efforts within the health sector. A significant portion of the pharmaceutical and health product industry's lobbying endeavours in 2022 were primarily directed towards the Inflation Reduction Act of 2022. This legislation, introduced as an amendment to the Build Back Better Act, was subsequently signed into law by President Joe Biden in August 2022. The bill encompasses various environmental and economic goals, including the provision for Medicare to engage in price negotiations for specific prescription drugs, the implementation of caps on out-of-pocket expenses for Medicare beneficiaries and initiatives targeting the costs associated with insulin. There were also those companies that benefitted substantially from the COVID-19 pandemic, with Pfizer, the manufacturer of one of the three COVID-19 vaccines authorised for emergency use in the US, spending the most amount of money on lobbying activities when compared with all other individual pharmaceutical companies. The company allocated a staggering US$14.9 million towards federal lobbying in 2022. In October of that year, Pfizer announced its plans to increase the price of its COVID-19 vaccine from US$30 to a range of US$110–130 per dose, anticipating a quadruple price surge (Erman, 2022). This decision coincided with the company's record-breaking revenue of US$100 billion and US$31 billion in profits, primarily driven by the ongoing pandemic. Other vaccine manufacturers shared such a move, indicative of the wider industry's attempt to ensure greater profits at the expense of society's most vulnerable. Such tactics were also used by the Sackler-owned Purdue Pharma and other oxycodonemanufacturers, which played a significant part in the US opioid crisis. Specifically, a joint investigation by the Associate Press and The Center for Public Integrity determined that over the course of 10 years, drug companies and their affiliated supporters allocated over US$880 million towards lobbying and political contributions at the state and federal levels. In stark contrast, a few organisations advocating for opioid restrictions spent a mere US$4 million. These funds were utilised for various political activities crucial to the drug industry, including creating legislation and regulations concerning opioids. More alarmingly, the opioid industry, alongside its allies, provided financial contributions to approximately 7,100 candidates running for state-level offices. The drug companies and affiliated groups maintained a substantial force of lobbyists, averaging around 1,350 annually, actively engaging in advocacy efforts across all 50 state capitals (The Center for Public Integrity, 2016). Such mingling between corporations and politicians regarding healthcare can also be seen in the UK. In 2022, the health secretary Steve Barclay appointed Lionel Zetter, a self-proclaimed 'renowned lobbyist' with ties to the insurance and private healthcare sectors, as an advisor. This instance highlights the interconnectedness between ministers, lobbyists and political advisers. Zetter served as Barclay's policy fellow at the Cabinet Office and subsequently became his political adviser in the Department for Health and Social Care, holding these positions from January to November. It is worth noting that Zetter simultaneously held two roles in the private sector (Wearmouth, 2023). Although this was not in violation of any legal regulations, it again speaks to the growing influence of the private sector on matters that were conventionally that of the state.

It is important to stress that the actual act of lobbying in itself is not illegal. However, we need to consider, as these few previous examples illustrate, the enormous influence that can be wielded by wealthy corporations that dwarf the resources available to ordinary citizens and non-profit organisations who attempt to highlight and address the harms caused by the actions of said businesses. However, it is not just the lobbyists that cause such issues but also the actions and economic interests of elected officials. For instance, according to an analysis conducted by *The New York Times*, it has been revealed that a minimum of 97 members of Congress engaged in the purchase or sale of stocks and bonds that intersected with their legislative responsibilities in 2022 (Parlapiano et al, 2022). There were members of Congress with investments in pharmaceuticals, banking, big tech, fuel and energy, and healthcare (to name but a few) while simultaneously sitting on various committees and subcommittees directly concerned with these various industries. Simply put, these politicians and their ability to act objectively and impartially were compromised due to their economic interests and investments in the industries they were supposed to review and provide an appropriate legislative review with citizens' interests in mind. Perhaps the most obvious example of this inherent conflict of interest is that of the politicians listed in the report who had sold stock related to tobacco companies while sitting on the subcommittee that has oversight over product safety, which held a panel hearing on e-cigarettes (Parlapiano et al, 2022). Such conflicts of interest can also be witnessed in the UK. For instance, according to an investigation conducted by The Ferret (Edwards, 2021), it has been discovered that 33 members of the UK legislative body, known as peers, hold shares valued at a minimum of £50,000 in 19 oil and gas companies. Additionally, ten peers serve as chairs, directors or advisors to 15 fossil fuel companies. The investigation also uncovered that 23 peers had invested in Anglo-Dutch oil giant Shell. In contrast, others held shares in prominent oil and gas companies such as BP, Chevron, ExxonMobil, Total and Equinor. Some of these peers also had affiliations with companies like Engie, Bahrain's Oil and Gas Holding Company, Canadian Overseas Petroleum and Pakistan Oilfields, either leading or advising them. Notably, two peers, namely Conservative Baroness Noakes and crossbencher Lord Burns, who have shares in Shell, served on the House of Lords Industry and Regulators Committee. In September 2021, this committee was involved in examining evidence related to climate policies aimed at achieving net zero emissions. In light of this investigation, campaign group Corporate

Observatory Europe's Pascoe Sabido stated that 'these are supposed to be the people holding the government's climate policies to account, and instead, they have direct financial links to the fossil fuel industry. How can a peer with shares in the industry also be on the committee that tries to regulate them?' (cited in Edwards, 2021).

The unawakenable nightmare

You may have noticed that many of the examples so far presented have been based in the US and the UK. This was intentional, as focusing on two of the most powerful countries in the world, both economically and militarily speaking, and that pride themselves on democratic principles of freedom, equality and justice for all, demonstrates just how powerful corporations have become and the corrosive impact this has had on these supposedly cherished ideals and values. While many may not be surprised to read of acts of blatant corporate corruption within politics in the Global South, including bribery, money laundering and other corruption-related activities (see Lawrence, 2016; Amundsen, 2019; Zysman-Quirós, 2019 for examples), what we are witnessing in the Global North often goes unnoticed and unchallenged. While the most important distinction here is the legality of the actions, the overall intended outcome is not so dissimilar when we consider growing corporate dominance across the planet. Ultimately, as demonstrated via this quick review of the importance of lobbying for corporations, politicians' susceptibility to conflicts of interest and corruption appears to be an inherent feature of the neoliberal state, which is defined by its fragmented yet interconnectedness to large corporations rather than an unintended flaw or side effect. Corporations, now untethered by the principles of neoliberalism and slowly capturing more and more power in the form of political influence, have now truly become the giants former President Rutherford B. Hayes warned against, and, despite what we may be told, governments are no longer for the people, but for the corporations.

Late capitalism is situated in a period defined by rising disparities and injustices fuelled by modern business and technological progress, and corporations have played a substantial role in manifesting such conditions. As the average person struggles to wade through the current environment of intense competition, culture and identity wars, and the next economic catastrophe and pandemic, corporations remain ever looming in the distance, only growing in economic power and influence over the foundations of democracy globally. Buoyed by economic liberalisation, technological advancement, lax regulation and nation-state manipulation, many corporations are the true winners in the current epoch. Perhaps the state has since become a mere subsidiary of the corporation, and the fears of long since dead presidents and the concerned contemporary politicians have become realised. When we consider their ability to lobby and gain political influence, the financial resources available, media ownership and regulatory influence due to conflicting interests from politicians, any hopes for any change seem to be ever out of reach. We may hear of a new regulation here or a new policy there, but the fundamental engines of the current economic system still remain unchecked. With that in mind, any future change would likely be akin to replacing a door or window in a house, all while keeping the underlying architecture intact. Perhaps, in the context of this chapter, a more suitable analogy would be the grand mansion situated on its own island, enclosed by fences.

4

Follow the Money: The Global Finance Industry

In the past few years, several leaks and scandals have brought to light the secretive financial dealings and extravagant luxury lifestyles of wealthy and politically influential elites. Among the notable events in recent decades are the MPs' expenses scandal, the financial crisis, and the revelations exposed by leaks such as the Panama Papers, Pandora Papers, Paradise Papers, Suisse Secrets, FinCEN Files and the Malaysian 1Malaysia Development Berhad scandal. These incidents have collectively revealed these individuals' hidden financial secrets and opulent excesses. These cases have confirmed that immorality and hypocrisy in the form of corruption, tax evasion, money laundering and kleptocracy are commonplace among the world's wealthiest and most powerful people.

Russia's invasion of Ukraine cast the global spotlight onto Russia's oligarchs, with particular attention being paid to their luxury assets dispersed across the world, such as real estate, superyachts, fine art, classic cars, vintage wines, jewellery and jets (Duncan et al, 2022; Milmo, 2023). Yet, corruption and its relationship to power, wealth and political influence have hardly been firmly on the political agenda. We could quite easily write a book alone merely detailing all the gory details of the relationship between the world's most corrupt actors and how the global finance industry seemingly sustains, enables and facilitates them.

We could look at how these elites have looted, embezzled, bribed and muscled their way to billionaire status and bent the rules to their own ends, and indeed, criminology all too occasionally does just this. Yet, few like Webster, in the book *Rich Crime Poor Crime: Inequality and the Rule of Law* (2023b), have noted in a sustained and holistic manner how contemporary Western (in his case British) society is founded on a legacy of past plunder and dispossession by elites against the rest. He demonstrates aptly how a centuries-long process has seen power and property consolidated in the hands of a few and coded in legal systems that favoured the rich and created extreme inequality (Webster, 2023b). We could, of course, attempt a blow-by-blow account of how such illicit wealth is enjoyed, laundered and stored through real estate in London (see Atkinson, 2020 for an in-depth account on this), superyachts in Monaco, auction houses in New York and freeports around Europe. We could also discuss how our political-economic system provides the legal and financial infrastructure to move illicit wealth freely throughout the global financial system and cast aspersions on the complicity of banks and luxury industries who act as 'enablers' in facilitating this activity. We also could and should rightly highlight how social stratification is often at the core of this, and the Global South and the poorest are the ultimate and main losers in this process. It is, after all, often difficult to comprehend the truly mind-boggling sums of money involved and see the impunity with which these elites with real power seem to thumb their nose at all forms of law, authority and ethics. However, focusing on the individuals themselves overlooks the systematic enablers and profiteers behind this and the importance of such understandings being systemic rather than individualistic. Yet, systems are, ultimately, always collections of individuals who act with some unity or purposeful cohesion.

Suppose the world operates with a global financial system, an international framework consisting of legal agreements, institutions, and formal and informal economic actors that facilitate global flows of financial capital for investment and trade financing. In that case, the network of individuals enabling individual avarice certainly deserves attention. Nevertheless, it is a collective of people. We need not pretend that the system exists without its people.

Wading through the murky waters

Since emerging in the late 19th century with the first modern wave of economic globalisation, the global finance industry's evolution has been marked by the establishment of multinational treatise, central banks and intergovernmental organisations whose stated aims were supposedly those of improving the regulation, transparency, accountability and effectiveness of international markets. However, while there is clear power here, these fields are rarely the stuff or focus of criminology. Is high-end banking fraud or political corruption how we conventionally conceive of serious organised crime? In what Christopher calls the 'asset manager society' (Christophers, 2023, p 7), the financially powerful who exert control over socially important sectors are increasingly driven by short-term greed imperatives. Due to privatisation and the financial crisis in the Global North, the ownership and management of essential social assets, such as housing, infrastructure and utilities, have shifted to secretive new owners. Asset management conglomerates like Macquarie, Blackstone and Brookfield Asset Management have replaced banks in acquiring ownership of critical resources like roads, water supply systems, farmland, energy utilities, schools, hospitals and residential properties. These assets are now part of the portfolios held by obscure entities prioritising quick profits and high investor returns over long-term investment and responsible stewardship. As Christopher suggests, these shadowy and little-known groups, such as Macquarie of Australia, own infrastructure on which more than 100 million people rely daily, and asset managers collectively own global housing and infrastructure assets worth more than US$4 trillion (Kumar, 2022).

Capitalism – and indeed the enterprise of money-making more generally – has never been entirely innocent and benign, and criminology has occasionally foregrounded it as a problem – a problem that is occasionally even understood, acknowledged and articulated by its supporters. During industrial capitalism's period in the 17th century, the rationale of political arguments favouring competitive free markets was that they could cure the ills of a society plagued by civil strife, religious tension and foreign wars (Hirschman, 1977; Dupuy, 2014). While economic self-interest and the desire for profit were seen as an extremely strong and powerful drive, it was also understood as calm, rational, calculated and predictable in contrast with the more base and violent urges that could be associated with military or political conquest or religious fervour. Economic avarice was still seen as a vice to a certain extent, but it was felt that such passions could be harnessed for the broader social good and benefit.

Certainly, criminal activities within the financial services sector span a wide range. They encompass instances like armed bank robberies, cybercriminals attempting to hack into bank computers for fund theft, and elaborate frauds committed by financial services entities against their own customers. Addressing these crimes requires a more intricate response. Traditional criminal justice agencies handle the prevalent volume crimes, while the financial services organisations employ a significant private sector to safeguard against crime. Additionally, multiple regulators address actions many might consider crimes but are not treated as such. While power might always be situationally and contextually constituted, it has long been recognised that money is a site of power. In American criminologist William Chambliss' seminal work *On the Take: From Petty Crooks to Presidents* (1978), which took place at the height of the controversy surrounding political corruption in the US, he noted that:

> Money is the oil of our present-day machinery, and elected public officials are the pistons that keep the machinery operating. Those who come up with the oil, whatever the source, are able to make the machinery run the way they want it to. Crime is an excellent producer of capitalism's oil. (Chambliss, 1978, p 1)

This simple fact is often forgotten as power becomes anything but the stuff of criminology. Occasionally, there may be discussions of the political economy that postulate the benefits of economic growth whereby favourable economic conditions help to keep future crime at bay, where an increase in observed GDP per capita, driven by higher labour productivity, can and will surely lower crime. The Global Financial Crisis, meanwhile, and the radical fall in liquidity as a primary catalyst in the exposition of the single largest episode of finance crime and financial fraud in generations, is regarded as a momentary and quickly forgotten exception (see Tooze, 2018a; 2018b). There was a momentary interest in how business ethics inevitably ebbs and flows as events in the financial marketplace draw attention to its flaws, but this was quickly supplanted and back to business as usual. Malpractice cases are held up as 'isolated episodes' or one-off 'exceptional' failures of individual morality and conduct or regulatory oversight rather than recurring malpractice patterns common in corporate and financial life. Many economic models of 'crime' see it as largely a threat that is ever-present but is the anathema of good finance. Just as the confident mechanistic models that tend to characterise economics, crime, when it appears in the economics literature, is an exceptional problem to be guarded against, not a routine part of the everyday. It is something of a utopian fantasy that the market is ever guarded against bad people cleaning their bad and dirty money. Following the 2008 financial crisis, Antonio Maria Costa, the head of the UN Office on Drugs and Crime, revealed that he had come across evidence suggesting that the proceeds of organised crime 'served as the sole available liquid investment capital' for some banks teetering on the brink of collapse during the immediate aftermath of the crisis (as cited in Vulliamy, 2011). Simply put, drug money worth billions of dollars kept the global financial system afloat as some US$352 billion (£216 billion) of drug profits was absorbed into the economic system. Ironically, it is often the same groups that claim to be staunchly committed to participating in international endeavours against money laundering, fraud, corruption and terrorist funding that facilitate these activities within their own jurisdictions. Criminology and social science, unfortunately, rarely delve into this aspect, partly because the prevailing focus on power often fails to align with the true realities of the situation.

Of course, crime is in and of itself necessarily and always an imprecise concept, and hence, financial crime, which often is not a crime at all, is no different. While we may have a global economy, there needs to be a more global consensus regarding the various legal characterisations of specific acts, such as money laundering, corruption and tax avoidance (or evasion). For example, considerable variation exists among countries regarding which crimes may give rise to proceeds that may be laundered. Indeed, a global financial system is, in many ways, the ultimate enabler of divisions. When immoral, unethical or criminal conduct in the global financial system is

CRIMES OF THE POWERFUL AND THE CONTEMPORARY CONDITION

encountered, it is often presented as eroding market integrity, quality and competitiveness and using financial systems. However, an alternative view is that it reflects the ultimate systemic logic of these. According to Mattei and Nader, the concept of the 'rule of law' is often portrayed as a positive force, but it disregards the fact that it has been employed as a potent political tool by Western nations to justify plundering weaker countries through acts of violent extraction by more powerful political actors (Mattei and Nader, 2008).

The concept of 'corruption' is also hardly uniformly defined. For example, in some countries, so-called 'facilitation' or 'grease' payments given to induce foreign public officials to perform their functions are quite the norm, while in others, these are treated as illegal bribes (Lopez-Claros et al, 2020). Agreement is also absent as to what constitutes financial crime. Some countries consider very low tax rates as abusive or harmful tax competition while others do not, just as there are also few agreements on what constitutes 'excessive' in terms of excessive bank secrecy. While on the one hand financial crime can be said to impede economic growth and undermine the global financial systems, so too the illicit proceeds from criminal activity are estimated to account for 2–5 per cent of global GDP (around US$2 trillion), yet less than 1 per cent is ever seized or frozen by law enforcement agencies (World Economic Forum, 2023). In the summer of 2012, a subcommittee of the US Senate released a report into the London-based banking group HSBC and discovered that it was awash in malpractice (see Committee on Homeland Security and Governmental Affairs, 2012). According to the 339-page report, the bank had laundered billions of dollars for Mexican drug cartels and violated sanctions by covertly doing business with pariah states. HSBC had also helped a Saudi bank with links to Al Qaeda transfer money into the US. Mexico's Sinaloa cartel, which is responsible for tens of thousands of murders (Council on Foreign Relations, 2022), deposited so much drug money in the bank that the cartel designed special cash boxes to fit HSBC's teller windows. On a law enforcement wiretap, one drug lord extolled the bank as "the place to launder money" (cited in Keefe, 2017). HSBC was not the only bank mired in controversy doing dirty business with less than wholesome people.

In 2018, it was revealed that around €200 billion of questionable money flowed through Danske Bank when its chief executive, Thomas Borgen, resigned (Milne and Winter, 2018; Pretorius, 2022). It was claimed that the Danish bank's Estonian branch had laundered the money between 2007 and 2015. To put that figure into perspective, the GDP of Estonia in 2017 was only €29 billion. Again, the case should have brought serious questions over the capacity of banks and governments to combat money laundering. The European Commission described it as the 'biggest scandal in Europe' (cited in Neate and Rankin, 2018), and Danske Bank and Denmark and

Estonia's financial watchdogs were investigated by the European Union's banking supervisor (though to little media commentary). The European Banking Authority ultimately closed its probe into Danish and Estonian regulators in relation to a money laundering scandal at Danske Bank, saying its board rejected a proposal to find the watchdogs in breach of European Union law. Danish authorities charged Borgen in May 2019 with neglecting his responsibilities. Additionally, charges against Borgen (along with fellow bankers Henrik Ramlau-Hansen and Lars Morch) were dropped in April 2021, and the former was acquitted in a civil lawsuit related to the Danske money laundering scandal in November 2022 (Wienberg, 2022). In December 2022, Danske Bank pled guilty and agreed to a US$2 billion fine to settle the case with the Department of Justice in the US (Office of Public Affairs, 2022). Today, Danske Bank proudly proclaims on their website that they are 'committed to fighting financial crime'.

A chronology of financial crime

The history of the global financial system being a site of exploitation and malpractice in pursuit of self-interest is tied to the very development of today's global financial system. The 1720 'South Sea Bubble' in Great Britain is often referred to as the world's inaugural financial crash, the first Ponzi scheme, a manifestation of speculative mania, and a cautionary tale illustrating the consequences of succumbing to 'groupthink' (Bruner, 2020).

The financial crash affected even some of the greatest thinkers of the time, including Isaac Newton and writer Jonathan Swift, who had initially supported the South Sea Company scheme. The establishment of the Bank of England in 1694 marked the creation of the first national debt, and it began issuing bills of exchange, which were paper notes bearing the words 'promise to pay' (a phrase that remains on banknotes today) (Kynaston, 2020). During this period, various financial practices experienced a surge in popularity, including lotteries, annuities, joint-stock companies, insurance firms and various money-making schemes. Financial news and investments from overseas, especially from Amsterdam and France, also increased notably. The City of London prospered and gained greater wealth and influence. London has remained a financial capital and powerhouse since. Yet, the South Sea Bubble is essentially a model for many similar frauds in the coming centuries.

The scandal originated with the establishment of a British joint-stock company known as the 'South Sea Company' in 1711 through an Act of Parliament (Carswell, 2001). The South Sea Company was a collaboration between the public and private sectors aimed at consolidating, controlling and reducing the national debt while promoting British trade and profits in the Americas. In 1713, it obtained a trading monopoly in the region, including the *asiento*, which permitted the trading of enslaved Africans to the Spanish and Portuguese Empires (Silva, 2016). The lucrative slave trade had generated immense profits, leading to widespread public confidence in the scheme. Expectations were high that slave profits would soar even further, especially after the conclusion of the War of the Spanish Succession, enabling trade to thrive.

The South Sea Company initially enticed investors with an extraordinary 6 per cent interest on their purchased stocks. However, the anticipated surge in trade following the end of the War of the Spanish Succession in 1713, marked by the Treaty of Utrecht, did not materialise (Teschke, 2019). Contrary to expectations, Spain only allowed Britain limited trade opportunities and imposed a share of the profits. Moreover, Spain imposed taxes on the importation of enslaved people and placed strict restrictions on Britain's 'general trade' ships. Nonetheless, in 1718, when King George I assumed control of the company, the stock prices soared due to the endorsement of the ruling monarch, instilling confidence among investors. Astonishingly, the stocks soon yielded a return of 100 per cent. Unfortunately, the company was not generating near the profits it had promised. Instead, it engaged in trading increasing quantities of its own stock, with those involved in the company enticing, and in some cases bribing, friends and associates to purchase stock to further inflate its price and maintain high demand (see McLynn, 1989).

In 1720, the British Parliament granted the South Sea Company permission to assume control of the national debt (Frehen et al, 2012), which amounted to over £30 million. The company acquired this debt for £7.5 million and received assurances that the interest on the debt would remain at a low level (Speck and Kilburn, 2006). The concept behind this arrangement was that the company would utilise the funds generated from the continually rising stock sales to cover the interest payments on the debt. Additionally, there was a plan to exchange the stocks directly for the debt interest. The stocks sold remarkably well, resulting in progressively higher interest rates, driving up the value and demand for the stocks even further. By August 1720, the stock price had reached £1,000. However, this surge was part of a self-perpetuating cycle without any substantial underlying fundamentals. The anticipated profitable trade that was supposed to support the stocks never materialised. Instead, the company engaged in a speculative cycle, essentially trading itself against its acquired debt (Walcot, 2019). This risky scenario eventually led to disaster in September 1720, as the bubble burst (Terrell, 2020). Consequently, stock prices plummeted drastically, dwindling to a mere £124 by December, representing an 80 per cent loss from their peak value (Marples, 2020). Countless investors were financially ruined, with many losing significant sums of money. The aftermath of the crash was grim, marked by a notable increase in suicides and widespread anger and discontent in the streets of London (Terrell, 2020). The public demanded an explanation for the catastrophic financial fallout.

Wise in their decision, the House of Commons initiated an investigation, which ultimately revealed the staggering extent of corruption and bribery involved, turning the situation into a parliamentary and financial scandal. To address such issues and prevent future occurrences, the Bubble Act was passed by Parliament in 1720 (Harris, 1994). This act effectively prohibited the establishment of joint-stock companies like the South Sea Company without the explicit permission granted through a royal charter. Remarkably, The South Sea Company continued its operations until 1853, although it underwent restructuring during that period (Paul, 2010). Around the time of the 'bubble', approximately 200 such companies were formed, and while many of them proved to be fraudulent schemes, not all were malicious or deceitful. The scheme's founders participated in insider trading by leveraging their prior knowledge of national debt consolidation timing to gain substantial profits from purchasing debt ahead of time. Additionally, they resorted to offering substantial bribes to politicians to secure the necessary legislative support for the scheme. Moreover, the company's funds were utilised for trading in its shares, while certain privileged individuals buying shares received cash loans backed by those same shares to further invest in more shares (Carswell, 2001). The prospects of profits from trade with South America were exaggerated to attract public investment, particularly concerning the slave trade (Boyce and Ville, 2002). However, the prices of the stocks in the speculative bubble far exceeded what the actual business profits, specifically those derived from the slave trade, could justify.

The example illustrates that classic Ponzi systems have existed since modern global financial markets were founded in London in the 1690s when the government sought new ways to raise funds for the Nine Years' War (between 1688 and 1697). Additionally, it highlights how such systems necessitate and involve powerful political actors. Indeed, separating the financial system from the realms of politics and state crime is problematic. During the reign of Charles II (1660–1685), the palace of Westminster bribes paid to MPs often came in the form of parcels of Guinea coins slipped under MPs' dinner plates at banquets (Doig, 1984). While bribery of political actors now might be slightly more subtle, it likely happens in every political system in the globe.

Conspiracy systems or conspiracy of elites

Across much of the globe today, there seems to be diminishing trust in political elites and Western political elites. At the same time, people more readily seem to identify with conspiracy theories and systems of othering and blame. The present world is flooded with a myriad of dangerous conspiracy theories. One of the most notorious is the bizarre QAnon conspiracy, which posits a global child sex-trafficking ring run by liberal, Satan-worshipping paedophiles and predicts its exposure through mass arrests orchestrated by President Donald Trump on a 'day of reckoning' (Roose, 2021). This surreal mass delusion is just one example of many infecting millions of people worldwide, including in the US. Yet, to treat all conspiracy theories as if only ever the preserve of the fantastic and mythical ignores the fact that even occasionally, the strangest conspiracy could be right or may have some grain of truth. For example, in the past, claims that the Dalai Lama was a CIA agent were dismissed as conspiracy. Nonetheless, it is evident that during the 1960s, he received a six-figure salary from the US government, and declassified US intelligence documents reveal that he earned US$180,000 as part of the CIA's funding of the Tibetan resistance, which amounted to US$1.7 million per year (Conboy and Morrison, 2002). The purpose of this funding was to disrupt and hinder China's infrastructure.

Of course, conspiracy theories are at least in part popular because the notion of power existing as secret plots coordinated by powerful and malevolent groups (see Goertzel, 1994) means a third of Americans believe global warming is a hoax (Swift, 2013). What is more, whatever the truth (largely unknowable as it likely is), the continual occurrence and acceptance by the public of what has been termed 'conspiracy theories' involving alleged corrupt political actors (Biden – Ukraine and Trump – Russia) founded around alleged engagement in corrupt activities (in the case of the former relating to the employment of his son, Hunter, by Ukrainian gas company Burisma, and in the latter business interests, corrupt payments and through blackmail with kompromat material) continue to frame political divisions and debates. However, the results of these conspiracy theories are that they help deflect people's attention from the real systematic damage billions of people around the world are suffering as a result of the powerful, including the very destruction of the living Earth, which, if unaddressed, may drive our entire civilisation to destruction.

Western political leaders, and the real truth or not of them, appear unknowable to the average person. However, many of the shadowy ways that power operates in conspiracy are not hidden at all, and people merely do not understand that the conspiracy is in plain sight. For instance, in 1947, amid the post-war reconstruction, a select group of free-market ideologists gathered at a luxurious Swiss resort to establish the Mont Pelerin Society. This organisation was dedicated to advancing and preserving the narrow ideology of neoliberalism on a global scale (see Monbiot, 2016). Their notions, advocating the almost complete dominance of the free market in all facets of society, the dismantling of regulations, and the prioritisation of individual liberty over concerns of fairness, equity or community welfare, were perceived as extreme and fanatical in their era. However, over a span of more than 30 years, fuelled by generous contributions from affluent patrons, they meticulously enlarged their strategy for global supremacy. They accomplished this by forming intricate networks of academics, businessmen, economists, journalists and politicians in influential centres worldwide (for a comprehensive overview of this process, see Mirowski and Plehwe, 2015). Their moment of opportunity arose when the stagflation crisis of the 1970s discredited classic Keynesian economics. By 1985, with fervent advocates of the free market like Ronald Reagan and Margaret Thatcher firmly established in positions of political and public power, they launched a concerted effort to systematically revolutionise nearly every aspect of life into an unregulated marketplace (Harvey, 2007). Their vision involved turning everything into commodities that could be traded without moral constraints, favouring the highest bidder.

They undermined trade unions, dismantled social safety nets, lowered tax rates for the wealthy, deregulated various sectors, and orchestrated a significant wealth transfer from society to the ultra-rich and politically influential elite (Cooper, 2012). As Graz (2010) points out, the annual gatherings of the World Economic Forum in Davos, Switzerland, have attracted the economic and political elite for over 30 years, establishing it as the venue for the world's masters. It is widely considered the hub of hyper-liberalism, the centre of globalisation and a stronghold of the prevailing *'pensée unique'* (p 321). Despite these observations, those closely affiliated with the Forum tend to downplay its influence.

Much of Davios is geared towards maintaining consumerist and highly marketised systems. Since the 1920s, when Edward Bernays (Sigmund Freud's nephew) used his uncle's insights into the subconscious to develop his new marketing method, the goal of constructing consumers, training the desire for an ever-increasing amount of goods and thereby converting their life's energy into profit for corporations has underpinned much of the global finance industry. Bernays' partner, Paul Mazur, had the aim to create a rampant desire for the want for new things, even before the old had been entirely consumed, and to shape such a mentality via marketisation and advertising. In his influential book *Propaganda* (Bernays, 1928), Bernays acknowledged how his techniques for mental manipulation had already enabled a small elite to control the minds of the US population. The book incorporated insights from social science and psychology to analyse the methods of public communication used at that time:

> The conscious and intelligent manipulation of the organised habits and opinions of the masses is an important element in democratic society. Those who manipulate this unseen mechanism of society constitute an invisible government that is the true ruling power of this country. We are governed, our minds moulded, our tastes formed, our ideas suggested, largely by men we have never heard of. ... In almost every act of our daily lives ... we are dominated by the relatively small

number of persons … who pull the wires which control the public mind. (Bernays, 2004, p 37)

Arguably, both corporations and governments have subsequently perfected the techniques he suggested. During the 1930s and 1940s, Bernays actively promoted cigarettes by presenting them as soothing to the throat and aiding in weight loss. He specifically targeted women, aiming to overcome their 'sales resistance' and increase the number of female smokers (Greene, 2010). Bernays orchestrated a staged demonstration at the 1929 Easter parade, where fashionable young women proudly displayed their 'torches of freedom' (Greene, 2010). Subsequently, the Nazi propagandist Joseph Goebbels became an avid admirer of Bernays and his writings, even though Bernays was a Jew. When Goebbels became the minister of propaganda for the Third Reich, he sought to fully exploit Bernays' ideas in creating the cult of the Führer and in the targeting of Jews by the Nazi regime (Johnson-Cartee and Copeland, 2004). Such ideas around propaganda and popularity and manipulation of the public mind have hardly disappeared in the realm of politics. The corporate and entrepreneurial class has learnt how to utilise 'triggers' like thumbs-up signs and 'likes' statistics to trigger short bursts of dopamine in our brains, leading to screen addiction. Social media has now pervaded various aspects of teenagers' lives, making the power of predatory corporate advertising, whether on platforms like Facebook or related to gambling and politics, even more potent in controlling their minds for profit. Similarly, Cambridge Analytica, the data analytics firm associated with Donald Trump's election team and the successful Brexit campaign, reportedly employed secretive methods to extract millions of Facebook profiles from US voters through significant data breaches. They utilised this data to develop a potent software program to forecast and manipulate voting decisions, thereby posing a threat to Western democracy. In January 2020, a release of more than 100,000 documents showed that Cambridge Analytica worked in 68 countries around the globe with operations to manipulate voters on 'an industrial scale', including in elections in Malaysia, Kenya and Brazil (Ekdale and Tully, 2020); global financial organisations and corporations do much the same with little concern.

Recently, criminology has belatedly turned its attention to environmental destruction and the Anthropocene, and how powerful multinational corporations are increasingly driving ecological harms and destruction. The multinational oil company Shell have long been seen as complicit in the arbitrary executions of the Ogoni Nine – a group of nine activists – hanged in 1995 (including the writer and human rights activist Ken Saro-Wiwa) at the bequest of the Nigerian military government to silence the protests of the Movement for the Survival of the Ogoni People (Amnesty International, 2017). The Movement for the Survival of the Ogoni People demonstrated that others had grown rich on the oil that was pumped from under their soil. At the same time, pollution from spills and gas flaring had 'led to the complete degradation of the Ogoni environment, turning [their] homeland into an ecological disaster' (cited in Amnesty International, 2017).

Such concerns about the damaging effects of the fossil fuel industry go back all the way to 1968 when the Stanford Research Institute alerted the American Petroleum Institute (the trade association that represents America's oil and natural gas industry) to the fact that CO_2 emissions were accumulating in the atmosphere (Robinson and Robbins, ND). The report issued a cautionary message, highlighting that increasing CO_2 levels could lead to dire consequences such as melting ice caps, rising sea levels and extensive global environmental damage. The potentially catastrophic effects of fossil fuel industries have been acknowledged for many years, with the understanding that climate breakdown could be a likely outcome. However, instead of addressing the issue, those accountable either deceived or misled the public.

Following the example of the tobacco industry, which condemned millions to early deaths through deception and obfuscation around the harms of smoking, the fossil fuel industries have lobbied experts and politicians alike, using selective data and false conclusions as to the harms caused and done (Oreskes and Conway, 2011). This situation arises because a select group of wealthy nations exercise control over the World Bank, International Monetary Fund and World Trade Organization, dictating international trade terms. Consequently, the South faces the consequence of wealth flowing to the North, amounting to around US$3 trillion annually, facilitated by illicit financial flows, debt interest payments and profit repatriation (Hickel, 2017). The income gap between Global North and South has quadrupled since 1960, so those countries that had the resources have seen little to no benefit as they have been extracted and plundered to the benefit of those in the West (see Hickel, 2020; Carrier, 2022).

Of course, global financial groups and multinational corporations have power, perhaps in many cases more power than nation states (for a more in-depth breakdown of this, see Chapter 3). In a footnote that went almost unnoticed amid the daily news, the World Wildlife Fund recently disclosed a staggering 68 per cent decline in animal populations worldwide over the last 50 years (World Wildlife Fund, 2020). This includes an 84 per cent decline in amphibians, reptiles and fishes and a staggering 94 per cent decline in animal populations in South America. This latest report is another alarming indicator of nature's decline, as it bows to the incessant expansion of human economic activity around the globe. A staggering three-quarters of all land has been appropriated for human use, transformed into farmland, covered in concrete or submerged by reservoirs (Watson et al, 2016). Approximately three-quarters of rivers and lakes are now utilised for crop or livestock cultivation, depriving several major rivers like the Ganges, Yangtze or Nile, which no longer reach the sea. About half of the world's forests and wetlands have vanished, and the Amazon rainforest, in particular, is disappearing at an alarming rate of an acre per second (Rain-Tree, ND). It is estimated that 5 billion people will face water shortages, and there will be more plastic than fish in the world's oceans (Earth Day, 2022). The root cause of this reckless pursuit towards disaster lies in our society's fixation with economic growth as the sole metric for gauging success. The Organisation for Economic Co-operation and Development (OECD), with only 18 per cent of the global population, accounts for 74 per cent of global GDP, and the richest 10 per cent of people are responsible for more than half of the world's total carbon emissions (Oxfam, 2020). We may not want the reckless system of unsustainable growth to continue, but do we have the power to change direction?

When he was in office as British Prime Minister, one of David Cameron's sternest predictions was that 'the far-too-cosy relationship between politics and money' was 'the next big scandal' (see Jenkins, 2021). However, Cameron himself was to come under criticism in the wake of the COVID pandemic for his own lobbying and advisory role for an Australian entrepreneur, Lex Greensill, whose multi-billion-pound business product, supply-chain financing, allows suppliers to big businesses to be paid earlier for a fee (Smith et al, 2021). In 2020, Cameron tried convincing ministers to include Greensill, his employer, as an adviser in the COVID Corporate Financing Facility scheme. This move would have allowed the company to issue government-insured loans to aid companies during the COVID-19 pandemic (Smith et al, 2021). Cameron and the company's founder, Lex Greensill, were ultimately unsuccessful in their attempts to secure this. While Cameron was found to have not broken any laws when Greensill Capital collapsed a year later with the loss of 440 jobs and possible billion-pound losses for investors, it was revealed that Cameron made £3.29 million after selling a tranche of Greensill shares in 2019 and made around US$10 million before tax for two and a half years' part-time work (BBC News, 2021). Indeed, sitting atop a secrecy jurisdiction that empowers bankers, lawyers and accountants to operate within it and actively facilitate corrupt practices by enabling illicit financial flows through an 'offshore interface' between illicit and licit economies raises more evident concerns about its morality. Cameron had an opportunity to address the issue of how financial market liberalisation contributes to the problem, but despite moral posturing, he, like his predecessors dating back to the 1970s, took little action to tackle the 'secrecy space' in the British financial sector. This 'secrecy space' includes banking secrecy, non-disclosure of corporate ownership, lack of accounting transparency for multinational companies and insufficient provisions for exchanging information between national authorities. As a result of this failure to ensure transparent financial flows, a criminogenic environment has been created, enabling illicit flows to be easily concealed among legitimate commercial transactions, leading to capital flight and widespread tax evasion. It rings fairly hollow, then, when his successors, such as Johnson and Sunak, postulated clampdowns on Russian oligarchs after the invasion of Ukraine (Kuldova et al, 2024, forthcoming).

The violence of financial turmoil

Unarguably, financial institutions and their stability matter. In 1931, it was the bankruptcy of Creditanstalt, Austria's biggest and most secretive bank, owned by the Rothschild family, that heralded the financial collapse of Central Europe and opened the doors for Adolf Hitler (Schubert, 1991). This marked the onset of one of the primary bank failures that triggered the Great Depression. Murder rates hovered around 9 per 100,000 when the Crash of 1929 occurred (Latzer, 2021). These rates rose even further in the early 1930s, the worst years of the Depression. By 1932, an estimated 28 per cent of US households (some 34 million people) did not have a single employed wage earner. The economy began improving after 1934, and crime fell sharply (Latzer, 2021). This suggests that economic improvement reduces violent crime. However, there was a major economic downturn in the US between 1938 and 1939 (the 'Roosevelt Recession') and nearly four million US people lost their jobs, boosting total unemployment to 11.5 million of the population. Yet, despite the widespread economic turmoil, violent crime continued to fall. However, financial crises can create violence in complex ways. Creditanstalt's bankruptcy, and its impact in producing a major global banking crisis, provided a major propaganda opportunity for Hitler and his Nazi party, allowing them to further blame Jews for German and international economic and social troubles (Kirk, 2013). Indeed, many power shifts in the global order have roots in financial turbulence and global markets.

Looking at more recent times, it is difficult to overemphasise the immense economic impact of the 2008 financial crisis. The crisis, spanning from 2008 to 2010, led to a combination of rising expenses and declining revenues, resulting in an estimated cost of over US$2 trillion for the US government. Remarkably, this figure surpassed double the cost of the 17-year-long war in Afghanistan (Horowitz, 2023). Alternative assessments indicate an even higher cost. By measuring the decline in per capita US GDP in comparison to the pre-crisis trajectory, it becomes apparent that the crisis had led to a loss of 15 per cent of the country's GDP, equivalent to over US$4 trillion by 2016 (Council on Foreign Relations, 2022). However, the most significant repercussions of the financial crisis might not be economic but political and social. In the aftermath of the crisis, there was a notable surge in political polarisation and the emergence of populist movements on both the left and right spectrums in Europe and the US. This culminated in events like Brexit in the UK and the election of Donald Trump as the US president. These instances ran concurrently across the globe. Alongside political instability, protests against joblessness, corruption and inequality raged in the West and globally; for example, the ousting of President Zine El Abidine Ben Ali in Tunisia in late 2010/early 2011 after an explosion of popular anger caused by the self-immolation of street vendor Mohamed Bouazizi. This culminated in the Arab Spring, which paved the way for a brutal war in Syria and a legacy of instability in the north of Africa that remains today.

There is growing evidence that recessions are associated with a sizable and highly significant increase in mortality. Specifically, recessions increase mortality rates primarily in emerging market economies rather than in the more affluent West and Global North and within child mortality rates. Several studies have indicated that the severity of a recession is linked to a notable rise in mortality rates among emerging market economies. It is crucial to note that recessions have long-lasting effects, as they result in significantly elevated death rates for as long as 10 years and increased child mortality rates for up to 12 years. It is not simply that recession increases mortality for the youngest and most vulnerable, but that it is a sustained process (Doerr and Hofmann, 2020).

Dirty, dirty money

In the 1970s in Europe, the crash of Bankhaus Herstatt in Germany, the Vatican Bank scandal in Italy and the collapse of Franklin National Bank in the US foreshadowed and gave early examples of how financial liberalisation and globalisation enabled the penetration of the international banking system by a network of secretive financiers, with political influence and links to organised crime (Block and Weaver, 2004). We should be careful not to embrace a simplistic narrative where, historically, banks, law firms and accountants stood as 'trusted institutions' against corruption. Conversely, we ought to be wary of the notion that all advances in compliance, regulation and oversight are to be understood merely through superficial reading of fact and without deeper reflection and questioning. Making just this point in a detailed way, Kuldova and colleagues note:

> US President Joe Biden has elevated corruption to a core national security issue for the United States. Some might write this off as mere political rhetoric, a PR exercise that makes it appear as if the administration is getting truly 'tough' on corruption. While this may be up to a point the case, we should be wary of being too hasty in our dismissal, as such cynicism can cause us to fail to ask important questions which might yield more prescient insights. We must ask why

corruption has been upgraded to a national security issue. Exactly what kind of threat is imagined here? The kind of corruption with which the Biden administration is concerned is primarily the kleptocracy of foreign political and business elites, rather than the more nuanced forms of corruption that pervade US and Western political economy more generally. ... For all of the hyperbole, we know that money laundering by Russian kleptocrats is not going to directly kill people in West Virginia, collapse the US economy, or disrupt its normal functioning. (Kuldova et al, 2024, forthcoming)

It is very much the same institutions that profess regulations that, ultimately, enable and facilitate the morally bankrupt wealth takers and are consequently the professional enablers of financial crime (and money laundering). I am reminded of having lunch in a Surrey hotel with a notorious British organised criminal who told me that the issue as he saw it was the nonsense that separated legitimate and illegitimate business. He said, "Anyone who has made a couple of million quid has bent a lot of rules and always broken a fair few". His view could be remarkably in keeping with Edward Gross's assertion that while all organisations are inherently 'criminogenic' (that is, prone to committing crime), they are not necessarily criminal (Gross, 1980), partly because what constitutes criminal and what constitutes morally right and defensible, as in the case of Cameron and Greensill, are often wholly different things.

The case of Britain today best illustrates the harms that financial liberalisation as a strategy driven by the government can have. In the wake of the Bretton Woods System's collapse, successive British governments, from Edward Heath to Margaret Thatcher, enacted radical financial liberalisations that dismantled social democratic limits on financial activity. The result was the tremendous expansion and globalisation of the City of London as a financial centre and global trading hub. However, this hub has shown little concern with regard to dirty money, estimated to be around £100 billion annually in the UK by the UK's National Crime Agency and up to US$2 trillion globally, according to the UN. While it might be suggested that this is a tiny proportion of the whole of global financial flows, the vast majority of which is 'clean' or legal money, the problem is there is absolutely no way to tell 'clean' from 'dirty' money. Money is simply money, whether existing as hard currency or mere digits on a spreadsheet. There is little ethics to money.

Additionally, because those with money often have significant financial resources and influence (if we look to those clients named in the case of Danske Bank, which is said to involve Vladimir Putin and his brother Igor), then the enhanced ability of such actors to create and use front companies in order to disguise the proceeds of illicit activities and, in the process, hide the ill-gotten gains is all too obvious (see Gricius, 2018). Such actors have access to substantial illicit funds, allowing them to subsidise the front company and offer its products and services below market rates. They have a range of competitive advantages over companies that source their funding from the financial markets. This makes it difficult, if not impossible, for legitimate businesses to compete. The main thrust of the regulatory response to money laundering has been to stop dirty money from entering the banking system and make sure it is traceable when it occurs. The introduction of the Criminal Finances Act 2017 brought forth new measures to combat asset recovery and money laundering in the UK. Among them, Unexplained Wealth Orders were introduced as an investigative tool to aid law enforcement in addressing corrupt assets (Shalchi, 2022). However, the UK's National Crime Agency has only utilised Unexplained Wealth Orders four times since its inception (Shalchi, 2022). This contrasts quite starkly with the supposed explosion of efforts in recent years to, on paper, police financial systems, industries and supply chains and to supposedly cleanse them of 'dirty money' and associations with bad people that include, but are not limited to, corrupt actors, kleptocrats and organised crime groups.

For example, the Basel Committee, a grouping of the world's leading bank supervisors, has so far come up with three guidelines for banks in combatting money laundering, namely 'The prevention of criminal use of the banking system for the purpose of money laundering' (1988), the 'Core principles for effective banking supervision' (1997), and the 'Customer due diligence for banks' (2001). Additionally, the Wolfsberg Principles came into force in 2000 and are an industry response to the threat of money laundering (Chatain et al, 2009). There is an agreement among 11 major international private banks (which account for at least a third of the world's private banking funds) to guide the conduct of international private banking. Essentially, these principles seek to control money laundering by cutting across the multiplicity of jurisdictional issues and addressing the serious reputation damage they suffered in the media because of money laundering. The Wolfsberg Group comprises 13 international banks with the primary objective of creating frameworks and guidelines for managing financial crime risks, specifically focusing on Know Your Customer, Anti-Money Laundering (AML) and Counter-Terrorist Financing policies. Formed in 2000, the Group convened at Château Wolfsberg in north-eastern Switzerland, where they collaborated with representatives from Transparency International, including Stanley Morris and Professor Mark Pieth from the University of Basel, to develop anti-money laundering guidelines tailored to private banking (Basel Institute on Governance, 2022). The Wolfsberg AML Principles for Private Banking were initially released in October 2000, later revised in May 2002 and most recently updated in 2012. However, the signatories include many of the same banks subsequently embroiled in scandals concerning corrupt money laundering. Perhaps this is unsurprising, as business ethics, as we have already suggested, have long been regarded by many as somewhat oxymoronic. In 2022, a huge trove of banking data was leaked, and secret owners of £80 billion held in Swiss bank accounts by an anonymous whistleblower to the German newspaper *Süddeutsche Zeitung* were revealed (Pegg et al, 2022). The said whistleblower suggested: 'I believe that Swiss banking secrecy laws are immoral. ... The pretext of protecting financial privacy is merely a fig leaf covering the shameful role of Swiss banks as collaborators of tax evaders' (cited in Pegg et al, 2022).

The leaked documents revealed that Credit Suisse had consistently provided banking services to a wide range of high-risk clients globally, including individuals such as a Hong Kong stock exchange executive convicted of bribery, a billionaire responsible for the murder of his Lebanese popstar girlfriend, executives involved in embezzling funds from Venezuela's state oil company and corrupt politicians from various nations (Pegg et al, 2022). Yet, while Swiss bank accounts have always been the stuff of secrecy and crime since the 1970s and financial liberalisation in the UK, the City of London has increasingly become the place for the super-rich. London today is essentially the 'world city' for high-net-worth and ultra-high-net-worth individuals. London now has the largest number of wealthy people per head of population. Taken as a whole, London is the epicentre of the world's finance markets, an elite cultural hub and a place to hide wealth, particularly in property, whether the money is clean or dirty (Atkinson, 2020).

Of course, London is also home to some of the world's most prestigious London companies, be it the elite corporate law firms headquartered in the UK or the big four accountancy firms – Deloitte, Ernst & Young, KPMG and PricewaterhouseCoopers – who all promote that they have established global networks of specialists who work to combat financial crime, be it in spheres of cybersecurity, fraud, money laundering, anti-bribery and corruption, or market abuse. However, these organisations have not convincingly demonstrated their impeccable business ethics or competence. The legal profession, in particular, is among the sectors that can enable malpractice and misconduct. Legal and accountancy work often involves facilitating real-estate transactions, managing company incorporations and trusts, providing business and financial advice, overseeing various transactions for individuals and businesses, and putting these individuals and businesses directly in the line of action. However, as Levi notes, the routine:

> Focus of the 'enablers' discourse is on lawyers using expert knowledge and legal professional privilege/professional secrecy to facilitate frauds and to conceal the criminal origins of the funds of others. Lawyer assistance may go little beyond doing the 'normal business': setting up constructions for clients that avoid external scrutiny is, of course, usually legal. It is implausible to fully resolve the extent to which

lawyer 'enablers' are, respectively, naïve, negligent, wilfully blind and/or intentionally criminal. (Levi, 2022)

In 2021, the financial services sector contributed £173.6 billion to the UK economy – 8.3 per cent of total economic output (Hutton et al, 2022). The sector was largest in London, where around half of the sector's output was generated. The UK's financial services sector was the fourth largest in the OECD in 2021 by its proportion of national economic output. Luxembourg's financial service sector was the largest in the OECD, contributing 25 per cent of the country's economic output (Hutton et al, 2022). The financial services sector encompasses crucial areas such as insurance, pensions, personal banking and commercial banking services. This sector has a notable global presence in the UK, drawing considerable foreign investment and in 2011 contributing to a trade surplus for the country (Button and Tunley, 2014). Financial crime is a multi-trillion-dollar business for criminal organisations for sure. However, it can also be big business for governments, not simply because of the cash that can come from doing a favour. As per the UN Office on Drugs and Crime, it is approximated that as much as US$2 trillion of illicit funds are laundered annually through global financial networks (European Union Agency for Criminal Justice Cooperation, 2022). This sum amounts to 2–5 per cent of the global GDP and continuously grows yearly. Naturally, politicians, being accountable to their constituents, hesitate to restrict economic flows that may benefit their respective regions.

Perhaps that is why it is estimated that only 1 per cent of illicit financial flows are intercepted globally (United Nations Office on Drugs and Crime, 2011). While it can be easy to create a binary where the offenders are shadowy and sophisticated offenders, the realities of crime in financial services and who are involved make them the perfect place to consider crime. Opportunist, innovative and agile, financial crime is continually evolving. Today, it includes cybercrime, fraud, bribery and corruption, money laundering, insider trading and antitrust schemes. Tomorrow will see it exploit emerging technologies such as AI, digital currency, open markets and borders, and domestic and international instability. Indeed, financial structures and products can be exploited to evade proper scrutiny and facilitate criminal activity. On the one hand, the state acknowledges that financial crimes, particularly high-end money laundering (involving substantial amounts of illicit funds through financial and professional services sectors), can jeopardise national security and prosperity and ultimately undermine the integrity of financial systems and international standing. On the other hand, it is also worth considering that some degree of questionable conduct may be embedded within financial systems. The very same financial mechanisms often create structures – often shell companies set up in so-called 'tax havens' or 'secrecy jurisdictions' – that are used by many of the world's wealthiest and most powerful people and corporations to shift and store money internationally, and largely legally. While such 'shell' companies or trusts, which do not really employ people (or carry out any real business themselves), may be notionally legal, they tend to be used to minimise liabilities to tax departments and others who might have a claim on those assets. To get some idea of the scale of the problem, the National Crime Agency has suggested that the cost of money laundering to the UK economy is in the billions (National Crime Agency, ND). Globally, it has been estimated that up to 5 per cent of global GDP – that is, £1.5 trillion – is laundered by criminals yearly (European Union Agency for Criminal Justice Cooperation, 2022). Of course, countries also have different legal characterisations of specific acts, such as money laundering, corruption and tax evasion. For example, considerable variation exists among countries as to which crimes may give rise to proceeds that may be laundered. The definition of corruption is not consistent worldwide. In certain countries, what is known as 'facilitation' or 'grease' payments, given to encourage foreign public officials to fulfil their duties, are not considered illegal. However, in other countries, such payments are deemed illegal and classified as bribes. Agreement is also absent as to other types of financial crime. Some countries consider very low tax rates as abusive or harmful tax competition, while others do not. There are also few agreements about what constitutes 'excessive' regarding bank secrecy.

London Interbank Offered Rate pains

In August 2014, Tom Hayes, a City trader, received a 14-year jail sentence, becoming the first person to be convicted by a jury for manipulating the London Interbank Offered Rate (LIBOR) interest rate (Hickey and Grierson, 2015). While the term 'LIBOR' might be an obscure one that people do not understand, the relevance of LIBOR to people is significant in so far as it determines a good deal of our financial lives: the interest rate consumers pay on their credit cards, student loans, mortgages or car payments. LIBOR stands for the LIBOR, which determines the interest rates on trillions of dollars in loans worldwide. Essentially, LIBOR is a benchmark rate, or rather a set of rates, that indicates how much interest would be paid by large banks when they borrow short-term funds from other banks on the money markets for a given period in a given currency. In 2012, following the financial crisis, numerous global banks were implicated in manipulating various trading benchmarks, revealing the industry's involvement in serious, widespread and organised corporate crimes (Council on Foreign Relations, 2016). At the time of the financial crisis, LIBOR was closely watched because it serves two key functions in the financial markets: it is a reference rate for a range of financial contracts and an indicator of the financial 'health' of systemically important banks. It, therefore, would stand to reason that its manipulation would be of interest to criminologists. However, with a few exceptions, LIBOR manipulation as criminal conduct by powerful actors has received scant attention. The rigging of the LIBOR (Wheatley, 2012) and Forex (foreign exchange) (Tillman et al, 2018) trading benchmarks by global investment banks indicate that the financial services industry was still affected by serious, pervasive and networked corporate crimes. The LIBOR came under public scrutiny at the height of the financial crisis with allegations that banks had deliberately misstated their LIBOR submissions to project financial soundness during market turbulence. The ensuing investigations revealed that the manipulations had preceded the crisis and uncovered various rigging activities undertaken by multiple systemically important participants in the financial markets. Nevertheless, those who have written about this, often journalists, have presented a picture that is far from the shadowy corruption of untouchable elites and stressed their normality. Hayes, a brilliant but troubled maths genius, became the linchpin of a wild alliance that included a French trader nicknamed 'Gollum'; a Kazakh chicken farmer turned something short of a financial whiz kid; a Swiss banker with a tendency to drunkenly accost women in bars; a karaoke-loving executive who would falsely boast about his role in a 1990s rock band; and a not-very-bright broker who spent much of his leisure time wiping out on his motorcycle (see Enrich, 2017). In October 2022, a criminal indictment against Hayes was dismissed by a New York court. Prior to this, he had served five and a half years in a UK prison for his involvement in rigging the LIBOR lending benchmark. Furthermore, in October 2019, the UK Serious Fraud Office (SFO) concluded its investigation into the LIBOR rigging scandal after a comprehensive review. The investigation incurred an estimated cost of at least £60 million during its seven-year duration. However, BBC Radio 4's programme, *The Lowball Tapes* (2022), questions whether the right individuals were convicted for rigging rates, alleging that during the height of the financial crisis, the Bank of England and political leaders in Westminster were instructing banks to manipulate LIBOR to a much greater extent than jailed traders such as Hayes ever did on their own account.

5

The Price of the Gun: The Arms Industry

On 17 January 1961, in a farewell address to the nation, US President Dwight Eisenhower warned against the establishment of a 'military-industrial complex'. His speech lasted less than 10 minutes, delivered on national television from the Oval Office of the White House. Those who expected the Second World War military leader to depart his presidency as a nostalgic former soldier were surprised at his strong warnings about the dangers of what has subsequently been termed the military-industrial complex:

> 'A vital element in keeping the peace is our military establishment. Our arms must be might, ready for instant action, so that no potential aggressor may be tempted to risk his own destruction. ... We have been compelled to create a permanent armaments industry of vast proportions. ... This conjunction of an immense military establishment and a large arms industry is new in the American experience. ... Yet we must not fail to comprehend its grave implications. ... In the councils of government, we must guard against the acquisition of unwarranted influence, whether sought or unsought, by the military-industrial complex. The potential for the disastrous rise of misplaced power exists and will persist.' (Congressional Record, 1970, p 4672)

The trade in arms, the smuggling of weapons, and the unlawful exchange of prohibited small arms and ammunition are frequently distinct from the ostensibly 'legitimate' military-industrial complex. This complex delineates the connection between a nation's military and the defense industry, involving influential figures in government and corporations focused on defense. This relationship traces its origins back to C. Wright Mills and *The Power Elite* (1956). In recent times, the systematic examination of how the availability of weapons impacts the rates, patterns and consequences of criminal violence has emerged as a significant area within criminology. This sub-field has gained substantial recognition and is experiencing rapid growth. However, the emerging criminological literature does not tend to focus so much on the harms of the industry but rather reinforces the dominant tendency to perpetuate the divides and focus on the lowest level 'illegal' transactions that arm dangerous offenders. This subsequently reinforces convenient binaries between illicit and legal arms. Of course, this is an understandable orthodoxy to some degree, given that guns are frequently legal commodities to be traded. However, making the issue only about the product's legal status is hugely simplistic.

Towards the end of the 1990s, Ian Taylor (1999) noted that for Western advanced capitalist and self-declared liberal societies, public anxiety over crime suddenly came to a head in a more specific agitation, focusing on the apparently increased use of firearms in crime. Taylor specifically charted the anxious public debates that emerged over firearms control in Britain in the 1990s, especially in the wake of the Dunblane massacre (Taylor, 1999). In the UK, at least, the mass murder of 16 people, mostly five-year-old children, perpetrated by a man using four licensed handguns in a primary school did drive firearms prohibitions that have seemingly effected change. These 1996 murders were not the first mass shooting in modern UK history. However, the reaction and decisive legislative action prohibiting handguns stand in contrast to the situation with shotgun regulation and licencing, where the fee for applying for a firearms licence did not fully meet the cost of processing it for police forces. Many forces (and now police and crime commissioners) have argued that the system of firearms licencing around shotguns in the UK should be overhauled. Furthermore, despite the absence of mass shootings involving handguns since the Dunblane incident, the discussion and discourse surrounding the tragic events of 2 June 2010 in Cumbria, where taxi driver Derrick Bird killed 12 people (prior to turning his legally owned but modified shotgun and .22 calibre rifle on himself) and the 2021 tragedy in Plymouth, UK, when 22-year-old Jake Davison fatally shot five individuals and wounded two others before taking his own life, largely overlooked the aspect of firearm licensing. It is worth noting that both of these incidents resulted from legally owned firearms.

In the UK, the control of firearms is notably stricter compared with several Western capitalist and European nations. However, there have been suggestions that police firearms licensing managers in the UK are sometimes hesitant to make decisions that might lead to costly legal actions when they refuse firearm licenses (Squires, 2014; also see Squires, 2000). A pro-gun lobby likes to present shooting as a hobby and as ethical, with shooters regarded as generally highly responsible. In the UK, shooting as a sport is often associated with rural and countryside life and is sometimes linked to the concept of 'natural conservation'. Some shooters opt for the 'non-toxic' steel shot in an attempt to address environmental concerns.

However, there is evidence that many sports shooters still prefer the 'more effective' lead shot, leading to contamination of woodlands, pastures and watercourses (Squires, 2014). Due to this, sports shooters and gamekeepers are often the same people convicted of offences such as killing protected wildlife in a climate where a lack of regulation and action allows individuals to retain their firearms despite criminal convictions (Nurse, 2020). Wilson and colleagues (2016) have suggested that the mass murders that took place at Dunblane in 1996 contained aspects 'prophetic of other mass murders, such as those that took place [much more recently] at Columbine, Sandy Hook and on Utoya Island' (p 55). The authors use what they describe as a 'criminological autopsy' of the shooting and consider why the Dunblane mass murder – still the worst in British history – has rarely been considered within criminology. However, even in this context, the scholarly examination of Dunblane primarily emphasizes the individual responsibility, mindset, and psychology of the mass shooter (killer). Yet, the acknowledgment that the potential for weapon-enabled violence extends beyond just the lone shooter is overlooked.

The prohibition on handguns in the UK does not mean that there are no weapon-assisted homicides; it simply means that since 1996, there have been far fewer killings with handguns and, fortunately, no mass shootings. Nevertheless, before we transition to the global context of the gun industry, it is important to perhaps situate some of these previously highlighted themes in a context that has also received significant media attention. Within a UK context, knife crime has developed into one of the most substantial and national debates related primarily to youth crime, with most examinations centred on exploring offenders' motivations, 'which then centre on commonly recognised tropes of protection, safety, ubiquity and normativity' (Harding, 2020, p 31). In providing a quantitative picture, the most common method of killing was by a sharp instrument, with 259 homicides by this method recorded in 2019 (Office for National Statistics, 2020). During the COVID-19 pandemic, levels of knife-enabled crime were lower during lockdown periods, but they returned to pre-coronavirus levels in the period from April to December 2021 (Office for National Statistics, 2022). The number of recorded offences related to knife-enabled crime decreased by 4 per cent to 46,950 offences in the year ending December 2021, compared with 49,152 in the year ending December 2020 (Office for National Statistics, 2022). Regarding the fatal outcomes, the number of homicides involving a knife or sharp instrument increased from 256 to 276 offences in the year ending September 2021, compared with the previous year. In 2021, the use of knives or sharp instruments accounted for 42 per cent of all recorded homicides, which marked an increase from 39 per cent in the previous year (Office for National Statistics, 2022). Among these cases, 50 homicides involved teenage victims (aged 13 to 19 years), and in

70 per cent of these teen homicides, knives or sharp instruments were the methods of killing. The latest figures also demonstrated that over half of sharp instrument homicide victims were identified as white (60 per cent). Just under a quarter (24 per cent) were identified as black, and of these 57 black homicide victims, 25 were aged 16 to 24 years. In the UK, the most frequent weapon used in homicide is a knife, and in street homicides, the Rambo knife seems particularly common. Such weapons can be bought for less than £10 and boast chilling names, including First Blood, Fantasy Hunting Knife and the Predator. Anglo Arms is run by Eddy Eliaz, a keen angler who also sells fishing tackle through his firms Next Generation Tackle and Sporting Wholesale. His Sporting Wholesale business had a turnover of £8 million in 2017, making a gross profit of £2.5 million. His companies are all based in a large warehouse in affluent Harpenden, Hertfordshire, just 30 miles but a world away from the London streets where his products are increasingly found. Until he closed, it has received a great deal of negative attention from newspapers in the spate of reports on the use of Anglo Arms weapons in London homicides. Eliaz's Facebook profile has used the picture of Michael Douglas in the role of Gordon Gekko in the classic film *Wall Street* (1987) – a character described by another in the film's dialogue as having "had an ethical bypass at birth".

The power of the gun

Of course, in stark contrast to the UK, guns are abundantly available in the US and taint every aspect of its criminal justice system. By 2020, the number of people incarcerated in the US for federal firearm convictions had increased tenfold over three decades. A significant factor contributing to the rise in numbers was the implementation of 'Operation Triggerlock', a Department of Justice initiative aimed at prosecuting individuals arrested by state and local police for gun possession in federal court, leading to more stringent prison sentences (Chang, 2022). The individuals subjected to prosecution are predominantly people of colour. Both Republican and Democratic politicians endorsed these prosecutions: the former as part of a law-and-order agenda and to prevent more comprehensive gun control legislation, and the latter to regulate firearms and shield against criticism from the right concerning inadequate law enforcement.

C. Wright Mills' tripartite of economic, governmental and military masters as combining the power elite did not specifically mention the power of the NRA. However, looking at where the powerful, political and economic come together to shape policy, the NRA is a case in point. Yet the criminal arms trade instantly conjures images of the illegitimate and criminal faces of shadowy foreign arms dealers and unethical actors, like Nicholas Cage's character Yuri Orlov in the film *Lord of War* (2005). In this fictional tale, a globetrotting arms dealer (inspired by the rumoured real-life figure Victor Bout) embarks on a perilous journey through some of the most dangerous war zones, constantly evading a relentless Interpol agent, rival traders and even some of his own customers, who happen to be some of the world's most ruthless and immoral warlords. That representation, the shadowy and powerful arms broker, is not an entirely fictional one. Such entrepreneurial brokers emerge in criminology, now at least in part because of the growth of acceptance that it is often criminal brokers and traders who supply weapons illegally for use in criminal ventures.

This then runs the full spectrum from the street criminal protecting his drug corner to using illegal weapons in regional wars and global terrorism. In both public discourse and academic discussions, arms dealers are often regarded as morally questionable individuals who capitalise on conflicts, given their prominent roles in the international arms trade. Debates surrounding the legitimacy and illegitimacy of weapon supply are prevalent. The issue here is that, for the most part, all weapons are made legitimately, and perhaps a logical starting point is to consider those making a profit from making weapons in the first place. Of course, the character of Victor Bout, the Russian former military translator turned arms dealer, who reportedly used his multiple air transport companies, including Air Cess, to smuggle weapons since the fall of the Berlin wall and the collapse of the Soviet Union, is one that criminologists should have some interest in. However, Bout's crimes received scant attention when, on 8 December 2022, the Biden administration in the US conducted a prisoner exchange, trading him for Brittney Griner, an American basketball player best known for playing with the Phoenix Mercury (Chisholm et al, 2022). Saudi Crown Prince Mohammed bin Salman also claimed to have 'played a leading role in mediation efforts' (Kirby, 2022). Russia's persistent pursuit of Bout's release was widely believed to have been motivated by his links to the country's notorious military intelligence and led some in the US to see the exchange as rather naïve. Certainly, when it came to the business of dealing in death, Bout was at the top of the metaphorical tree. His business dealings were global, ranging from Eastern Europe to Africa and the Middle East, and led to him becoming infamous with state law enforcement and security personnel in the 1990s and early 2000s. Bout earned the moniker 'Merchant of Death' due to his alleged extensive operations, diverse clientele, and readiness to circumvent weapons embargoes and humanitarian restrictions (Yilek, 2022). This includes claims that he made around US$50 million from sales to the Taliban in the late 1990s, and he had spent almost a decade flouting international law, living openly in Moscow and dining at his favourite restaurants even though an international arrest warrant from Interpol existed for him. In March 2008, he was apprehended in Thailand by the Royal Thai Police, and the US ambassador sought his extradition, which was ultimately ordered by the Thai High Court in August 2010 (Walker, 2008). Bout faced accusations from the US of conspiring to smuggle arms to the Revolutionary Armed Forces of Colombia, which could potentially be used against US forces. He denied the charges in November 2011 but was convicted by a US jury in federal court and sentenced to 25 years. While Bout can be cast as an immoral entrepreneur willing to arm despots for self-profit through the 1990s and 2000s, his companies received 'federal funds totalling millions of dollars from the US companies the likes of FedEx, Kellogg and Brown and Root' (Stohl and Grillot, 2009, p 110), and both the British and US military confessed that they had inadvertently used his company to transport cargo in Iraq (Stohl et al, 2007). Western media sources have also suggested that 'Bout's relationship with Russia's political elites is as murky as his arms-dealing career' (Sauer, 2022b).

A core issue in such a framing of individual arms dealers as the 'evil actor' is highlighted by Victoria Collins and Melissa Pujol, who, having analysed the various documents involved in the prosecution and trial of Bout in the US, note that such a perception tends to paint a partial picture. Indeed in looking at Bout's arms trafficking prosecution and the documents associated with it and subjecting them to analysis, they argue that the case fitted well within the realm of what they regard as a 'neo-liberal crime control policy' where the focus is on 'hyper-individualism, and the protection of state legitimacy', and such framing in and of itself allows for the maintenance of the flourishing arms market (Collins and Pujol, 2016, p 93). Of course, what complicates the picture is that the global arms industry is much wider and much more complex than many people initially recognise. The arms industry (or arms trade) is a global one that manufactures and markets not only weapons but military technology that can connect and intersect in complex ways with a wide range of commercial industries and practices. Occasionally the arms industries and its harms become the target of criminology, where academics the likes of Rob White have explored the use of depleted uranium munitions and armour in wars in the Gulf, work that still is not given nearly enough recognition in criminology generally (White, 2008) but might be useful in focusing a criminological lens on harm.

The arms industry

The arms industry spans a wide array of processes that connect in complex ways, overlapping and intersecting with everyday consumerism in ways we do not recognise, some of which can be beneficial and for the social good. Almost all sectors of global trade, encompassing commodities like bananas, petroleum, timber and minerals, are subject to regulations that bind countries into agreed-upon conduct. Surprisingly, before the UN General Assembly adopted the Arms Trade Treaty (ATT) in April 2013, there was no comprehensive set of global rules governing the trade in conventional weapons. The ATT, it is often suggested, sets in place robust international standards to help guide governments in deciding whether or not to authorise arms transfers. The ATT facilitates cooperation and assistance to support countries in developing effective regulatory systems and safe weapons stockpiles. Its adoption represented a pivotal moment in the international community's endeavours to regulate the global trade in conventional arms and advance peace and security.

However, despite this ATT, gun-related deaths are tragically common. In 2019, more than 250,000 people died due to firearms worldwide (World Population Review, 2020). Nearly 71 per cent of gun deaths were homicides, approximately 21 per cent were suicides and 8 per cent were classified as unintentional firearms-related accidents (World Population Review, 2020). Gun-related violence is widespread globally, even in countries with stricter gun ownership regulations. In 2019, out of the approximately 250,227 gun-related deaths worldwide, 65.9 per cent occurred in six countries: Brazil, the US, Venezuela, Mexico, India and Colombia (World Population Review, 2020). Among these, gun deaths are considered an epidemic in the US, leading the world in civilian gun possession, as many acknowledge. In 2019, the US was second only to Brazil regarding gun deaths, where some 83,451 people lost their lives due to a gunshot.

The arms industry stands out as one of the most thriving corporate enterprises on a global scale. Not only has it created an economic system that almost guarantees growth and sustainability (everyone wants the latest, more developed and refined weapon, while old models are rendered obsolete), but arguably, it has also normalised war and security responses to every social crisis. This is something we see if we look at recent examples such as the migrant crisis, themselves often shaped and forced by disorder resulting from armed conflict, the COVID-19 pandemic or even our responses to climate change, where military advocates are already warning that military capacities will be increasingly overstretched as the crisis intensifies (Tucker, 2021).

Most mainstream politicians, media and corporate leaders regard those involved in financing, inventing, manufacturing, buying and exporting arms as participants in a respectable industry that fosters progress, employment and security. Globally, individuals engaged directly or indirectly in the manufacturing, sale and spread of arms are involved in activities largely seen as legal and legitimate and deemed a 'normal' and beneficial business practice, despite their significant negative human impact. Furthermore, this unquestioned and unchallenged stance has led to the normalisation of war and the utilisation of armed forces to pursue political and, at times, humanitarian objectives. Of course, that can doubtlessly be the case. For example, research and development of goods and technology, from transportation to communication equipment and the internet as engineering production, and servicing of the military, equipment, technology and facilities, cannot be easily separated from more widespread processes of marketisation. Furthermore, many arms-producing companies, those that could be legitimately referred to as 'arms dealers' or as the military industry, produce not only arms for the armed forces of individual states and their civilians but a wider range of products and respond to all manner of commercial opportunities.

As a political issue, it tends to be the case that people agree on the supposed benefits of the arms industry (and its necessity). Yet, the economic and social impacts of the arms sector are hardly debated in the public arena and often escape any scrutiny because of the complexity and lack of transparency in the sector. The UK Defence and Security Exports estimates that the UK is the second largest exporter of defence items worldwide based on the value of orders/contracts signed. Between 2011 and 2020, the majority of UK defence exports (60 per cent) went to the Middle East, followed by North America (17 per cent) and Europe (15 per cent), but very often now to repressive regimes such as Saudi Arabia (Stone, 2021). The UK government often claims that it has one of the most robust and transparent export control regimes in the world (Feinstein and Smidman, 2021) and publishes the cost of arms sold abroad and subsequently authorised under what is referred to as permanent standard individual export licences (SIELs). In 2021, the UK government issued 12,600 SIELs, of which 10,600 (84 per cent) were for permanent exports. The total value of SIELs issued was £10.7 billion. Around £6.5 billion (40 per cent) of this was for military goods, and £4.2 billion (60 per cent) for non-military goods (Kirk-Wade, 2023). The government also details what kinds of weapons were sold and to whom they were allowed to be sold. Despite this seemingly transparent façade, the government also manages a corresponding and less transparent 'open licence' system, which provides a more open-ended means of approval to manufacturers to sell particular armaments to a specific country without a monetary limit (Stone, 2021). For instance, between 2014 and August 2019, the UK operated an open licence for bombs and air-to-surface missiles to Saudi Arabia, a type repeatedly used in the war in Yemen (Action on Armed Violence, 2018). Researcher Katie Fallon of Campaign Against Arms Trade states that "the use of open licences also offers the government a convenient sleight of hand when it comes under pressure over arms sales to a particular country due to events such as wars, military coups, or well-publicised human rights abuses" (cited in Stone, 2021).

Fallon continues, noting that "so much of the arms industry takes place in secret, and that's how the arms dealers like it" (cited in Stone, 2021). The use of such open licences naturally conceals and obfuscates the realities of such trade involving armaments, along with where and how such arms are ultimately used and against whom. As such, the realities and extent of the

UK's involvement in the arms trade are consequently concealed and thus free from any significant oversight.

Since March 2015, Saudi Arabia and the United Arab Emirates have spearheaded a coalition of states in Yemen against Houthi forces, which, in alliance with former Yemeni President Ali Abdullah Saleh, gained control of Yemen's capital, Sanaa, in September 2014. The involvement of these states in the armed conflict in Yemen has led to the most significant humanitarian crisis globally, with thousands of Yemeni civilians killed and injured by the parties involved. Since 2015, over 17,000 people have been killed and injured, with a notable proportion of civilian casualties in air raids being women and children, accounting for a quarter of the total (Human Rights Watch, 2019). Over 20 million people in Yemen are facing food insecurity, with a staggering 10 million of them at risk of starvation, as reported by Oxfam (2016). Since March 2015, the coalition has carried out numerous indiscriminate airstrikes, resulting in the deaths of thousands of civilians and targeting civilian structures in clear violation of the laws of war. These airstrikes have been conducted using munitions supplied by the US, the UK and other countries. Between January 2021 and February 2022, a further 87 civilians were confirmed to have been killed in Yemen by weapons supplied by both the UK and US (Sabbagh, 2023), indicating that such tragedies will continue. Upon being confronted with such a tragic loss of life, a spokesperson for Britain's Department for International Trade, unsurprisingly, said it operates "one of the most robust and transparent export control regimes in the world" (cited in Magdy, 2023). Alongside this, on a geopolitical level, Oxfam also notes that the British government failed to effectively respond to the Saudi-led coalition attacks in Yemen while providing such responses in other instances. For instance, the charity said the UK 'imposed sanctions on Russian officials over attacks on civilians in Ukraine, while continuing to defend arms sale to the Gulf monarchy to use in Yemen's war' (Magdy, 2023). In referencing this apparent contradiction, Oxfam stated this is 'a clear demonstration of double standards and politicisation of the law for reasons of national interest' (cited in Magdy, 2023).

According to Human Rights Watch, at least 90 airstrikes conducted by the Saudi-led coalition appear to be unlawful, including deliberate attacks on civilians and civilian objects, such as Yemeni fishing boats, resulting in dozens of casualties. These actions are in clear violation of the laws of war. As of the time of writing, the Yemen Data Project records that the Saudi-led coalition has carried out more than 20,100 airstrikes on Yemen since the start of the conflict, averaging approximately 12 attacks per day (Human Rights Watch, 2019). The coalition has bombed hospitals, school buses, markets, mosques, farms, bridges, factories and detention centres (Human Rights Watch, 2019). It clearly would be of no great comfort to women and children under the falling bombs in Yemen to know that they are legally procured, but even here, the reality is much murkier still. Nevertheless, with rare and notable exceptions, criminology little considers this sphere (Taylor, 1999).

The arms trade can make wealth for powerful people and is open to abuse and exploitation. The media should have access to the information necessary for a democratic debate to fulfil its role in monitoring government actions. However, crime stories concerning armament and controversy centred on the arms industry are limited. The role of arms exports is rarely subject to scrutiny. One notable case that stands out is the Arms-to-Iraq scandal in the early 1990s, which involved four directors of the British machine tools manufacturer Matrix Churchill (Norton-Taylor, 2012). The directors faced trial for providing equipment and knowledge to Iraq, but the trial fell apart in 1992 when it emerged that the company had received advice from the government on how to conduct arms sales to Iraq (Hellier, 1995). Despite this, corruption in the arms trade rarely receives the attention that infamous and more conventional crimes do. The SFO charged British civil servants Jeffrey Cook and John Mason for sanctioning corrupt payments totalling £7.9 million to senior Saudi officials between 2007 and 2012 to secure lucrative contracts for a British firm, GPT, in the Saudi military equipment sector, with the British government's awareness (Evans and Pegg, 2022). In July 2022, Judge Simon Bryan dismissed the jury sitting at Southwark Crown Court in, which imposed reporting restrictions on the reasons for halting proceedings (Beioley, 2022). Before the trial was halted, it had been claimed that Cook, a former Ministry of Defence (MoD) civil servant, and Mason, who worked for an offshore firm, Simec, were accused of funnelling millions of pounds in bribes to the Saudis. It was claimed in court that the MoD organised the original deal based on what the MoD 'called at the time, "the deniable fiddle"' (Evans and Pegg, 2022). The prosecuting QC claimed 'they actually recorded that phrase in reports and file notes at the time' and alleged that the UK government facilitated the payments (some might call them bribed) to Saudi royalty amounting to £60 million to be made from the late 1970s to 2020 (Evans and Pegg, 2022). The case received little attention in any media sources outside broadsheet newspaper reporting and *Private Eye* and no attention at all in academic criminology.

Of course, what the above cases also highlight is the complexity and obscurity of what happens in the arms trade, and this in and of itself means that it is difficult to obtain figures on arms and arms dealing, particularly because governmental and industry classifications specifically covering arms production do not exist as such. In statistical data, weapons production figures are often divided between aeronautical, naval, space and other sectors, which may include civilian products and employment. Hence, it is impossible for analysts to verify details on the trade's scope, scale and actuality. Hence, a lack of transparency and information on the actual size of national arms industries becomes the norm and can serve to impede and obfuscate any meaningful debate. Additionally, the regulation and control of arms exports (reformed by the Conservative government between 2015 and 2017 with the creation of an Export Control Joint Unit), which is said to provide a coordinated cross-government operation of export controls while maintaining a prompt and high-quality licensing service for UK exporters, removed the Department of International Development representation, the section some deem the more moral and ethical conscious against representatives from the Department for International Trade, Foreign, Commonwealth and Development Office, and the MoD expertise. This is especially the case when the government's stated aims are to provide an 'efficient, rigorous and customer-friendly export licensing and compliance service' (GOV.UK, ND) of what are, essentially, tools intended to kill people.

The banality of evil: the arms trade and genocide

From 1941 to 1945, Nazi Germany, with the assistance of local collaborators, carried out a systematic genocide that resulted in the murder of approximately six million Jews, accounting for around two-thirds of Europe's Jewish population. The government of Nazi Germany also targeted other groups for various discriminatory reasons due to their ethnicity, religion, political beliefs or sexual orientation. In total, including the six million Jewish deaths, the total number murdered during the Holocaust is estimated at 17 million. Sixteen years after this tragic event occurred, Adolf Eichmann, the Nazi operative responsible for coordinating the transportation of millions of Jews and others to various concentration camps as part of the Nazi's Final Solution, stood trial at the Supreme Court of Israel. Hannah Arendt, a political philosopher, author and Holocaust survivor, travelled to Jerusalem to report about Eichmann's trial for *The New Yorker*. It was here that she began questioning the nature of evil and, more pertinently, whether someone can be complicit and enable evil acts without being evil. Her observations of Eichmann instigated such deliberations, who, according to Arendt, was 'neither perverted nor sadistic' but 'terrifyingly normal' (cited in White, 2018). Arendt elaborated further, noting that standing before her was not a monster or ideologically motivated tyrant but an amoral bureaucrat with a seeming lack of evil intentions and a general 'thoughtlessness' behind their actions (Arendt, 1963). Specifically, Arendt noted that 'the longer one listened to him, the more obvious it became that his inability to speak was closely connected with an inability to think, namely, to think from the standpoint of somebody else' (p 49). Arendt is not suggesting that Eichmann was unable to think per se, but that he was instead motivated by what she refers to as 'an idea'. As such, she characterises Eichmann as a 'perfect "idealist"' who 'had of course his personal feelings and emotions, but he would never permit them to interfere with his actions if they came into conflict with his "idea'" (p 43). By utilising this ability to detach oneself from the consequences of their actions, he 'commit[ted] crimes under circumstances that made it well-nigh impossible for him to know or to feel that he [was] doing wrong' (cited in White, 2018).

While Arendt's observations and philosophical ruminations have been critiqued and elaborated on since her work was published, it raises interesting questions related to those who perhaps do not engage directly with acts of mass murder but instead are complicit and enable such crimes against humanity in other ways. For instance, returning briefly to the Holocaust, some benefitted financially, including certain businesses and manufacturers whose bought-and-paid-for services facilitated such brutal acts. Adolf Hitler, upon implementing his 'Final Solution', realised that he would have to find more economical and time-efficient ways to carry out his plan, so he enlisted the help of a corporation called Topf and Söhne to build crematoriums, gas chambers and other machinery (Schüle and Sowade, 2018). Alongside these lethal industrial components, this same company made weapons, shells and other military vehicles during World War I. In World War II, it made armaments, including weapons shells and aircraft parts for the Luftwaffe. Alongside this, it is important to note that this company was not the sole provider related to weapons or instruments used in the Holocaust, with the Berlin-based company H. Kori GmbH being its primary competitor for military bids (Lepiarz, 2020). Attempting to capitalise on Hitler's and the Nazi party's plans for mass extermination, the company ensured that it outbid its competitors that were also attempting to gain lucrative contracts, while designing ever more powerful machinery designed to cremate victims. Here, we can perhaps see traces of Arendt's banality of evil – a 'normlessness' and indifference to others while driven by an almost singular 'idea' that, in this instance, serves the ideology of profit over all other considerations. Perhaps this is best articulated within the company's correspondence with the Nazi party, in which the letterheads read: 'Always a pleasure to do business with you' (cited in Lepiarz, 2020).

It seems that even with the world coming together through the Universal Declaration of Human Rights in 1948 to prevent the recurrence of a tragedy like the Holocaust, the Political Instability Task Force revealed a disturbing reality. Between 1956 and 2016, the world witnessed a staggering 43 genocides, resulting in the loss of approximately 50 million lives (Anderton and Brauer, 2016). The UN High Commissioner for Refugees also approximated that these episodes of violence had displaced an additional 50 million people until 2008 (Anderton and Brauer, 2016). This is only further compounded when we consider that there are currently, according to Genocide Watch – the Coordinator of the Alliance Against Genocide – active emergencies in countries such as Afghanistan, Central Sahel, China, the Democratic Republic of the Congo, Ethiopia, Myanmar and Nigeria

(Genocide Watch, 2021). There is also little doubt that Russia's invasion of Ukraine and the reports of mass graves being uncovered at the time of writing will result in this also being added (Johnson, 2022). A 'genocide emergency' is declared when the genocidal process has reached the stage of genocidal massacres and other acts of genocide. At the time of writing, these listed countries were engaged in exterminating certain groups that exist and live within them yet are routinely ignored in the face of more 'newsworthy' stories and headlines designed to maximise sales and profit (Jewkes, 2004).

The UN has established the ATT and the UN Office for Disarmament Affairs concerning weapon manufacturers and the arms trade. The former aims to control the trade in arms, asserting that one of its fundamental elements is to regulate and prevent any transfer that could breach Security Council arms embargoes or be utilised to perpetrate acts of genocide, crimes against humanity or war crimes (United Nations: Office for Disarmament Affairs, ND). According to the UN, the latter is designed to coordinate the UN system on all issues related to the arms trade, along with building 'synergies with related topics such as the illicit trade in small arms and light weapons and weapons stockpile management' (United Nations: Office for Disarmament Affairs, ND). Such regulatory policies are perhaps not surprising when we consider, for instance, the role of imported arms in the lead-up to the Rwanda genocide that took place in 1994. The majority of the mass murders that began in Rwanda on 6 April 1994 were executed using local agricultural instruments such as machetes. However, the killings were largely instigated or overseen by members of the security forces who had more light weaponry, including automatic rifles and grenades. Such arms, shockingly, were traced back to the UK and, more specifically, to a drab office above an aromatherapy shop in North London just two years after the massacre. Upon initial inspection, the office, located on Vivian Avenue, Hendon, was the home of Travelour (UK) Ltd, a travel agency and import-export business, but it was 'locked and its operators had vanished' (Boggan, 1996). Boggan continues, stating that:

> Attention focused on the address because it was from there four years ago that a man called Anoop engaged a firm of accountants to act for another company, Mil-Tec Corporation Ltd. Mil-Tec was the company name on invoices for arms, totalling some pounds 3.3m, found on a bus abandoned at a Hutu refugee camp in eastern Zaire on Sunday. (Boggan, 1996)

These findings were pertinent, as they suggested that a British company had violated a UN embargo imposed in May 1994 while soldiers of the Rwandan army were killing Tutsis and moderate Hutus. It was subsequently revealed that Mil-Tec, a company that was registered in the Isle of Man, had supplied millions of rounds of ammunition, thousands of rifles, grenade launchers, and tens of thousands of mortar bombs and grenades up until July of 1994. It was also uncovered that Mil-Tec was fronted by a nominee company, Business Management Services Nominees Ltd, and 'a professional company secretary, John Donnelly, of BMS Company Secretaries, based in Sark, in the Channel Islands' (Boggan, 1996). Human Rights Watch (1999) reported that five shipments were reportedly arranged. Alongside this, National Westminster in the UK and banks in Belgium, France, Switzerland, Italy and the US 'were also said to have handled financial transactions involved in purchasing weapons for the regime' (Todd, 2017). Anoop Vidyarthi, reportedly the 'manager' of the operation, was a Kenyan Asian who ran a travel consultancy from the mentioned London office. He was also associated with a UK arms dealer, Paul Restorick, who operated another arms brokering company, Mil-Tec Marketing, based in Ashford, Kent (Todd, 2017). At that time, the UK government was responsible for ensuring that UN sanction measures were applied to the Isle of Man. Although such UN Security Council measures should automatically apply to all member states, they still required formal implementation through Orders in Council under the United Nations Act 1946 of Parliament. These orders would establish offences and corresponding penalties. Even with the UN sanctions and embargo in place, the oversight for implementing the UN Security Council resolution fell under the Foreign and Commonwealth Office, which seemed to experience a breakdown of communications with the Home Office (Todd, 2017). Consequently, the required order to extend the sanction controls for Rwanda to the Isle of Man was not issued until December 1996. As such, no charges were brought to the company or Anoop Vidyarthi.

This one example from almost 30 years ago is by no means an isolated incident, with individuals, corporations and even governments providing arms used in mass atrocities. For instance, the government of Charles Taylor in Liberia provided weapons and troops in exchange for diamonds to the rebels of the Revolutionary United Front, who killed thousands of civilians in the Sierra Leonean capital, Freetown, in 1999 (Anderson, 2012). So too, the genocide in Darfur, Western Sudan, whereby an estimated 80,000 to 400,000 civilians were killed, was also facilitated and enabled by arms from both China and Russia. Brian Wood, an expert on military and policing for Amnesty International, noted that "China and Russia are selling arms to the Government of Sudan in the full knowledge that many of them are likely to end up being used to commit human rights violations in Darfur" (cited in Amnesty International, 2012). The genocide in Myanmar, in which over 25,000 civilians were killed in 2018, was also facilitated by UN member states, including two permanent members of the Security Council, who provided arms to the Burmese military. Specifically, it was identified that China, Russia and Serbia had supplied the culprits of the atrocities with weapons used to attack and kill civilians. The Special Rapporteur on the situation of human rights in Myanmar, Tom Andrews, stated that:

> It should be incontrovertible that weapons used to kill civilians should no longer be transferred to Myanmar. These transfers truly shock the conscience. ... Stopping the junta's atrocity crimes begins with blocking their access to weapons. The more the world delays, the more innocent people, including children, will die in Myanmar. (UN Human Rights Council, 2022)

Alongside this, a French court convicted the son of late President François Mitterrand and others who were once among France's elite of crimes related to illegal arms sales to Angola during its civil war in the 1990s (Shirbon, 2009). Referred to as 'Angolagate', the trial centred on US$790 million in arms sales to Angolan President Eduardo dos Santos' People's Movement for the Liberation of Angola between 1993 and 1998, when it was fighting National Union for the Total Independence of Angola rebels led by Jonas Savimbi (Shirbon, 2009). When this conflict finally ended, the death toll stood between 500,000 and 800,000 people, and over one million were internally displaced. These illicit acts of arms trafficking were deeply intertwined with the systematic killings, mass rape and torture of civilians in the Democratic Republic of Congo. Amnesty International (2005) shed light on the significant role played by arms dealers, brokers and transporters from various countries, including Albania, Bosnia and Herzegovina, Croatia, Czech Republic, Israel, Russia, Serbia, South Africa, the UK and the US.

Ultimately, acts of mass murder and genocide need to be facilitated and enabled by arms that, similar to the complicity of private corporations that profited from the Holocaust in World War II, are primarily driven not by the ideology or motivations of direct perpetrators, but by a seeming banality that does not consider the sheer tragedy of their actions. Returning to the work of Hannah Arendt and her observations at the trial of Adolph Eichmann, she notes that such banality of evil is, in essence, an abyss: 'A lack of common measure between the gigantic scale on which the crimes (the evil) were committed and the insignificance (the banality) of the persons who were among those most responsible' (cited in Martine, 2007). In examining Eichmann, Arendt could not assign him to 'any particularity of wickedness, pathology, or ideological conviction of the doer' (Arendt, 1971, p 417). Instead of the typical characterisations found in definitions of 'evil', this individual was characterised as someone willing to do anything to advance in the Nazi bureaucratic ranks. We can perhaps see traces of this banality of evil within the cases previously discussed. There are no traces of apparent wickedness to those who assisted in arming the perpetrators, but instead a form of cognitive disconnect of their role within such atrocities, which, from

CRIMES OF THE POWERFUL AND THE CONTEMPORARY CONDITION

illicit individual arm dealers to corporations and states, is instead driven by a singular 'idea' of the pursuit of profit over all other considerations.

Weapons of the powerful

The MoD's Saudi Armed Forces Projects has 200 staff supporting the UK's arms sales to Saudi Arabia (Jones, 2022). It also advises those considering export licences on the possible diversion of the exports to third countries and the potential risk of the export to the UK or its armed forces. As an illustration, the Al Yamamah arms sales, where the UK sold arms to Saudi Arabia in exchange for up to 600,000 barrels (95,000 m³) of crude oil per day to the British government (Pallister, 2006), involved BAE Systems (and its predecessor British Aerospace) as a prime contractor. BAE Systems pleaded guilty in a US court to charges of false accounting and misleading statements concerning sales (Leigh and Evans, 2010).

After facing political pressure from both the Saudi and British governments, the British SFO decided to discontinue its investigation into the deal. This again received almost no attention in criminology, and only some of the public would have heard of it. Currently, the trial of Jeffrey Cook and John Mason has garnered minimal attention from media, political commentators and academic criminologists, despite featuring testimonies that allege the British government's involvement in payments of up to £60 million to a future Saudi Arabian king and his son as well as other high-ranking officials as part of a massive arms deal, with attempts to conceal them under the guise of a 'deniable fiddle' (Evans and Pegg, 2022). This is a long-established pattern. In the extensive academic literature on crime and criminal justice, one would be hard-pressed to find references to the South African Arms deals of the 1990s, despite the calls for decolonisation of the curriculum. The more significant issue, involving European arms companies and prominent South African politicians, revolves around the manipulation of the procurement process for a US$5 billion arms deal at the time, where bribes as high as US$300 million were exchanged from the seller companies (BBC News, 2018; Corruption Tracker, 2020).

Moreover, the corruption was hardly simply capitalist Western business hampered by ethics. The African National Congress (ANC) and their government in South Africa, which took power in 1994, faced a country with great poverty, a population ravaged by AIDS and a deeply divided country with the legacy of violence that came about through Apartheid. Under President Nelson Mandela, the ANC government committed to reducing spending on arms. However, following Mandela, when South Africa resumed spending on military equipment, that spending became mired in controversy and self-gain for black ANC figurehead politicians like Jacob Zuma. In search of new fighter planes, South Africa's air force chiefs had initially tendered for new planes and selected Italian aircraft as cheaper and more modern. However, the defence minister, Joe Modise, then amended the tender specifications and decided to exclude cost as part of the procurement process, a move that tipped the balance in favour of the ageing British Hawks that BAE Systems and Saab had tendered to supply (initially shortlisted as the third-place bidder) – at nearly double the price. The Hawks were part of a £1.5 billion package BAE and Saab put together to supply 24 Hawk fighter trainers and 28 Gripen light fighter aircraft to South Africa (McGreal, 2007). It was at the time the single biggest contract that the new South Africa, which was still emerging from the violent and militarised repressions of the Apartheid system, had ever signed.

It was alleged that Modise manipulated contract processes by taking bribes (some US$50,000) from European companies, such as British BAE Systems, to manipulate contract processes to favour them as bidders and, further, to change procurement processes so that cost was not a foremost consideration in determining who won tenders. In essence, arms deals worth US$5 billion at the time were subject to manipulation by European arms companies and prominent South African politicians, who received bribes of up to US$300 million from the seller companies. Jacob Zuma, who served as deputy president of South Africa from 1999 to 2005 during the negotiation of the deal, was involved in this scandal and later became president from 2009 to 2018. Zuma allegedly took bribes to facilitate the deal. His imprisonment in July 2021 for contempt of court at the Zondo Commission (Eligon, 2021) and the allegations that he took corrupt payments from the arms industry are rare instances of the powerful being held (perhaps partially) to account.

6

Making a (Corporate) Killing

On 19 July 2023, the day we sat down to write this chapter on corporate harms and deaths caused in the perpetual pursuit of profit, news broke of how energy firm BP was fined £650,000 after an offshore worker's death when he plunged from an offshore platform into the sea (Banks, 2023). Upon investigation, it was revealed that on 4 September 2014, 43-year-old Sean Anderson accidentally fell through an uncovered grating located on the Unity installation, approximately 112 miles (180 km) northeast of Aberdeen. Although BP initially pleaded not guilty to the health and safety charges, the company was ultimately found guilty of neglecting to implement appropriate control measures for open gratings on the lower deck of the platform and was handed the aforementioned monetary fine. Graham Buchanan, Sheriff of the Scottish Courts Service, said that although what happened was "tragic and devastating", it had been an isolated incident (cited in Banks, 2023). He subsequently added that a man had died and that a fine on a profitable company such as BP must have "some economic impact" (Banks, 2023). This story, while tragic, is unfortunately indicative within the context of corporate harm and, in the most serious of instances, death.

This is not a new story for criminology, as such forms of corporate harm have been well examined. The harms of the North Sea oil industry, for example, were highlighted by W. G. (Kit) Carson as far back as 1981, well before the Piper Alpha disaster (Carson, 1982). Thus far, we have examined the enormous scale and influence of some corporate 'giants' and the way they have infiltrated and gradually chipped away at the very foundation of democratic principles, both in the developing world and in advanced capitalist and consumerist nations such as the US and UK. When discussing power as a resource that can be harnessed to influence others, corporations now challenge or even surpass the more conventional state, or public, power that many consider when examining the 'crimes of the powerful'. This, as described in Chapter 3, has been made possible by the emblematic nature of neoliberal ideology, poor regulations and criminal justice responses, the ability to lobby for favourable policies, generous donations towards political candidates and parties, the entangled and shared economic interests of politicians and corporations, and, as will be discussed in Chapter 7, media ownership.

Alongside this, within the remit of criminal justice and law-making, we must consider how corporations have significant influence through financial support towards think tanks and policy institutes engaged in research and policy formulation (McGann, 2016). This backing, naturally, allows corporations to mould the prevailing discourse and sway public sentiment on matters, thereby exerting an indirect influence on the legislative process. There is also the matter of the 'revolving door' phenomenon, which entails the transition of individuals between governmental roles and corporate positions (LaPira and Thomas, 2017). This phenomenon indicates how former legislators, government officials and regulators regularly join corporations or lobbying firms, utilising their expertise, networks and clout to advance corporate interests. Considering all these points, it creates a bleak picture regarding the supposed objective and impartial manner of law-making that is supposed to uphold the values of a society, protect citizens and provide avenues of recourse for potential damage(s) inflicted by such organisations. As we have alluded to in other chapters and will come to see later in this chapter, corporations are behind some of the most harmful and destructive conditions we currently face for individuals and the environment. Many of these, though, are not necessarily 'crimes' in the legal sense due to the potent combination of the aforementioned points regarding corporate influence.

However, of course, there are those harmful actions committed by corporations that are indeed classed as criminal, and we will also examine some of these in due course. First, it is worth briefly examining and questioning some prevailing orthodoxies about the representation and narrative often presented to us via mainstream media.

A few rotten apples

To have a more comprehensive and nuanced understanding of corporate crime more generally, we need to recognise the importance of how cultural representations of crime, specifically violence, shape society's understandings. Specifically, as we move beyond the arguments and concepts presented in this book, it is important to continually question and critique why certain forms of crime and violent content are continually presented to us via a multitude of media platforms (films, television, mainstream media news coverage), while other forms are barely mentioned, researched or ignored entirely. We are in an age where serial killers and mass shooters dominate the headlines and screens. However, we rarely consider the devastating impact of corporations in some of history's most tragic moments. While we can lament criminological imbalance, it is also true that some crimes and corporate harms have been much more extensively covered than others. The prevailing narrative of imbalance only takes us so far. While it is understandable that people tend to focus on those extreme acts of violence that disrupt normality (such as serial killers, knife crime and acts of terrorism) due to the perceived news value, we should also consider those acts of violence if we were to take a Žižekian perspective, which is inherent within normality itself. Despite this need to re-orientate this discussion, we continually fail to correctly identify, articulate and critically discuss the normalised forms of violence. But why is this the case?

We must turn to innovative theoretical developments within the discipline to answer this question and make sense of this preoccupation with spectacular displays of physical violence at the expense of less visceral yet more destructive actions of corporations. Kelly et al's (2022) 'Graze' theory suggests that Mark Seltzer's notion of a 'wound culture' – a collective that is addicted to physical manifestations of violence and 'torn and open psyches' (Seltzer, 1998, p 109) – struggles to make sense of the public's fascination with violence within the era of late-stage capitalism. Specifically, Kelly et al (2022) initially frame their critique on Seltzer's ontological and epistemological understanding of violence. In particular, the authors suggest that Seltzer formulates his theory based upon more direct or physical conceptualisations of the term, thus negating the importance of more critical strands of the 'violence tapestry', including structural and symbolic manifestations (Lynes et al, 2021; Kelly et al, 2022). By utilising more critical strands of violence, namely objective violence (Žižek, 2008), the authors argue that a more nuanced and critical relationship emerges between the media and representations of violence, and thus the general public. This relationship was demonstrated via an overview of serial murder media representations (in both its consumer and prosumer manifestations), in which it was suggested that such offenders have become 'familiar monsters' the public consumes as a means in which to 'fetishistically disavow' the nature and thus reality of violence within late capitalism (Fisher, 2009). This individualising tendency in relation to violence can also be translated to acts of corporate criminality. Subjective (or physical, direct) violence is directly experienced intersubjectively in relationships of dominance (for example, being a victim of a physical assault). This is what we experience most overtly; therefore, we have an inherent assumption that all violence is subjective in nature. Consequently, according to Žižek, we subjectivise forms of violence by attributing them to one person or group, when really this person or group is being motivated by a much larger structure of violence.

While we have so far considered the primacy of physical acts of violence within media and subsequent consumption, we also have to consider another central theoretical underpinning of Graze theory: Žižek's notion of the 'disavowal'. More specifically, the fetishist disavowal, which Žižek summarises as 'I know, but I don't want to know that I know, so I don't know' (2010).

This, in essence, is a process of denial, the denial of one's position in the world relative to others. He argues that life functions on the basis of such denials. Žižek (2008) discusses the treatment of animals so that large swathes of the population can eat meat and how many people are indeed aware but do not want to ponder or consider the actualities of such conditions these animals find themselves in before being cut up, packaged and bought for our convenience. Taking this concept further, not only do we know that other people or (as demonstrated in the previous example) animals are treated badly, but that our entire system of life is founded upon such moral and ethical concessions. For instance, we buy clothing, electronics and one of the most important symbols of status, iPhones, which are made in China despite knowing the horrendous conditions suffered by the workers that make them (Li et al, 2016), though more on that later.

The ever-increasing popularity of mainstream media accounts of physical violence – violence committed by an identifiable agent – serves as a distraction from the objective violence that has proliferated throughout the era of late capitalism. Corporations, which have only grown in size and influence within our current economic model and are profoundly influential regarding the perpetuation and maintenance of our collective sense of 'normality', are indicative of this objective violence and thus often under-acknowledged and thus understood within the general public. This tendency to 'brush up against familiar monsters' (Kelly et al, 2022, p 315) as a form of comfort and a channel in which to disavow objective forms of violence can be somewhat comforting. However, it also presents a barrier in which both the public and, to a degree, academia struggle to penetrate and move beyond. As such, Graze theory is a contemporary critical framework that synthesises key Žižekian concepts in order to articulate how, as a collective, we generally struggle and fail 'to disentangle ourselves from the fascinating lure of this directly visible "subjective" violence, violence performed by a clearly identifiable agent' (Žižek, 2008, p 1).

However, such a culture captivated by visceral violence does not mean that corporate crimes and harms are omitted entirely, though only a few instances demonstrate concentrated media coverage (Lynch, 2020). For example, significant media coverage arose following the tragic Grenfell Tower fire in London, England, where 72 lives were lost due to a string of cost-saving measures. There was also widespread attention on the fraudulent activities of Silicon Valley aspirant Elizabeth Holmes and her failed start up, Theranos, resulting in investors losing over US$600 million. Additionally, the collapse of the North American energy giant Enron due to poor corporate governance and efforts to conceal substantial losses garnered substantial scrutiny, along with the Deepwater Horizon oil spill in 2010, which caused severe environmental damage by releasing 210 million gallons of oil into the Gulf of Mexico.

While there has been some attention to the actions of corporations, it should be noted that such attention is primarily provided to the most serious of cases and often focuses on the actions of the individuals responsible rather than acknowledging the broader systemic factors that enabled such actions to occur in the first place. For instance, a great deal of attention was given to the life and history of Elizabeth Holmes when Theranos' illegal activity became known, going through the typical vilification processes often seen in mainstream news reporting and in which her nefarious actions were presented in precise chronological order (see *The Economic Times*, 2023, for instance). Enron's CEOs, Jeffrey Skilling and Kenneth Lay, also dominated news headlines upon the company's collapse, with a particular focus on their lack of ethics, lack of compassion for workers, and general disregard for regulations and the law (Barlow and Barlow, 2010). Such attention to the actions of a few 'rotten apples' or immoral agents can also be seen in the film *The Wolf of Wall Street* (2013), whereby Leonardo DiCaprio portrayed Jordon Belfort. The film charts Belfort's rise and eventual fall, who pleaded guilty to fraud and related crimes concerning stock-market manipulation in 1999. While the film introduces other unethical agents surrounding Belfort, it does not spend much time pondering the broader context and corporate environment in which these actions were committed. What we have here, in essence, is the presentation of 'sacrificial lambs' offered up to demonstrate that justice is working and encouraging the public not to ponder on more substantial questions related to the actions of the corporate world. This world is heavily presented as being, at a political level, a source of economic progress and social good, no matter what their failings are (Tombs and Whyte, 2015).

This narrative is much easier to maintain when such examples of corporate wrongdoing are portrayed as isolated and marginalised instances whereby responsibility is laid primarily on the actions of a few immoral and unscrupulous agents acting in self-interest. Such sentiments are echoed by Levi (2006), who argues that the mainstream media tend to favour corporate crime cases associated with an individual's transgressions and the ineptitude of the 'establishment' at the expense of more serious and nuanced examinations into the system itself. This is further compounded when we consider the work of Slapper and Tombs (1999), who argue that often-used terms such as 'abuse' and 'scandal' generate notions of unethical and immoral practices at the expense of signifying the actual crimes committed and again obscure the systemic and routine nature of such behaviour.

Even when responsibility is seemingly established, there is also a pattern of diminishing the seriousness of such conduct and actions, especially concerning the more senior members of a corporation. For instance, Machin and Mayr's (2012) case study on the reporting of the Paddington rail crash in 1999, whereby 31 people lost their lives as a result of cost-cutting measures, determined that while issues of corporate responsibility were raised, there were several questions related to how the language of crime and criminality were used. In demonstrating this, the authors present a quote from an article stating: 'No one is suggesting that board members actually expected that there would be any tragic reckoning for their rejection of the new system on the grounds of cost.' The authors discuss the language employed here, noting that:

> Here actual responsibility is again mitigated. We are told 'no one is suggesting' that board members did think there would be a crash. On the one hand, this is a presupposition that assumes that there is a possibility that someone might make this suggestion. On the other hand, it allows the writer to provide a sense of what everyone thinks. And in the next line this is described as a 'gamble' which had paid off for over four years. In this sense the use of the world 'gamble' loosens the connection to intentionality. (Machin and Mayr, 2012, p 74)

We must also question when responsibility appears straightforward or intuitive at first glance. Let us consider, for instance, the growing 'gig economy' and the documented cases of delivery drivers who have caused injury and even death during the course of their work. While there are laws designed to capture a range of behaviours and scenarios related to vehicular homicides, the shift to zero-hour contract transient work, which operates under a 'payment by number of deliveries' (Morrell, 2016), poses serious questions with regard to responsibility and culpability. For instance, let us take the death of Telesfora Escamilla, who was struck down and killed in 2016 by Amazon delivery driver Valdimar Gray as she attempted to cross a street in Chicago (Ward, 2016). At first, the mainstream media narrative framed the death of Telesfora Escamilla around individual responsibility, stating that:

> A witness told ABC7 that the driver drove around a car in front of him and made a left, hitting Escamilla, who was in the crosswalk. "He knew he did something. He was just screaming: 'I can't believe I did this! I can't believe I did this!'" the witness said. (Ward, 2016)

The Amazon driver was arrested and charged with vehicular homicide. However, while such a sentence may appear justified, it is essential to consider how this move to a gig economy is slowly removing corporate responsibility from both the point of view of the law and media representations. For instance, an undercover investigation by the BBC News (2016) into the conditions of an Amazon delivery driver showed that those working for one of the many agencies supplying Amazon with drivers could earn less than the minimum wage and face significant stress in getting their deliveries done on time. It also found incidents of drivers speeding to meet their deadlines and even going to the toilet in their vans simply because they were pressured to complete their deliveries in the expected time. So too, drivers routinely did 11-hour shifts and were expected to be available at least six days a week. Workers within the courier service sector have caused several injuries, and the typical reaction from corporations is one of ambiguity. Take, for instance, Amazon's response to the death of Telesfora: 'Amazon says these drivers are not their employees, and the company hires independent contractors to handle most deliveries. … "We have high standards for our delivery service partners and investigate claims made about inappropriate driver behaviour and take the appropriate actions, which may include no longer delivering for Amazon"' (Savini, 2018).

Of course, within media reports on such cases, such discussions pertaining to working conditions that may create the conditions for unsafe practices and potential death are omitted, and we are instead served the individual as the sole agent responsible for the events that transpired. This process is nicely elucidated by the work of Gray (2009), who notes that workplace safety is experiencing a shift towards 'responsibilisation'. While employers have traditionally been the primary focus of health and safety regulations, there is a growing trend of assigning workers greater responsibility for their own safety. They are now held accountable, evaluated and subject to consequences through this perspective. As we can see in both the Paddington rail crash and the death caused by an Amazon driver, responsibility is diminished for the more senior members of the corporation while simultaneously increasing for employees, but both ultimately ignore the broader context of corporate behaviour and activities.

It is important to stress that corporate crime is also often categorised as 'victimless'; however, this could not be further from the truth (Croall, 2001). Through the manipulation of values and false class consciousness, the 'crimes of the powerful' are often dismissed by society as an unavoidable social fact rather than a preventable crime (Pearce, 1976). The media, official statistics and government soundbites often help to perpetuate a 'carnival mirror' image of reality that corporate crime is isolated rather than structural and institutional (Reiman and Leighton, 2013). The architect of the 2008 financial crash has been theorised to be financial malpractice (Will et al, 2013; Mayer et al, 2014). Financial institutions and investment banks were involved in a game of high stakes with money that did not belong to them. When it all crashed around their expensive handmade shoes, they left thousands of their investors in economic ruin, as in the Lehman Brothers case (Ward, 2010). Furthermore, the effects of their recklessness and financial crimes have had a lasting effect on the global economy that has caused misery to millions and continues to do so (Abdul, 2009; Varoufakis, 2016). Yet, society's chagrin only fleetingly focuses on criminals within the banking industry and instead fixates on the criminals offered up to them in the *Daily Mail* et al (Tyler, 2013). Just as the banking industry is not the only player in the world's economy, financial crime is not the only nefarious act committed by unscrupulous executives; they are vast and varied, covering a spectrum of malpractices. Furthermore, the victims of these crimes are diverse, from employees forced to work in conditions that violate many health and safety laws to the wildlife impacted by chronic exposure to illegally disposed toxic waste (Hartley, 2008). Crime committed by companies that would rather cut corners than their profit margins has caused some of the world's most devastating disasters with long-term effects (Peterson et al, 2003). This not only includes the human or animal victims, such as in the cases of the Deepwater Horizon oil spill and the Herald of Free Enterprise ferry disaster, but also the world's ecosystems and competitors. Moreover, the plethora of health and safety laws that are globally imposed in an attempt to curtail these devastating practices often do not apply to the multinationals that are seemingly immune. However, as in the case of Trafigura's ship of death, when held accountable for flouting these laws, it often results in tokenistic a punishment, while indigenous populations live with the chronic repercussions for generations.

When researching corporate crime beyond the few cases reported in the media, it soon becomes apparent that the unethical business practice seems almost systemic rather than a few localised incidents and immoral agents (Valukas, 2010). However, holding businesses to account for their illegal actions continues to be problematic, even with new legislation, such as the Corporate Manslaughter and Corporate Homicide Act 2007. Through legal loopholes, lobbying for the decriminalisation of corporate offences and holding nation states to ransom, perpetrators of even some of the most harmful corporate crimes often go unchallenged (Michalowski and Kramer, 2006). These businesses often move production to countries where practices classed as criminal in the West are minor infringements under their civil law (Ross, 2006). Furthermore, the effects of these malpractices usually are hardest felt by those who lack the financial means to exact any retribution within a court of law. Thus, many corporations commit a plethora of human rights violations with little to no reprisals (Croall, 2001). This suggests that corporate crime is substantial, state-sanctioned, institutionalised and a perpetual consequence of late-stage capitalism (Michalowski and Kramer, 2006).

The drive for healthy profit margins habitually outweighs the power elites' moral and legal obligations. Furthermore, their crimes often have disastrous and long-lasting global ramifications. To suggest that the countless numbers of workers who are maimed or killed every year at work due to their employers' criminal negligence or the children fighting diseases linked to the dumping of toxic waste are not victims of corporate crime is unfathomable. However, they often remain overlooked or seen as a necessary by-product of a healthy economy, and any retribution for their conditions is counterproductive and damaging to our collective economic stability and way of life. Thus, the victims of corporate crime are relegated to less than a footnote in capitalism and eventually forgotten.

Killing them softly: the pervasive harm of contemporary life

We have so far determined that despite the media depicting acts of corporate criminality as generally isolated and due to the actions of a small number of unethical agents, corporate crime is, in fact, far more pervasive and systemic than previously thought. Criminology has provided some examination into corporate activities that have resulted in considerable harm and deaths, with those examining it within the broader context of homicide (see Brookman, 2005), the well-documented 2017 Grenfell fire (Cooper and Whyte, 2018; Hodkinson, 2018; Tombs, 2019; 2020; 2021); the Bhopal disaster in India where, in 1984, 16,000 to 30,000 people died and 500,000 others were injured due to a chemical leak caused by a series of cost-cutting measures (Pearce and Tombs, 1989; 2012; Matilal and Höpfl, 2009); the Paddington rail crash of 1999 (Machin and Mayr, 2012); and the 2010 Deepwater Horizon oil spill (Ruggiero and South, 2013; McClanahan et al, 2015; Gottschalk, 2019). Such academic attention is important and raises important questions regarding the broader enabling political and economic contexts that can result in such tragedies. However, such events are indicative of cases that receive a great deal of media attention due to their dramatic and visceral nature and are often examined within a critique of current laws and regulations (such as the Corporate Manslaughter and Corporate Homicide Act 2007). While such critiques are valid and important, there has been a general lack of attention towards those cases that are so mundane and embedded within our consumer-oriented way of life that they often go unnoticed. The point here is to highlight that while such previous academic attention on corporate homicide and harm has been important in shining a light on such injuries, we often fail to consider the everyday, normalised injurious conditions that powerful corporations exploit and profit from. We will primarily explore this by examining a series of case examples of how corporations outsource a myriad of harms across the globe.

Let us start with an item that we are (mostly) all familiar with: Apple's iPhone. Many may be familiar with or even have participated in the countless lines of eager early adopters excited to possess the latest iteration of Apple's flagship smartphone series. Despite the only incremental or, for the laypeople, hardly noticeable improvements, the buzz and excitement for Apple's latest phone only seem to intensify each year. As one article reporting on the release of the iPhone 13 noted, 'as the following photos and tweets illustrate, consumers were ready to line up at Apple stores again to get their new device' (Molina, 2014). In one of the more memorable images included in the report, a man wearing a face mask due to the current COVID-19 policies is seen holding up the latest phone in triumph for being the first customer to get his hands on the device, complete with an adoring and clapping crowd. For many, the iPhone is a clear signifier of ornamental consumerism – a sign that they are living up to the desire to be immersed in consumer indulgence by not just the acquisition of the item but also its display (Hallet al, 2008). However, many may not or, more importantly, choose not to learn how that pristine and ergonomically pleasing device is manufactured. For the average consumer, their knowledge begins by being greeted by an Apple 'genius' in one of the many immaculate and well-lit Apple stores. In fact, Apple prefers for you not to consider these as stores at all but rather 'more like a town square, where the best of Apple comes together and everyone is welcome' (Angela Ahrendts, Apple's senior vice president of retail, cited in Grabar, 2017). It is not only the environment that is carefully considered, but also the staff, who are taught the APPLE technique as part of their customer-centric training. This acronym stands for: Approach customers with a personalised warm welcome; Probe politely to understand the customer's needs; Present a solution for the customer to take home today; Listen for and resolve any issues of concern; and End with a fond farewell and an invitation to return (cited in Gallo, 2015). Such attention to detail is even given to the packaging itself, particularly the opening of said packaging. Those readers who have ever owned an iPhone may recall first opening their brand-new device, casting their eyes over the aesthetically pleasing box and revelling in how the phone is slowly revealed with the so very satisfying pulling away of plastic sleeves to expose their shiny brand-new device. This deliberately crafted experience is actually the result of years of research into human psychology, with Isaacson's biography on Apple founder Steve Jobs (2011) noting the three key pillars of Apple that influenced this approach to packaging. The first principle was empathy and the drive to create an intimate connection with the customer based on understanding their needs and wants. The second pillar was that of focus and the need to eliminate unwanted or unimportant distractions. The third pillar, and arguably most important, is that of 'impute', which was Jobs' belief that any products sold had to be presented in the most creative and professional of manner due to the belief that consumers will judge an item by its presentation despite how good the product actually is. As far as the average consumer is concerned, Apple represents the pinnacle of commodity fetishism (Marx, 1867), whereby a commodity appears as if by magic. Its appearance, crucially, is divorced from the labour that produced it. Of course, such desirable consumer goods do not simply appear by magic, and we will now chart the various steps of production of the iPhone and how this is far removed from the shiny veneer presented to us, the consumer.

Most may be aware that the iPhone and most other Apple products are not manufactured in North America, where the company was founded and where the CEOs and software engineers live. However, the specific reasons as to why this is the case may be somewhat less known. The most obvious starting point is simply a factor of economics, with the cost of labour being far higher if the products were manufactured in the States or other Western nations. Tricontinental: Institute for Social Research (2019) noted that if the iPhone were to be produced in the US, the phone would have to have a retail value of US$30,000 due to increased labour costs. Alongside these increased costs, Apple would have to contend with much more stringent health and safety measures, pre-defined working hours and labour unions. Fortunately for Apple, some countries give little consideration to factors, such as China. Before we examine where the phone is assembled, let us trace our steps back to where the material is sourced. As we will come to learn, the exploitation of labour commences long before the phone is actually built.

Among the raw materials you will find in your iPhone, you will find cobalt, carbon, iron, platinum, copper, gallium and tin (to name but a few). Let us take cobalt as an example. This raw material is used in various electronic devices, and other companies covet this resource, including Google, Tesla and Microsoft. The reason this material is so valued is due to the fact that it is used in the cathode of rechargeable lithium-ion batteries, and the Congo, situated in Central Africa, continues to be the world's leading source of mined cobalt, supplying approximately 70 per cent of world cobalt mine production (United States Geological Survey, 2020). While Apple and the other aforementioned companies continue to pledge to use ethically sourced cobalt as part of their carefully crafted PR efforts, the reality is far from this. In fact, in 2019, Apple (along with the aforementioned examples) were named in a US lawsuit regarding the deaths of children who were subject to forced labour in the Democratic Republic of Congo (Kelly, 2019). Cobalt mining is incredibly harmful to the environment due to devastating landscapes, polluting water sources and contaminating crops (Davey, 2023). Unfortunately, it also significantly impacts children due to how their smaller hands are used to mine for this precious resource. Amnesty International and Afrewatch (2016) accused Apple, along with other tech giants, of insufficient control of their cobalt supply from mines, whereby it was reported that children as young as 12 years old were being forced to dig this precious but poisonous (it can be damaging to eyes, skin, heart and lungs) material. As documented by Siddharth Kara in the book *Cobalt Red* (2022), the conditions of mining cobalt can only be described as hellish, with the average worker only earning a few dollars a day despite experiencing a multitude of harmful working conditions, including the touching and breathing in of toxic substances, grinding manual labour, and threats and acts of violence (Kara, 2022; Murray, 2022). ABC News spoke to former child labourer Yannick from Kolwezi, a city of more than 500,000 people in the south of the Democratic Republic of Congo, who left school at the age of seven and went into full-time work in one such cobalt mine: "When I was going to the mines, it was to look after my family, because there was a lot of suffering. ... People died in the mine, and you could suffocate when you are deep in the mine" (cited in Lavoipierre et al, 2018). Returning to the work of Kara, he pertinently states that 'the ongoing exploitation of the poorest people of the Congo by the rich and powerful invalidates the purported foundation of contemporary civilisation and drags humanity back to a time when the people of Africa were valued only by their replacement cost' (Kara, 2022, p 1).

Significant environmental consequences also arise from mining operations. The southern regions of the Congo possess cobalt and copper reserves and considerable amounts of uranium (Nkulu et al, 2018). Within these mining areas, scientists have observed elevated levels of radioactivity. Moreover, mineral mining, like other industrial mining endeavours, frequently generates pollution that trickles into nearby rivers and water sources (Otamonga and Poté, 2020). Such a discussion about the environment extends to many of the numerous rare chemical elements in the device. David Cole-Hamilton, Vice President of EuChemS and Emeritus Professor of Chemistry at the University of St Andrews, stresses that Apple, along with other tech giants mining of precious elements, including aluminium, copper, lithium, silver and gold, "create major problems leading to waste and element depletion" (cited in Dayaram, 2022) and impact key climate goals as the world faces ever more severe weather events each year (United Nations Office for Disaster Risk Reduction, 2020).

This is, of course, only the beginning of the supply chain for smartphones and other technological devices, and attention will now shift to further up the production sequence. While the overall manufacturing process of an iPhone consists of sourcing numerous materials from across the world (the previous overview of cobalt mining is only a small fraction of this), it is one of the final phases of assembly that is carried out in Zhengzhou, China, that will be examined next.

The Foxconn (a Taiwanese multinational electronics contract manufacturer) factory in the central Chinese city of Zhengzhou houses 200,000 workers as of November 2022 and is often described as 'iPhone city' due to its sheer size and scope (Liu, 2022). For most employees, days commence by entering a workshop devoid of windows and the air permeated with the scent of chlorine. They then need to carefully don an antistatic gown and a face mask before taking their place on the assembly line, each employee's individual and distinct features removed as they join

CRIMES OF THE POWERFUL AND THE CONTEMPORARY CONDITION

a sea of similarly clad workers. Whenever they have required a restroom break, they are monitored and have to compensate for the time lost. Behind the assembly line, supervisors, referred to as 'line leaders' or *xianzhang*, keep a watchful eye on the workers' productivity through a computer system, frequently admonishing those who fall behind. Alongside this, workers at Foxconn often face long shifts, with reports of employees working more than 60 hours per week, exceeding legal limits in China (China Labour Watch, 2015). Overtime is frequently required, sometimes unpaid, and workers have experienced immense pressure to meet production targets, especially in the lead-up to peak seasons. As previously alluded to, the factory environment is characterised by strict rules and discipline, with workers being closely monitored by supervisors and security personnel. One worker even recalled how a fellow employee's pay was reduced for drinking too much water (Zhou, 2023). Such an action is only further compounded when we consider that up until 2022, the average wage for employees was 21 yuan per hour before being raised to 24 yuan (US$3.32) due to production disruptions caused by the COVID-19 pandemic (Deng and Feng, 2022). We also must consider the tasks these low-paid and overworked employees must complete daily, with workers on the assembly lines performing repetitive tasks for extended periods. One such worker documented how it was their responsibility to retrieve the back cover and a miniature charging cable for an iPhone before scanning the QR codes on both items. He would then have to remove the adhesive tape backing and securely fasten the two components together with two screws. Afterwards, he would place the partially assembled phone on a moving conveyor belt that transported it to the next workstation. This same worker stated that they were expected to accomplish this task within 1 minute. Over the course of a standard 10-hour shift, his objective was to connect 600 cables to 600 cases, utilising a total of 1,200 screws. Each day, an additional 600 disassembled iPhones awaited him (Zhou, 2023). Unsurprisingly, such repetitive tasks lead to physical strain and repetitive motion injuries. There have also been reports of inadequate safety measures within such Foxconn factories. This is perhaps most aptly illustrated by the company's response to the outbreak of COVID-19, whereby management made the decision to lockdown the facility with 300,000 workers in unsafe working conditions. Foxconn, it was reported, prevented employees from leaving the factory while they worked within a 'closed-loop system' prior to thousands of staff members fleeing the 'plant on foot' (China Labour Bulletin, 2022). One worker, who posted a video online, which has since been removed, conveyed their experiences of working within such a system during the pandemic: "I thought coming here would be a new start, but I didn't expect it to be like jumping into a big fire pit. Now, I'm here amid the fire and water. No matter how we struggle, it's to no avail" (cited in China Labour Bulletin, 2022).

The Chinese government's position on this incident, which resulted in thousands of staff leaving (with some climbing over the factory fences) the facility and impacting the delivery of iPhones to the West, solely blamed the employees (China Labour Bulletin, 2022). Foxconn refuted claims that 20,000 of its staff tested positive for the virus as it attempted to maintain business as usual (CNBC, 2022). Despite the government and Foxconn's stance on this, the numerous now-deleted online accounts of workers have survived to provide the human experiences of the labour that goes into ensuring that lines continue to grow whenever a brand-new iPhone is released:

'We know that production always comes first in Foxconn's eyes, but we really want to live a normal life. We don't want to be worried and cautious all day long. We just want to eat a normal meal, take off our masks and sleep, take a look at the outside world and restore the beauty of life.' (Anonymous Foxconn worker cited in China Labour Bulletin, 2022)

This snapshot into some of the documented harms of supply chains and labour production is by no means unique to Apple and the iPhone. Almost all of our technological devices, from televisions to supposedly environmentally friendly electronic cars, perpetuate many of the previously discussed conditions.

Alongside this, we also have to reflect on our relationship with consumerism more generally, and clothing, particularly fast fashion, made popular by Primark, Boohoo, H&M and Zara, needs to be considered. Similar to the glossy veneer of the iPhone masking myriad harms into its production, many do not consider the exploitation that goes into the next trendy set of trainers or garments. The fast-fashion industry depends on globalisation, and it is fuelled by cheap labour used to generate enormous profits with low production costs. Let us take Primark as an example. Primark made headlines in 2014 when shoppers found messages written on labels sewn into summer dresses. Some of these messages, sewn in with the other normal labels, contained text reading 'sweatshop conditions' and 'forced to work exhausting hours' (Aspinall, 2014). In response to these messages, the company launched an investigation. It stated that "to be clear, no prison or other forced labour of any kind was found during these inspections. ... Primark is committed to making working conditions safer for those who manufacture its products" (cited in McDonald, 2014). However, despite making strides in recent years with the company being a signatory to the Bangladesh Accord on Fire and Building Safety and the Cotton Pledge, which commits to boycotting Uzbekistan cotton, supply chains still have evident issues. For instance, it does not control its supply chain and can therefore effectively remove any responsibility for factory workers and any labour issues that may be occurring. Due to this, it received a score of 31–40 per cent in the Fashion Transparency Index (Fashion Revolution, 2023), and it has been highlighted that the company took inadequate policies or safeguards to protect suppliers and workers in its supply chain from the impacts of COVID-19. Specifically, Primark's supply-chain workers have protested in Bangladesh, Myanmar and Cambodia over unpaid wages, reduction in pay and mass dismissal due to the company's response to the pandemic. In Bangladesh, one of Primark's suppliers, which usually employs 6,000 people, only had 500 people working while the rest were on unpaid 'holiday' during the pandemic (Clean Clothes Campaign, 2020). In Myanmar, another Primark supplier closed its factory, resulting in 2,000 workers losing their jobs and receiving only partial compensation (Clean Clothes Campaign, 2020). Primark CEO Paul Marchant stated they had been "left with no option but to take this action". Yet, for a global brand with a net worth of £1.1 billion in 2019 (Smith, 2023), Primark could have taken the decision to protect the most vulnerable workers in their supply chain by 'honouring their orders from the beginning of the Covid-19 crisis' (Clean Clothes Campaign, 2020). Primark is by no means the exception here, though, with 88 per cent of major brands still not disclosing their annual production volumes despite mounting evidence of overproduction and clothing waste, along with just 12 per cent of brands publishing a purchasing code of conduct, suggesting that most are still unwilling to reveal how their purchasing practices could be affecting suppliers and workers (Fashion Revolution, 2023). These statistics impact the ability to fully understand the risks of exploitative conditions and forced labour within the fashion industry, along with the clear impact of such an industry on the environment despite the greenwashing often asserted by such companies and brands.

These are but two examples of how corporations, in an attempt to satiate our never truly satisfied consumer habits, essentially 'outsource' harm to decrease costs and increase profits. There is also the added benefit for such companies in the form of avoiding the more stringent employment and health and safety regulations often found in the West, along with decreasing the risks of the consumer confronting the realities behind their coveted purchases. While these two cases serve as examples of highly sought-after commodities, it is important to stress here that similar harmful practices can even be found in more mundane products, including a cup of coffee, in which our regular 'to-go' cups play a significant part in deforestation whereby an average of 10 million hectares are lost each year – roughly the size of Portugal (Food and Agriculture Organization of the United Nations, 2020) – alongside plantation workers who often labour under intense heat for up to 10 hours a day, with many also facing debt bondage and serious health risks due to exposure to dangerous agrochemicals (Chen, 2020).

Of course the powerful can control through and with food, and academics such as Jon Davies have highlighted the harms of exploitation of migrant workers in routine forms of exploitation in the UK food industry (Davies, 2019). The broader food industry of course has been considered, and the fast-food industry has long been known to be devastating to both people and the environment, with companies such as McDonald's being one the largest users of beef, which exacerbates the climate crisis due to methane production, along with the use of environmentally destructive chemicals (Elgin, 2021; Pomranz, 2022). This is not even considering the incredible amount of packaging waste that ends up littering our streets or added to the ever-mounting landfills full of non-degradable materials (Surfers Against Sewage, 2022), or poor wages and working conditions of staff and, at the time of writing, the reports of racial and sexual abuse experienced by workers in the UK by members of management (BBC News, 2023). We also need to consider how McDonald's, and the fast-food industry more generally, increases the risk of obesity, insulin resistance, type 2 diabetes and various cardiovascular conditions (Bahadoran et al, 2015). What is even more sobering here is that due to prevailing and increasing inequalities and the low prices such companies set their products at, along with the increasing costs of healthier alternatives (Herforth et al, 2020; Lewis et al, 2023), such health risks are increased for the poorest who, as noted in Chapter 3, have the least access to healthcare provisions, especially in the US, in which about half of all deaths are from heart disease, stroke and type 2 diabetes (Micha et al, 2017).

Sugary drinks also play an integral role in such health issues, but if we take a closer look at the most famous fizzy drink, Coca-Cola, the harm does not just begin at the point of consumption. According to the Brand Audit Report (Break Free From Plastic, 2021), Coca-Cola was named the world's worst plastic polluter for the fourth year in a row. Coca-Cola, boasting over 500 brands, distributes over 100 billion plastic bottles annually, equivalent to approximately 200,000 bottles per minute (Plastic Soup Foundation, 2022). Unfortunately, a significant portion of these bottles becomes waste, often ending up in the environment, particularly in areas where waste collection and processing are inadequate or non-existent. Of course, such companies often boast about caring for the environment and make all manners of pledges; however, according to a report by the Conservation Law Foundation, Coca-Cola has a poor track record in meeting any of its pledges as it continues to place profits before the environment (Pecci et al, 2022). As an example of the company's priorities, we only need to consider that in 2019, they spent US$4.24 billion on advertising and marketing purposes and only US$11 million towards a river clean-up initiative (Break Free From Plastic, 2021). The human cost caused by sugary drinks such as Coca-Cola has also been heavily documented in the developing world. In Mexico, for instance, where for some towns, Coca-Cola is more available than water (Perlmutter, 2022), tens of thousands of deaths nationwide can be attributed to these easily available and affordable sugary beverages (Braverman-Bronstein et al, 2020). The devastating impact on the citizens of Mexico is only further compounded when we consider how the corporation, along with other sugary and alcoholic drink producers, continues to plunder the country's natural water resources as it faces increasingly devastating climate crises, with numerous cities having reached a state known as 'day zero' – indicating a critical level of water scarcity – in 2022. Speaking of water, it should also be noted that Nestlé, with its slogan 'good food, good life', has been harvesting millions of litres of water across multiple countries, including the US, Canada, the UK and Nigeria (to name but few), and has been embroiled in controversies including the taking of water from public land, to leaving locales with limited to no access to drinking water (see Shimo, 2018).

All of the examples so far discussed are likely familiar to you, the reader, and that is likely to stay the same for the next: Amazon. Amazon is a prominent American multinational technology corporation specialising in various sectors such as e-commerce, cloud computing, online advertising, digital streaming and AI. It has gained recognition as a highly influential force in both economic and cultural realms worldwide and is widely regarded as one of the most valuable brands globally. As one of the five major technology companies in the US, commonly referred to as the Big Five, Amazon joins the ranks of Alphabet (the parent company of Google), Apple, Meta (formerly Facebook, Inc.) and Microsoft. Founded by Jeff Bezos in Bellevue, Washington, on 5 July 1994, Amazon initially operated as an online marketplace solely for books. Over time, it has expanded its reach into numerous product categories, earning it the nickname 'The Everything Store' (Stone, 2014). So influential is Amazon in terms of market dominance and influence that 'Amazon capitalism' has been created to portray this phenomenon (Alimahomed-Wilson and Reese, 2020). It is estimated that the company's global user base exceeds 310 million active users, with approximately 80 per cent of them (amounting to over 230 million customers) hailing from the US (Campbell, 2023). As of 2020, Amazon has sold and shipped over 600 million products across the UK (Strugar, 2023).

With the move to online shopping, there is the false perception that the lack of immateriality on the consumer's side is similar for the seller, thus creating a 'consumer capitalist utopia' of seamless transactions. This has only been exacerbated by the creation of Amazon Prime, in which members can routinely expect their order to arrive the very next day (Amazon, ND). The convenience and speed in which items arrive at our door are likely, for the average person, not to raise questions pertaining to the experiences of those who ensure our orders reach us in such a timely manner. However, studies have shown that Amazon employees often perceive their jobs as physically demanding and alienating, imposed by strict management and surveillance (Alimahomed-Wilson and Reese, 2021). This was found to be the case in the investigative podcast *Megacorp* (Hanrahan, 2022), where numerous people were interviewed, including an undercover journalist and an ex-prisoner who compared the working environment to be worse than the prison in which he served his sentence. The journalist revealed that workers could be given 'idle points' each time they took too long to go to the bathroom. If an individual accumulated idle points, they could receive a 'disciplinary point', and too many of these would result in termination. The rising targets and expectations have also significantly impacted workers' mental health, with 55 per cent of employees reporting that they have suffered depression since working at Amazon in the UK (McCarthy, 2018). Such demands have also resulted in 'backaches, knee pain, and other symptoms of constant strain [that] are common enough for Amazon to install painkiller vending machines' (Newton, 2020). Deaths have also been reported, with the National Council for Occupational Safety and Health's report (2019) citing six US Amazon worker deaths between 2018 and 2019 (p 12). In one incident where a man died after suffering a heart attack, workers were "forced to go back to work. No time to decompress. Basically watch a man pass away and then get told to go back to work" (cited in Sainato, 2019). An investigation conducted by O'Connor (2013) utilising employee accounts likened working in the warehouse in Rugeley, UK, to 'a slave camp'. Another employee revealed that he advised workers "to smear their bare feet with Vaseline" to reduce blisters and sores from the work boots Amazon provides. A worker at the Coventry warehouse, UK, articulates such issues centred on working conditions, stating that the robots in the warehouse "are treated better than us" (Jordan and Conway, 2023). Since 2018, data obtained through a Freedom of Information request by the *Mirror* revealed that ambulances had been dispatched 971 times in response to emergency calls at Amazon's UK 'fulfilment centres'. The *Mirror*'s report indicated that these ambulance callouts occurred at 24 different Amazon warehouses. Notably, the company's Tilbury warehouse in Essex, the largest in Europe, accounted for 178 of these visits (Tiernan, 2021). A whistleblower from Tilbury told the *Mirror*, "Amazon sees people just like numbers, just like rats" (cited in Tiernan, 2021). Despite these documented accounts of working for Amazon, the company, in the first quarter of 2023, generated US$127.4 billion in revenue, up 9 per cent year over year (Amazon Investor Relations, 2023), as we continue to indulge in the low prices and speedy delivery the company offers.

Oppression in three monthly instalments

To understand the significance of consumer culture with regard to the generation and maintenance of particular powerful interests involved in the production of consumer goods, it is important to acknowledge the impact of such ideology on the individual's conscious and, more importantly, unconscious mind. Here, we will briefly touch upon the work of psychoanalyst Jacques Lacan's three orders, particularly his notion of the symbolic order (Lacan, 1997). Lacan's theories on these elements are, in essence, concerned with the normal developmental stages of infancy and are fundamentally based on the senses experienced from the moment of birth. The first order, referred to as the 'imaginary', is grounded in the visual representation of reality we acquire by seeing ourselves as objects. This is associated with the 'mirror stage', which is the young child's identification with his own image (Homer, 2004). The 'symbolic' refers to the words (signifiers) that we use to comprehend the world and ourselves – our development of language (Lacan, 1973). The 'real' is what is left from our pre-language selves, and what Lacan suggests creates the subconscious (Julien, 1995) and is momentarily revealed when language cannot be shaped to clarify nor define it – we are forever severed from the real by our entrance into language. Referring back to the symbolic order, this is, in essence, the collective narrative structure that the subject is entrenched in. Culture, law and language are important factors that comprise and provide structure to the symbolic. The symbolic is the register of language, but importantly, it is the register of language as this mediates our social relations by providing categories in which we are placed and so which we take to be formative of what we are and what our values should be. In essence, a rigid ideological system provides ontological security to the subject and moves the individual beyond the juvenile misidentifications of the imaginary (Johnston, 2008). However, while previous ideological systems have been founded on positive beliefs, when today's subject emerges to pursue a clear and coherent symbolic order, it encounters a system established on: 'The fundamental negative belief that nothing beyond the current system is possible. This negative belief is not hegemonically reproduced solely by the dominant elite but also by the sub-dominant elite who have neutralised any genuine political opposition' (Hall and Winlow, 2018, pp 43–57).

The current deaptative ideological order of symbols is based on capitalist realism (Fisher, 2009; see Winlow and Hall, 2019) – the negative principle that we have reached the 'endpoint of economic history and no alternative to liberal capitalism will ever be possible' (Hall and Winlow, 2018, pp 43–57). Neoliberal capitalism's accompanying consumer culture – predicated on material wealth as the sole signifier of status and identity affirmation – strengthens the subject's sense of looming social irrelevance and a return to the terror of the real (Hall, 2012b). Therefore, it does not pacify but overstimulate the secondary form of objectless anxiety in the subject (Hall, 2012a), which means that the overdriven subject's determination to contest against others and integrate itself into the social order is unwavering. The capitalist imaginary of a potential life of excess and material opulence operates as a prevailing ideological milieu, modelling the wants and imaginings that energise and strengthen consumer culture, but it also thoroughly upsets and thwarts symbolic connections with 'social, economic and environmental realities' (Hall and Winlow, 2018, pp 43–57). We live in an age where we can no longer imagine an alternative to the socio-economic reality in which we reside, and, as Hall and Winlow point out, it does not even ask us to believe in capitalism but only to refuse to believe that anything beyond capitalism is possible. The rich will always be so. The powerful will always be just that. We are, in essence, locked in. We exist in an era where our sense of self, identity and status are wrapped up and predicated upon material wealth and the failings of others (Rousseau, 1990), and we cannot consider a way of life beyond such negative value systems. Instead of a positive value system related to morality, community, traditional commitments and responsibilities of collective identity, the symbolic order we find ourselves within and vital to our very sense of self and identity is now predominately based on the principles of neoliberal consumer capitalism, supported and reproduced through mass media. As such, consumerism gives rise to a perpetual state of anxiety, fear of cultural irrelevance and an enduring sense of lack, which in turn serves to perpetuate desire (Hayward and Smith, 2017). These previously alluded to capitalist imaginings, transmitted via mass media, promise that we can 'fix' such anxieties and insecurities via consumption, though any feelings of fulfilment are fleetingly short (Hayward and Smith, 2017). Instead, it results in a society filled with competitive interpersonal relations fuelled by envy and deep-rooted dissatisfaction (Hall and Winlow, 2018, pp 43–57).

Under such societal forces, we 'fetishistically disavow' (Žižek, 2010) the various harms such practices and lifestyle cause, which is only further compounded given the legal status of many such activities. From the rich to the poor, consumerism and its detrimental characteristics and influence cannot be ignored, and the breakdown of societal values has created psychological distortions that produce personalities less and less capable of relating to others except as consumer items or as trophies (Currie, 1997). In essence, the practice of consumption now transcends all over more traditional forms of self-expression (Campbell, 1989). In essence, we are conceptualizing the ways in which power wielded by economically affluent transnational corporations is nurtured, sustained, and endorsed. This stems from previous discussions about how consumerism has fundamentally transformed our perception and relationship with the external world.

While it may be relatively simple to identify forms of state and legitimate power bestowed by some sovereign or dominant order, these forms of power are instead reliant upon our perceived need to buy consumer goods in order to feel like we are 'winners' in the current social order we find ourselves existing within. For example, companies involved in big tech and fast fashion are involved and responsible for a multitude of harms in the process of production. Yet, this knowledge appears to mean very little to most who will actively line up outside a store in the hopes of being an 'early adopter' of the latest smartphone or fashion trend. The harms related to such form of consumer-based activities are further explored in the emerging deviant leisure perspective (Raymen and Smith, 2019b), which explores normalised and accepted forms of leisure that generate a range of harms due to the subject's unwavering commitment to consumer ideology. For instance, such a perspective critically examines the injurics caused by engagement with the night-time economy and the legalised gambling industry, as well as the ecological damage caused by the tourist industry.

Contemporary consumerism is an ideology that fundamentally generates and yet hides harms due to our own inability to imagine a world in which our status and identity are not reliant on material displays of wealth. So too, the inherent individualism of consumerism, which turns former communities into atomised individuals in which competition is paramount over all other social considerations, further compounds the subject's difficulty to recognise such harms and relate to those subjected to them (Hayward and Smith, 2017). Returning to previous discussions pertaining to the use of force as a demonstration and instrument of the powerful, this example presents how we can be complicit and support current power relations and the harms generated due to prevailing consumer ideology in which the current status quo is important to the maintenance of these ideologies and lifestyles. In essence, little in the way of the use or threat of force is required to ensure such powerful interests continue operating. For instance, we examined how the ever-pervasive consumer culture and ideology have fundamentally impacted positive belief systems and instead predicated the symbolic order on negative principles in which our very fear of irrelevance and insignificance maintains the status quo and further 'props up' the elite class in both the economic sustenance of our purchase activities, but also our buying into the perceived symbolic importance of such goods – goods they have and flaunt to the masses.

Rotten to the core

This chapter has likely been a rather depressing read, and it was, if we are being honest, a rather sombre and, at times, disheartening process researching and writing it. However, the central argument presented here is that despite the attention towards corporate harm and death within the discipline of criminology, it is not a phenomenon relegated to a small number of nefarious organisations or immoral agents, but rather a systemic and everyday feature of our modern way of life. The victims of Grenfell were an avoidable tragedy; the citizens and workers in Bhopal were indeed victims of greed at the hands of their politicians and the US company that sought cheaper labour; and those lives lost by the Deepwater Horizon oil spill and the Paddington rail crash could have been avoided if profits were not put before people. However, such cases received extensive media attention and clearly disrupted our collective sense of 'normality' as defined by Žižek. Much academic attention has been spent critiquing (quite rightly) the current laws, the punishments (or lack thereof) and the inability of current regulations. However, as hopefully demonstrated here, considerable harm, even deaths, is a routine occurrence that happens daily throughout the world, now shaped by the ever-increasing power and influence of corporations to satisfy our never-ending desire to indulge in the contemporary consumer way of life.

7

The Remote Control Over the Masses: The Media

At the time that we wrote this chapter, we were inundated with news stories that succinctly demonstrated each of the points that we not only showcase in this chapter, but also give a panoramic view of the corruption and contempt the global elites have for the populous that keeps them in the lifestyle that they have always been accustomed to. The stories will range from reports of entanglements with Russian spies and prominent political actors having their accounts frozen, to the media circus involving five missing billionaires seeking some sense of purpose in the wreckage of yet another triumph of capitalism. For this chapter, these individual stories are less important than how they are reported.

As with the Titanic, whether figuratively or not, in all instances where capitalism fails, the rich are given seats on the lifeboats while the rest of society is left to drown in their failures. This is where the media attempt to soften the blow, with the prevailing narratives that our suffering is 'unavoidable' and 'necessary' while shareholders retreat to their ivory towers built on dividends. Each story that either emerges or resurfaces has the same prevailing narrative woven through the media reports: unscrupulous individuals have violated the benevolent system of free enterprise and ethical trade. This leads to a murmur of discontent and then silence as our eyes are diverted to the safe and welcoming news stories of working-class villainy and aggression.

As discussed in Chapter 6, the false dichotomy of the unethical minority is built into the fabric of society. Unlike the proverb, we blame the players and not the game. All pillars of society help to reinforce this paradigm: laws that coddle the rich and abuse the economically disenfranchised; financial institutions that fiscally punish the non-consuming poor and reward the hoarding habits of the rich; a political system that asset strips society's basic needs and politicians so far removed from the societies that they exploit; and religious dogma that promotes an awkward tolerance of oppressors and a meagre existence to reap divine reward. And then we have media that, in all its forms, makes a spectacle of all of it and all of us.

Eyes are turned so rapidly from one story of corruption to the next, interspersed with dance crazes, wholesome stories and tales of shirkers attempting to take from the system that which does not belong to them, that focusing becomes an arduous task. This has become the epoch of information, misinformation and hyper-information. News is on tap. A never-ending stream of information that can be accessed 24/7. Before the technical revolution of the 1980s/1990s, the news was printed and projected at limited times of the day. Fast forward through the early MTV years and society's new-found appetite for 24-hour entertainment to the brave new world of social media. Today, whether we want to disengage from the information superhighway constantly in our hands or not, we will be subjected to an amount of news media that would have been unprecedented before the introduction of the third-generation smartphone in 2001.

When the RMS Titanic sank in 1912, newspapers from around the globe ran stories of how the liner had hit an iceberg on her maiden voyage. Undoubtedly, many debates were held in homes and workplaces in the days and weeks following the disaster. In juxtaposition, when the submarine carrying five wealthy elitists lost communication with the surface from the watery grave of the souls lost on RMS Titanic, the whole world watched in real-time. Social media platforms speculated. Memes circulated, and the whole world became invested. For many watching the disaster unfold, it was an embodiment of opulent dark tourism; for others, it was a Father's Day tragedy. As with all prominent stories from our progressive epoch of history, the conversations transcended the homes and workplaces, and the result was a cacophony of opinions vying for attention on media platforms across the globe. In the 21st century, it is no longer enough to engage with the news passively; we consume it and become invested in it. Each story feels a little more personal than the next, with the expectation that our own thoughts must be shared, and these thoughts must align precisely with prevailing popular opinion.

One of the central themes discussed in the opening chapter was that, among a variety of factors, one of the distinguishing characteristics of power was those who hold relatively high levels of trust or positions of influence. In an age in which media has seemingly saturated all facets of our lives, from mainstream media organisations, social media platforms and web media – now available at our fingertips via smartphones – the media's power to influence has never been greater.

By no means are we suggesting that there is some form of media hegemony that is motivated by the same ideas and motivations designed to monopolise and consolidate power while influencing audiences via ideological principles. Within such discussions concerned with media, it is perhaps easy to imagine a media-like monolith or, to use a Hobbesian term, 'leviathan' that uniformly and actively seeks to shape our notions of reality and understanding of the world around us in order to maintain some form of control and conceal the actions of the powerful. While such musings may be easier to apply to conventional forms of the mainstream or consumer media (in essence defined as the 'few to the many'), newer forms of 'prosumer' media in the forms of blogs, social media posts and videos certainly challenge some of these orthodoxies as it, in essence, democratises media. In Chapter 1, it was briefly acknowledged that a defining component of power is that it has the capacity to shape and influence larger dynamics like social groups, professional organisations and, of course, governments. It was also noted that notions of power do not necessarily imply an inherent 'good' or 'evil', and this is perhaps best illustrated in how newer forms of prosumer media can be harnessed by those seeking to challenge perceived injustices and inequalities. For instance, we can consider how social media played a potentially significant role in facilitating communication and interaction among participants of political protests during the revolutionary wave of demonstrations and protests in the Middle East and North Africa between 2010 and 2012 (Wolfsfeld et al, 2013). So too, we can witness how video recordings shared via social media platforms have the capacity to spark movements, such as the filming of George Floyd's death at the hands of police officers in the US. Such movements instigated and later fuelled by the communication potential of such mediums assisted in transforming the statistics of police brutality by naming the victims and putting in motion the act of more media outlets to take it upon themselves to look into the issue of how certain police officers are misusing their discretionary powers (King, 2018).

It is important to acknowledge that, similar to examining the elite and their use of power, not all latent potential of social media has been used for the social good. Perhaps the 6 January storming of Capitol Hill in Washington, DC, provides one such example. Leading up to the riot, on social media sites used by the far-right, such as Gab and Parler, 'directions on which streets to take to avoid the police and which tools to bring to help pry open doors were exchanged in comments' (Frenkel and Feuer, 2021). Upon breaking and entering the halls of Congress, individuals would subsequently upload celebratory photographs of themselves while also encouraging others to join them (Frenkel and Feuer, 2021). It has also been documented that social media-related protests, such as the Capitol Hill storm, can influence and encourage violence. For example, as the Atlantic Council's Digital Forensic Research Lab (2021) reported, a mixture of 'disinformation about the results of the 2020 election and extreme support of Trump, often amplified by Trump himself, intensified the overall movement's actions toward violence'. Five people ultimately died, including capital police officer Brian Sicknick, who died two days after the riot from suffering two strokes with 'all that transpired play[ing] a role in his condition' (Viswanatha, 2021). Despite this, though, these newer forms of media perhaps hold the most potential when it comes to empowering those who lack conventional forms of power and evidently have the capacity to challenge mainstream forms of consumer media, which will be discussed later in this chapter. Before examining crimes of the powerful within the context of the media, though, it is also worth a brief mention of those journalists that, similar to some of the aforementioned examples of prosumer media, have attempted to shed light on injustices and the damaging behaviour of those in positions of power.

'Speaking [some] truth to power': the investigative journalist

There are those journalists, an integral component of news media, who risk their lives and safety in order to reveal injustices and harms committed by powerful agents, organisations and even governments. For instance, Ida Tarbell, an American writer, lecturer and investigative journalist who sought to 'expose the ills of American society' (McCully, 2014), brought down an oil monopoly and the reputation of the man who established the company. John D. Rockefeller, the man in question, used his considerable resources in an attempt to stop Tarbell's investigation, which included using one of his banks to threaten the financial status of Tarbell's magazine, and her own father was reported as trying to prevent the investigation due to Rockefeller's ruthless reputation as an oil tycoon. Tarbell, who transformed the practices of journalism at the time to include the inclusion of documents and interviews with corporate executives, competitors, government regulators and academic experts to triangulate findings, became one of the earliest examples of what is now known as investigative journalism. Upton Sinclair, an American muckraker (reformed, progressive journalists and writers) novelist, also investigated the corruption of those in power by examining the conditions of the meat-packing industry in 1906. Sinclair's accounts paint a bleak picture of the working environment, highlighting themes of poverty, despair and unpleasant circumstances in which workers found themselves – a stark contrast to the meat-packing owners' wealth, decadence and opulence. Sinclair, specifically, provides an interesting account of the various levels of corruption operating at the turn of the century, including police practices and government officials, who enriched themselves via the unfettered capitalist system of the time.

Ultimately, such early pioneers of investigative journalism have paved the way for subsequent journalists to uncover the exploitative practices of others, including, for instance, the now famous 'WikiLeaks' founded by Julian Assange and Josh Young, in which 251,287 secret American

State Department cables were uncovered and released in 2010. Such leaks questioned the long-standing assumptions of the US's approach to foreign affairs and relations via the uncovering of various human rights violations, secret operations and subsequent cover-ups, all in an effort to expand American interests along with cultural, economic and political hegemony. Such leaks also included what is known as the 'Afghan War Logs' and the 'Iraq War Logs', which described the thousands of civilian deaths caused by these respective wars, along with the torture of prisoners at the hands of Iraqi security forces. In 2015, it was also revealed by WikiLeaks that there was evidence of American surveillance of former German Chancellor Angela Merkel, French President François Hollande, UN Secretary-General Ban Ki-moon, along with two prime ministers, Israel's Benjamin Netanyahu and Italy's Silvio Berlusconi. Two years later, in 2017, it also released what was referred to as 'Vault 7', which they stated was a collection of thousands of internal Central Intelligence Agency documents that revealed a clandestine hacking program undertaken by the agency that targeted smart TVs, the operating systems of the majority of smartphones and web browsers. As of writing, Assange has been confined in Belmarsh, a category A prison, in London since April 2019. In December 2021, the High Court in London ruled that Assange could be extradited to the US to face charges related to violating the Espionage Act of 1917. On 17 June 2022, Home Secretary Priti Patel approved the extradition.

In addition, it is important to take into account the involvement of *The Guardian*, a British daily newspaper, and Edward Snowden, a former computer intelligence consultant who leaked highly classified information from the National Security Agency (NSA) in 2013.

His revelations, which were published in *The Guardian* and other American-based newspapers, exposed various global surveillance programmes, most of which were operated by the NSA and the Five Eyes intelligence alliance in collaboration with telecommunication companies and some European governments. Snowden's decision to leak NSA documents developed gradually as he grew disillusioned with the agency and the, in his opinion, unethical and deceitful data-gathering practices they engaged in. Afterwards, he reached out to Glenn Greenwald, a journalist employed by *The Guardian*. Using the alias 'Cincinnatus', he anonymously contacted Greenwald and expressed his intention to share sensitive documents. On 20 May 2013, Snowden travelled to Hong Kong, where he resided, while the initial articles based on the leaked documents were published, starting with *The Guardian* on 5 June. Greenwald later said Snowden divulged between 9,000 and 10,000 documents. Perhaps one of the most significant revelations was that of XKeyscore, an analytical instrument that permits the collection of virtually everything on the internet, with Snowden stating: "I, sitting at my desk [could] wiretap anyone, from you or your accountant to a federal judge or even the president, if I had a personal email" (Greenwald, 2013). Due to the classified and sensitive information they shared, Snowden subsequently fled the US and is now currently residing in Russia, where President Vladimir Putin has since granted him citizenship and thus, it is impossible to extradite him (Sauer, 2022a).

There are also entire organisations that specialise in forms of investigative journalism, such as, for example, the Netherlands-based group known as Bellingcat. In the age of 'post-truths' and 'alternative facts', Bellingcat prides itself on fact-checking information and being transparent in its journalism techniques. It was founded in 2014 by former British journalist Elliot Higgins, and the organisation predominantly focuses its attention on conflict zones, serious organised crimes and human rights abuses – all areas that powerful actors, businesses and states are in some shape or form involved in and responsible for. Higgins perhaps best personifies the core principles of what we consider to be fundamental to any investigative journalist, sharing many of the attributes of the early pioneers such as Tarbell and Sinclair – individuals who risk much, including their personal safety, in order to 'speak truth to power' in a very real sense. For instance, Higgins, in 2013, set up a blog in order to report on the previously ignored use of cluster munitions and chemical weapons by the Syrian regime by the mainstream media (Weaver, 2013), and in 2014, Bellingcat first caught mainstream attention with their investigation into the downing of Malaysia Airlines Flight 17. This particular investigation, accomplished mainly with the use of volunteers, uncovered that Russia was responsible – a report that later confirmed the Dutch-led international joint investigation team (Bellingcat, 2019). Since launching in 2014, Higgins and Bellingcat have reported on other notable cases, including the Yemeni civil war and the 2018 Hajjah government airstrike by the Saudi Arabian-led coalition that used weapons manufactured by the American company Raytheon, which specialises in aerospace and defence (Elbagir et al, 2018). They are also well known for reporting on the 2018 poisoning of former Russian double agent Sergei Skripal in Salisbury, England; the coverage of the Christchurch shooting in New Zealand in 2019; and the 2021 attack on the US Capitol by supporters of Donald Trump in the aftermath of the 2020 presidential election.

These aforementioned examples of investigative reporters, driven by a strong sense of ethics and notions of justice, are by no means indicative of journalism in general. In fact, a range of factors serve as a deterrent and hindrance to such approaches towards journalism. For instance, the very prosumer forms of media previously touched upon – from tweets to video recordings – have resulted in a change in journalism from active investigating and data collating to the recycling and repurposing of information generated by others online (Bunz, 2010; Broersma and

Graham, 2012). In the age of constant news cycles, competitive headlines vying for the audience's attention, the constant seeking of advertisement investment, and the simple logic of capitalism and profit-making have, it is argued, worked to de-incentivise such forms of journalism. Instead, it promotes the repurposing of already published user content in order to keep up with the competitive landscape in which breaking news stories, in general, have an extremely short shelf life where 'there is little activity after 3 or 4 days' (Castillo et al, 2014, p 219). Alejandro (2010) stresses the potential pitfalls of such an approach to social media, noting that inaccurate and misleading reports have been published based on such sources. Alongside this, Arguedas et al (2022) note that such a preoccupation with the reuse of social media content runs the risk of providing reports encouraging biased and highly polarised attitudes and, in effect, resulting in social 'echo chambers'. Despite these factors, though, for every potential dead end or fabricated social media post, there may also be the seeds for a flourishing breaking news story, which could give a media organisation an edge in the hyper-competitive news market.

We also have to consider that powerful actors and organisations own and control many of the mainstream media outlets, with the likes of Rupert Murdoch, who owns *The Times*, *The Sunday Times*, *The Sun*, *Fox News*, *The Wall Street Journal*, the *New York Post* and several Australian titles, and Amazon's Executive Chairman Jeff Bezos who owns *The Washington Post*. Claire Enders, founder of Enders Analysis – an organisation that publishes independent research based on technologies and media – was cited by *The Guardian* as stating that you can now "count on one hand the big media brands that aren't owned by an oligarch or other billionaire" (cited in Neate, 2022). Indeed, the prosumer media platforms, previously noted for their subversive potential and latent ability to empower those who may lack other forms of power and influence, are now primarily owned by billionaires. For instance, Mark Zuckerberg, with a net worth of US$66.4 billion, owns Facebook, Instagram and WhatsApp, and more recently, the once richest person in the world with a net worth of US$191.4 billion, Elon Musk, bought Twitter for US$44 billion in 2022. Returning to Claire Enders, she continued to state that:

> 'It's another sign that the super-wealthy wish to control assets that give them an extra level of power. ... Whatever they may say, that's the reason why they buy them. ... It is now unusual for major news media not to be owned by a billionaire, and that is why the Guardian [owned by the independent Scott Trust], the Financial Times [owned by the employee-owned Japanese media group Nikkei] and the BBC are consistently shown to be the most trusted news brands.' (Cited in Neate, 2022)

Naturally, such powerful actors generate certain conflicts of interest regarding the actions of such owners and their organisations acting on their behest, and the difficulties such ownership and influence create when it comes to reporting said actions. While we will be exploring such themes throughout the course of this chapter, we will also be challenging this perception of 'trustworthiness' via an in-depth examination of the BBC and, in particular, the history of the chair of the corporation. Ultimately, though, such dynamics and influences of power impact upon the ability and potential of the 'rouge' investigative reporter – characterised by integrity and a code of ethics – to operate efficiently, if at all, given the potential damage they could cause to their company's owners, including their investments and interests.

We have so far examined the role and importance of investigative journalism, its role in exposing the harmful and criminal practices of those in power, and how, in the West, both consumer and prosumer forms of media have gradually come under the control and thus influence of extremely wealthy individuals who encapsulate the antithesis of the likes of Turbell and Sinclair and push particular agendas that are deeply entwined with the principles of capitalism. But what is the importance and role of the media in authoritarian regimes such as China and North Korea, and kleptocracies like Russia? Attention will now move to these more apparent and visible examples of how power can be used by such states to influence, obfuscate and control populations via media.

Social credit systems and great firewalls

Black Mirror (2011–2023), a science fiction television series that adopts the anthology format in which each episode is a self-contained story, is often characterised by its creative yet dystopian themes of the potential dangers of technological advancements. Stand-out episodes include 'The National Anthem' (2011), whereby the British Prime Minister is forced to have sex with a pig on live television in order to prevent the execution of a beloved kidnapped princess; 'Hated in the Nation' (2016), which revolves around robotic bees that become involved in a murder plot; and 'Crocodile' (2017), whereby insurance companies tap into people's memories in order to settle claims. However, perhaps the episode aptly titled 'Nosedive' (2016) is most prescient when examining the potential impact of newer media. This episode examines how media changes human behaviour through the lens of a world where social media ratings dominate every aspect of life. In this world, individuals are persistently rated on a scale of one to five stars based on their social interactions, with the highest-rated individuals receiving significant privileges such as access to exclusive locations, opportunities, employment and career progression prospects. The protagonist of the episode, Lacie Pound, is a woman consumed with her social media rating. She is determined to boost it to gain access to a luxurious consumer lifestyle continually promoted and shared by others on social media. She spends her time carefully curating her social media posts and interactions, attending social events purely to network and gain ratings, and obsessing over her rating to the point of it becoming all-encompassing. As the episode progresses, Lacie's obsession with her rating causes her to become increasingly desperate, leading to her downfall and eventual arrest. The episode illustrates how media, particularly social media, can profoundly impact human behaviour. By creating a system of constant evaluation and comparison, the social media platform's ratings appear to incentivise individuals to prioritise their online persona over their true selves, leading to a loss of authenticity and individuality.

The episode arguably personifies Foucault's argument that power is not just something individuals or groups possess but rather a pervasive force embedded in all social relations and structures (1998). In particular, it parallels his notions of disciplinary power, which operates through surveillance and control systems, and biopower, which involves regulating and managing populations to maximise their productivity and efficiency (1977). In 'Nosedive', we see how social media ratings function as a form of disciplinary power. They create a system of constant evaluation and surveillance that shapes individuals' behaviour and reinforces social norms. The rating system displayed during the episode depicts a hierarchy of social status, with those with high ratings enjoying privileged access to resources and opportunities. In contrast, those with low ratings are excluded and marginalised. The episode also touches on the idea of biopower, as the rating system is presented as a way of regulating and managing individuals to create a more efficient and productive society. 'Nosedive' demonstrates how power can potentially operate in subtle and pervasive ways in a technologically advanced society and how new technologies and forms of media can be used to reinforce social control and regulation. What is of note here, though, is that the episode takes place in what is clearly some future form of the US and, like most episodes, during an unspecified period during the 2040s/2050s. However, we can already see how such technology is already being implemented in more authoritarian regimes, including China.

China's social credit system is a technologically developed and expanded iteration of the risk assessment credit rating systems that were introduced in China in the 1980s (Cash, 2019). The initial system was designed to reportedly develop a financial credit rating system aimed primarily towards those living outside of major urban areas, along with small companies requiring official documentation (Hoffman, 2017). This more recent iteration is a government-led initiative to assess and rate the social and economic behaviour of individuals, companies and other organisations (Donnelly, 2023). It is important to note here that there are currently multiple social credit systems in China, with some managed by the state and others by private companies. These include the business trustworthiness system, which creates a blacklist system for discredited businesses and is regulated by the People's Bank of China; the government trustworthiness system, which evaluates civil workers and institutions; the social trustworthiness system, which forms a blacklist system for discredited individuals; and the judiciary public trust system, which also runs a similar blacklist system but is regulated by the Supreme People's Court (Liu, 2019). The systems are designed to create a centralised database that collects and analyses a wide range of information regarding individuals' financial history, criminal records, employment records and social media activity (Botsman, 2017; Chen and Grossklags, 2022). These various systems rate individuals, businesses and institutions based on the accumulation and analysis of data. 'In some trials, this has involved a single numerical score (usually between 1 and 1000, like a FICO score), or a letter grade (usually from A–D)' (Donnelly, 2023). The system, which is still in its infancy and continually evolving (Drinhausen and Brussee, 2022), is anticipated to draw data from sources including governmental records, registry offices and school documents, along with internet sources including search histories, shopping habits and interactions with others on social media (Wong and Dobson, 2019). Details from the various pilot schemes suggest that the higher the score, the more trustworthy the government considers the individual or business. There is currently no unified, numerical or otherwise credit score for businesses or individuals; rather, national and local platforms use different evaluation or rating systems (Brussee, 2021). A high score can result in such 'privileges' as priority for school admissions and employment, easier access to loans and credit, free gym facilities, cheaper public transport, shorter wait times at hospitals, tax breaks and a fast track for promotions (Canales and Mok, 2022). Conversely, those with low scores may face various penalties and restrictions, including denial of licences and access to some social services; exclusion from booking flights and high-speed train tickets; less access to credit; no access to governmental positions; limited schooling prospects; and forms of public shaming, including names and photos aired online in public spaces (Ma, 2018). In 2019, it was reported that China banned approximately 23 million citizens from buying travel tickets due to this system, echoing the words found within a government document from 2014 in which such a system 'allow[s] the trustworthy to roam everywhere under heaven while making it hard for the discredited to take a single step' (cited in Kuo, 2019). So too, a journalist who was blacklisted by the social credit system was publicly shamed by a local court in China (Wang, 2017). Von Blomberg and Yu (2023) note that shaming plays an important role within such a system to inform members of the public of the actions of others, along with providing an important means of deterrence. This public shaming had a powerful impact on the journalist's reputation and social standing and on his ability to conduct business and travel freely (Vanderklippe, 2018). Such an example echoes back to previous discussions highlighted in this chapter and the various ways in which powerful organisations and institutions, including the state, can detrimentally impact the ability of journalists to investigate and report on several injustices, inequalities and actions of the elite. Regarding companies, those with high scores may receive favourable treatment from the government, such as access to loans or preferential tax rates. In contrast, those with low scores may face increased regulatory scrutiny or penalties (Lin and Milhaupt, 2021). Points can reportedly be gained via such actions as performing charity work, helping those less fortunate, having a good financial history and caring for elderly family members. Equally, points can be deducted for various reasons, including traffic offences, 'illegally' protesting against the authorities, not visiting elderly family members frequently, posting anti-government messages on social media, participating in anything deemed to be a cult and cheating in online games (Donelly, 2023).

A substantial amount of reporting in English-language media has been observed to rely on linguistic misunderstandings and policy proposals that remain unimplemented (Matsakis, 2019). Nonetheless, the parallels between the themes depicted in the *Black Mirror* episode 'Nosedive' (2016) and China's social credit system, which rewards and penalises individuals based on their behaviour's alignment with or deviation from societal norms, are not hard to discern. 'Nosedive' was originally devised as a satire on the perils of social media, but as previously outlined, the consequences presented in the episode are increasingly becoming a reality. As previously mentioned, such a system (or currently systems) is continually being refined, and there currently exists a lack of uniformity across various jurisdictions and cities. However, the creator of *Black Mirror*, Charlie Brooker, replied, when asked about this very system, "They're going to do the system from 'Nosedive' for citizens! It's incredibly sinister. Am I right in thinking that your ranking is affected by your friends, so if you hang with the wrong crowd, your social ranking will go down? Wow. It's completely mental" (cited in Stern, 2016).

Outside of the aforementioned social credit systems, China has also been documented as utilising many more conventional forms of media control to shape public opinions and, conversely, ensure minimal potential dissent. With a combination of the internet and carefully crafted and controlled news media, the government's ability to create narratives and shape citizens' minds has become increasingly sophisticated, enabling the government to exert even greater control over the population. For instance, China has one of the most extensive censorship systems in the world, with the government using a combination of legal regulations and technological tools to control both the scale and flow of information (Han and Shao, 2022). The government actively blocks access to foreign websites, social media platforms and news sources that it deems politically sensitive, and it also has a host of internet censors, or 'cleaners', who monitor and delete content that is critical of the government or challenges its policies (Sharwood, 2022). As an illustration, if you were to search for 'Tiananmen Square massacre' on a computer or smartphone within China, which pertains to the incident where hundreds of people were killed on 4 June 1989, during the People's Liberation Army crackdown on pro-democracy protesters in and around Beijing's Tiananmen Square, you would not find any information or mention of this event (Griffiths, 2019). Such censors have even begun revealing users' locations in an effort to further regulate and control what information is shared online (Dong, 2022). Furthermore, Chinese social media and web video platforms are required to pre-approve all news-related comments before they are posted online, and they have intensified training for censors to prevent the dissemination of 'harmful' content (Zhang, 2022). These myriad online techniques and policies ultimately ensure that the 'great firewall' of the Chinese internet is maintained and that the latent subversive potential of this communication technology is never unleashed to challenge the elite's rule. We can already witness how such use of sophisticated censorship has transformed large swaths of the youth, with 'now young online Chinese, once conduits for new ideas that challenge the power structure, [becoming] increasingly part of Beijing's defence operation' (Wang, 2020). Wang (2020) elaborates further, stating:

> Widely popular movies, TV shows and books portraying Chinese society in a critical light are attacked for being 'unpatriotic'. The 2001 comedy Big Shot's Funeral, critically acclaimed in China at the time, a stinging satire of China's fledgling capitalists, is now deemed 'a smear on national entrepreneurs'. Once a hero for making Chinese innovation global, TikTok's founder, Zhang Yiming, is denounced as a U.S. 'lapdog' for negotiating to sell TikTok's U.S. operations—despite the fact he didn't actually have a choice. Chinese scientists who question the scientific proof, clinical validation and effectiveness of traditional Chinese medicine are labelled 'Han traitors'. (Wang, 2020)

We also have to consider the creation and use of propaganda – a classic 'go-to' in the authoritarian playbook (Schneider, 2014). The Chinese government has an extensive propaganda system that seeks to promote its own version of events and shape public opinion. State-controlled media outlets like China Central Television and People's Daily are the primary sources of news for many Chinese citizens, and they often promote government policies. The Chinese government has also spent a great deal of time and resources in an effort to portray the country's leadership in a good light, both internally and abroad. It has reportedly spent approximately US$6.6 billion since 2009 to improve its global media presence (Kumar, 2021). A significant component of this initiative includes exchange programmes for foreign journalists, in which China provides training for journalists in China. The government also provides state media content free of charge, pays for entire supplements in respected foreign newspapers and launches bilateral cooperation agreements with local media outlets (Kumar, 2021).

On the social media front, the Chinese government has also begun to implement social media influencers in an effort to censor information and, importantly, reduce the level of critical attention from other nations. For example, research conducted by Ryan et al (2022) for the Australian Strategic Policy Institute determined that a 'small but increasingly popular set of YouTube accounts featur[ing] mainly female China-based ethnic-minority influencers from the troubled frontier regions of Xinjiang, Tibet and Inner Mongolia' were being employed by the government. Xinjiang, in particular, has been under intense scrutiny due to the Chinese government having arbitrarily detained more than one million Uyghur Muslims since 2017 in 're-education camps' and subjected those not interned to severe surveillance, religious restrictions, enforced labour and involuntary sterilisations (Maizland, 2022). While information on what transpired or is currently taking place in these 're-education' camps is limited, many detainees who have since left China described bleak conditions. For instance, the United Nations Human Rights Office of the High Commissioner (2022) published a report that included interviews with 26 individuals who were detained, determining conditions consisting of 'patterns of torture or other forms of cruel, inhuman, or degrading treatment' (p 25). Within the report, it was also revealed that 'instances of sexual and gender-based violence in VETC (Vocational Education and Training Centres) facilities, including of rape' (United Nations Human Rights Office of the High Commissioner, 2022) transpired. The report concludes this examination into human rights abuses by stating that 'the government's blanket denials of all allegations, as well as its gendered and humiliating attacks on those who have come forward to share their experiences, [has] added to the indignity and suffering of survivors' (United Nations Human Rights Office of the High Commissioner, 2022). Returning to the work of Ryan et al (2022), the government has denied such accusations and has also turned to more subtle means to control narratives. The authors found that when compared with the more rigid and direct messaging and dissemination of more traditional forms of propaganda, influencer-produced content was described as being 'less polished', and the presentation 'has a more authentic feel' (cited in Davidson, 2022). These social media videos, in terms of content, predominantly shared positive lifestyle content and presented Xinjiang and other regions as peaceful and economically and culturally flourishing. One such influencer stated in one video: "Xinjiang is the same as other places in China. ... People live and work in peace and happiness. There is no genocide and no forced labour. ... People from all over the world are welcome to Xinjiang" (cited in Davidson, 2022).

Away from the conventional use of propaganda and strict surveillance systems, it is clear that China is adapting its use of newer, prosumer forms of media in order to challenge any perceived dissenting voices and even use individuals from within these very victimised communities with the aim to construct and legitimise their carefully crafted narrative. As witnessed, we are clearly seeing a transition away from solely conventional forms of propaganda, such as posters and carefully crafted films that were used by the likes of the Nazi party and Stalin's Communist Party, and towards a more technologically sophisticated multi-lateral approach with an eye towards a global reach and influence.

China is by no means the exception when we consider how the powerful use the tool of media to censor, hide and obfuscate the realities of their regimes to prevent any challenge to their rule. For instance, we only need to look to China's neighbour, North Korea, to witness even more overt forms of censorship and barriers to information. North Korea, a communist-controlled state since 1949, prohibits independent journalism, which, as previously discussed, is one of the most important avenues of shining a light on the injustices brought on by powerful actors or, in this case, institutions. It is important to note that, according to the law, Article 67 of North Korea's constitution theoretically protects the freedom of the press (Socialist Constitution of the Democratic People's Republic of Korea, 2014), but the regime continually ignores and acts against this law. This has manifested in journalists being arrested, expelled from the country, forcibly moved to labour camps, and even killed for deviating from or opposing the regime's carefully orchestrated narrative (Committee to Protect Journalists, 2017). Alongside this, the Korean Central News Agency is directly affiliated and directed with the government and is the only legitimate news source for North Korea's media, according to said authority. The regime tightly controls the production and dissemination of information via this channel and strictly prohibits any form of information that would challenge the approved content. It is important to note that there are a 'few foreign press agencies such as Agence-France Presse (AFP) and Kyodo News' that are permitted access in North Korea, 'but operate under close surveillance, which impairs their reporting ability' (Reporters without Borders, ND). Propaganda is also under the control and direction of the Propaganda and Agitation Department, in which posters, art, music, films and leaflets are produced and disseminated with the overarching aim of reaffirming the ruling elite's political stance, the unquestionable rule of the Kim dynasty, and the existential danger posed by North America and its allies (Lim, 2015). Such use of propaganda is not limited to conventional forms of media, with reports of an entire village supposedly designed to project an image of economic strength and prosperity, yet is simply a shell designed to obfuscate reality. Kijong-dong, or 'peace village', is situated not far from the demilitarised zone between North and South Korea and upon closer inspection, this seemingly perfectly crafted spectacle is brought into question with the numerous painted-on windows and hollow buildings lacking floors and even walls (Wharton, 2018). For a country with continuous humanitarian crises and human rights violations, such a village serves as an apt metaphor for the hollow image of strength and wealth North Korea's regime attempts to depict. On the internet front, North Korea utilises predominantly a form of intranet, which is a local or restricted communications network that is not connected to the internet or the World Wide Web, to which many of us have access. The Kwangmyong (Korean for 'bright star') intranet system is primarily used to link libraries, universities and other government organisations within the country but does not go further than the 'country's borders' (Williams, 2015). Despite this significant restriction to information, it should also be noted that for the majority of North Korean citizens, even access to this highly restricted intranet is incredibly difficult, with only a few thousand individuals being granted access (Burgess, 2023). While the internet is tightly regulated in countries such as the aforementioned China and others such as Iran, Belarus, United Arab Emirates, Myanmar and Turkmenistan (see Bischoff, 2023 for a breakdown of internet restrictions per country as of the time of writing), what makes North Korea distinct is that for millions 'the internet simply doesn't exist' (Burgess, 2023). Those fortunate few who can access the country's intranet, often in libraries, are also consistently monitored regarding activity and, more specifically, what they are searching for. Regarding access to the internet itself, this is firmly delineated by power, and, within the context of North Korea, this is top governmental positions. To demonstrate how rare such access to the internet is, one only has to consider the billions of IP addresses in the US for a country of approximately 579 million people, compared with less than 2,000 IP addresses in a country of 26 million in North Korea (Fisher, 2015). Alongside these members of the elite who are granted access to all the information of the internet (albeit rather slowly due to infrastructure), those working in government positions concerning propaganda and intelligence are also granted such access in order to engage in misinformation and hacking activities where relevant. Such strict control of access to either the intranet or the internet is also tightly controlled via the sales and distribution of hardware, with such ownership allowed via government approval and 'registered with the police as if they were shotguns' (Fisher, 2015). This is, of course, not factoring in the fact that even smuggled laptops from China on the black market cost approximately between 270,000 and 450,000 KPW (US$300 to $500). At the same time, the average worker's monthly salary is approximately the equivalent of US$2 a month (Lankov, 2022). Similar to

China, North Korea has also recently begun harnessing the potential of more prosumer forms of media, with YouTube and other platforms being utilised to promote the regime and counter criticisms, though lacking the same level of 'authenticity' found within similar Chinese content and betraying a high level of scripting and editing. Park Seong-Cheol, a researcher at the Database Center for North Korean Human Rights, stated that such videos "look like a well-prepared play" scripted by the North Korean government (cited in Yeung and Bae, 2023).

This overview of authoritarian regimes has only scratched the surface of the myriad of ways such states control media via legal, technological, economic and cultural channels. What is evident is that the more orthodox systems of propaganda are still very much at play while, simultaneously, there is a concerted effort to synthesise these methods with newer forms of information technology. In doing so, the primary aim of shaping the hearts and minds of the populace is actively sought while also attempting to prevent outside and potentially dissenting voices from challenging these carefully manufactured narratives. However, are more Western and democratically structured states the pinnacle when it comes to freedom of the media? Is the influence of the state and powerful actors and organisations limited when attempting to reveal and report the 'truth' when compared with these more authoritarian states? Such questions and deliberations will be discussed next.

A not-so-national treasure

Although thus far, we have concerned ourselves with the in-your-face practices of some of the global media, known for their nefarious ways, can we really suggest that our own national media corporation is beyond reproach?

As Mills (2016) succinctly discusses in his book that sets out to demystify the myths surrounding our not-so-national treasure, the BBC is not the mouthpiece for the establishment but is, in fact, an integral part of it. The accolade-collecting benevolent 'auntie' is, in fact, the creepy 'uncle' whose interests have always been intrinsically linked to that of the establishment. To start to attempt to unravel how intertwined our supposedly impartial national broadcasting corporation is to politics and, moreover, the financial sector, we must look at its 'appointed' chairs.

We will start with Richard Sharp, who was appointed chairman in February of 2021. Sharp, a former investment banker with a career spanning 40 years with elite financial institutions such as JP Morgan and Goldman Sachs, has strong links to the Conservative Party. Sharp, who classes himself as a friend to Rishi Sunak, has sat on the Conservative think tank the Centre for Policy Studies and has been a party donor for a number of years. Baroness Wheatcroft, who sits on the House of Lords Communications and Digital Committee, was cited in *The London Economic* newspaper stating that:

'Mr Sharp may be a very honourable man but there's no getting away from the fact he helped to organise an £800,000 loan that would get the prime minister out of financial trouble, he did him a favour just when he wanted the prime minister to give him the top job at the BBC.' (Cited in Peat, 2023).

With murmurings of cronyism stirring within the media, this is not the only scandal that has been gnawing at the ex-banker's heels. While in the post, Sharp had donated thousands of pounds through his personal charity to a group that has persistently called for the privatisation of the BBC. Eventually, public scrutiny forced Sharp to resign from his position. However, this was not some one-off 'rotten apple' but is indicative of the BBC's appointed custodians. Hailing from wealth and privilege, those appointed to this role are members of the elite British establishment.

Since the initial appointment of Lord Gainford as the inaugural chairman of the BBC in 1922, a precedent was set for individuals from the landed gentry and former politicians to secure this coveted position. Lord Gainford, a member of Lloyd George's government who held roles like Postmaster-General and President of the Board of Education, initiated this trend. Additionally, the pattern extended to include the recruitment of notable figures from the UK financial sector.

In recent years, much has been discussed regarding the illusion of impartiality of the BBC. While all sides of the political spectrum attempt to highlight left or right-wing bias, one prevailing assumption is that the BBC reflects and reinforces the interests of the powerful groups with which this book concerns itself (see Mills, 2016). The Cardiff University Study (2004) commissioned to look into anti-war rhetoric and bias actually found that the BBC was, in fact, displaying the most pro-war stance than any broadcaster during the Iraq War. The report demonstrated that the BBC was reliant on government and military sources to construct their news bulletins and paid little attention to Iraqi or other independent sources, such as the Red Cross. It can be argued that this may not be an indictment of establishment bias; however, this approach to war correspondence does demonstrate a less than panoramic overview of the war in Iraq.

However, when their presenters take to their social media to criticise government policy, the BBC take 'proportionate action'. In early 2023, BBC sports presenter Gary Lineker (2023a) re-tweeted a tweet from the British Home Office with the comment, 'Good heavens, this is beyond awful'. The tweet that makes reference to immigration policy garnered 88.4 thousand likes and thousands of retweets. This was the start of a debate that would rage across all forms of media and Parliament. This polarising tweet was then doubled down on by Lineker (2023b), who likened the language used by the Home Office to being akin to 1930s Germany. Accused of breaking editorial guidelines, Lineker was suspended from his position at the BBC as Match of the Day presenter. The outcry was deafening. For many, the BBC had finally shown its true establishment face. This debate soon spilt over into Prime Minister's Questions. Heated exchanges between the Prime Minister and Labour Party leader Keir Starmer demonstrated a more 'muscular approach' to the subject of BBC bias. However, this latest inception of the Labour Party, according to some academics and political pundits, has benefitted from this less-than-impartial approach to news broadcasting; media coverage of the tribulations of the former Labour Party leader had been less than favourable and paved the way for a new leader and a complete overhaul of the party. Dr Justin Schlosberg (2016) of the Media Reform Coalition and Birkbeck, University of London described the broadcaster as 'a mouthpiece for the right-wing press' after they had taken umbrage with a report into the 'clear and consistent bias' against Jeremy Corbyn. The report found that the BBC had a 'strong tendency' within the main evening news for their reporters to use pejorative language when describing Jeremy Corbyn and his supporters. When evidence points to a blatant bias against political opponents of the government, it is a logical conclusion that opponents of the West would provoke a similar response in the UK media.

It is at this point that we turn our attention to a haircut. In 2021, news stories emerged of North Korea's haircut police enforcing despotic hair standards, with media outlets discussing the outlawing of mullets and socialist haircuts. This media fascination with the enforced grooming standards of the Democratic People's Republic of Korea started with a story that started to gain traction in 2014. Seemingly originated from Radio Free Asia, a non-profit funded in part by the US government, the story that a law that men must wear their hair in the style of their leader, Kim Jong Un, was picked up by various news outlets, including the BBC. Not only did this make the evening news in multiple countries across the West, but comedy sketches and memes were shared across social media. Not only did academics such as Aidan Foster-Carter at Leeds University, who dismissed the story as 'bull shit', refute these claims, but so did YouTube content creators Boy from Australia, who travelled to North Korea for a haircut.

Complicity via a tweet and a share

Although much of this chapter has been dedicated to the way that both traditional and new media conduct their exploitative business practices, it is equally important to look at how the Western public consumes this media. We live in an epoch where we are under more digital surveillance than ever before. Again, we have looked at the Eastern media practices and their overt state surveillance practices. Often, the West clings to its moral high ground, with much of its media denigrating these practices and stories of

North Korean Stasi constantly watching its oppressed populous and enforced haircuts. Undoubtedly, this type of panoptic gaze has been woven into the fabric of their societies, but these technological advances that have been used to root out enemies of the state are a global (mis)adventure. However, unlike North Korea, which cites the Western menace to ensure that its citizens endure the Orwellian monitoring of their daily lives, the prosumer populous of the West is not just enduring but enjoying contemporary surveillance capitalism (Zuboff, 2020). As noted by Debord, 'When the real world is transformed into mere images, mere images become real beings' (2005, p 10). According to Debord (2005), societies dominated by modern conditions of production present life as an immense accumulation of spectacles. Hitherto, these spectacles were glossy advertisements, and the beautiful people who adorned the large and small screens provided us with an amusing glimpse into a world converted by most – a world of superficial capitalist opulence that acts as both sedative and aphrodisiac. These visual representations of the ruling classes serve not only to ensure complete compliance with commodity fetishism but also to entrench the ideology of production and productivity further.

Fast forward to a world where the big screen is making way for the very small screen. Alongside these spectacular representations of human life and achievement are the new breed of prosumer ambassadors: the influencer. These contemporary specialists of 'apparent' life project the rewards of the capitalist system as ultimate life goals – wealth, power and beauty that can be obtained for as little as US$9.99 and the complete submission to the social media platforms that they represent. They reign supreme on TikTok and Instagram, acting out a plethora of capitalist identities, lifestyles and socio-political views. While they are, for many of us, selling inaccessible results of social labour, and they themselves are what Debord referred to as 'superficial' objects, they are objects that we can not only identify with but aspire to become.

With influencers that appear overnight earning millions of dollars per year by posting images of whimsical consumption, many of us have started to document all aspects of our lives in the hope that Amazon et al will see our potential and will facilitate our transcendence from the drudge of the material self to digital celebrity. All interactions are reduced to a hashtag; we trudge through social media with zombie-like optimism and managed #glee. While we, the next crop of influencers, wait impatiently to usurp them to be the next 'big' thing, social media trend, representative of the system, they trade more of their privacy. Surely, this is a small price to pay. The rewards of this transaction are apparent to see, and those who somehow manage to avoid the allure of social media will be given valuable insight into the fiscal rewards in the life of an influencer and a step-by-step guide on 'how they can join them' from the traditional media outlets.

It is easy to oversimplify social media and its effects on society and not give adequate consideration to this ubiquitous unification in pursuit of capital, both social and economic, as a mere by-product of the advancement of new technologies rather than another powerplay of the economic elite. Gramscian discourse often refers to the velvet glove of consent that entraps societies into capitalist servitude. However, this glove is now worn by influencers across the globe and comes with a hefty price tag that many pay without question. The images that we accept as our own material reality create a longing and a sense of belonging almost simultaneously; we assume our carefully chosen identities and begin a journey of consumption that then replicates and reinforces the modern conditions of production that swaddle us in this season's must-haves.

These contemporary new media platforms have been under much scrutiny, with industry insiders such as Jaron Lanier (2019) offering compelling arguments as to why we need to delete our social media. These arguments tend to focus on how, as a society, we are becoming more polarised and more disconnected from our material realities. However, should traditional media be under the same, if not more, levels of scrutiny? Moreover, as traditional media becomes more and more intertwined with social media, further discussions must be had regarding the powerful reach of news media. Hitherto, those of us who had an interest in current affairs would purchase a newspaper or sit and wait for the News at Ten. Now, the news is constantly disseminated through our mobile phones. This news now comes targeted to us through social media platforms, with polarised debate from an infinite number of users all primed for outrage.

Warring factions from all sides of the political spectrum fight for space. On the battlefield of social media, moderate voices begin to silence themselves in the fear that by aligning themselves with one narrative or the other, they will become caught up in the crossfire. This pool of discontent is not limited to the fringes of social media; everyone with a keyboard is expected to have an opinion. However, this must be the right opinion. Wendi Jade Jensen (2018) wrote that 'an environment that is not safe to disagree in is not an environment focused on growth – it's an environment focused on control'. This succinctly holds a mirror to social media. Users are expected to have a fully formed social consciousness and one that aligns perfectly with dominant societal narratives; they should have amassed enough social capital to be 'relevant' in their profession and pursuits. A meticulously kept social media presence that highlights their citizenship, achievements and positive social interactions must be cultivated and maintained. This is the capitalist West's insidious version of the Chinese Social Credit System, where one ill-thought opinion or off-colour joke can manifest in social and economic ruin (Hart, 2018). From high-profile celebrities to Joe Bloggs, who downloaded Twitter to see what the fuss was about, all became under the scrutiny of algorism and users searching for the miscreants in their midst. Moreover, even academics who once freely shared their philosophical musings on Twitter, often at the behest of their institutions, have begun to feel the harsh reality of this Western credit system. The system, as quickly as it bestows the promise of unlimited capital rewards, is the same system that can rapidly remove the legitimacy of the disgraced user, leaving them to face the reality of a virtual firing squad and the death of a carefully crafted digital identity.

The sun always shines on TV

> Surveillance capitalism unilaterally claims human experience as free raw material for translation into behavioural data. Although some of these data are applied to product or service improvement the rest are declared as proprietary behavioural surplus, fed into advanced manufacturing processes known as machine intelligence and fabricated into prediction products that will anticipate what you will do now, soon and later. … Surveillance capitalists have grown immensely wealthy from trading these operations, for many companies are eager to lay bets on our future behaviour. (Zuboff, 2020)

In the 1990s, surveillance-based reality television emerged as a resurgent programming genre in the US and Western Europe, with early forerunners of this terrestrial revolution, such as The Real World and Big Brother, commanding worldwide audiences into the millions along with high ratings and viewing figures that succinctly demonstrated to the network executives audiences emerging pallet for the unscripted chaos of reality TV. Bell-Metereau, cited in Murray and Ouellette (2004), argues that it is the one genre that has completely remade television culture. Production companies scrambled over themselves to provide viewers with hyperbolic depictions of social identities and interpersonal relationships. From dysfunctional families to bright young things living it large in Greek holiday resorts, there was something for everyone, and those who opened up their lives to the spotlight of prime TV found fame, fortune and notoriety. Like Ferrell's (1999, p 397) depiction of the hall of mirrors where one image bounces endlessly off another, multiple inceptions of the reality format loop replicate and evolve into an ever-expanding boxset of social voyeurism.

This normalisation of being watched changed society's notions of the Orwellian gaze of the omnipresent 'Big Brother' from a chilling prophecy to a much-coveted prosumer lifestyle. As much of this chapter has discussed, society has entered a time when the online economy is becoming increasingly reliant upon surveillance as a form of economic exploitation, and the need for a society that feels in control of 'invasions' of their privacy is heightened since MTV first broadcast The Real World in early in the 1990s (Andrejevic,

2002). This new breed of celebrity became famous for being famous, often without any obvious talent; these 'stars' were catapulted into the public eye. The new sweethearts, heartthrobs, comic relief and those that the baying public loved to hate. Their lives are broken open for all to see on a variety of platforms, with celebrity correspondents salivating for the latest gossip. While many crave this media frenzy to capitalise on paid partnership opportunities, others will find themselves casualties of their own infamy.

In season three of the British Big Brother, a young naïve girl walked in front of the 24-hour surveillance cameras and unbeknown to her, every aspect of her previous life was sold to tabloids who ran 52 front page stories on the 20-year-old from a socio-economically deprived background. From stories denigrating her behaviour in the house to 'kiss and tells', the tabloids were relentless in their pursuit of polarising content to feed to their insatiable audiences. Not only does Jade Goody's reception hold a mirror to the predatory nature of reality TV, but it also succinctly demonstrates how embedded the class system is within the UK, as Jade, the epitome of the working-class stereotypes, drank, swore and engaged in a sex act with a fellow contestant. The disdain that the middle-class media showed for Jade was palpable. The depiction of working-class villainy not only piques the interest of the viewing populous but also serves to give a visage to the scrounging shirkers that politicians tell us are destroying society and our economy. This media management of societal emotion works in tandem with the corporate surveillance model to relegate independent thought to a relic of the past and replicate social and class divisions. In a genre that incites judgements on all its participants, willing or otherwise, the working classes are often depicted as classless and worthless (Skeggs and Wood, 2008). The projection of the neoliberal agenda of self-growth is encapsulated in many adaptations of this genre as the middle-class host offers the extending hand of support to the feckless working-class protagonist to offer them encouragement with what should be their ongoing identity work, for example, to make the right lifestyle choices. How to dress, eat, clean, bring up their children, conduct their relationship and do their weekly shopping is just a fraction of the TV support guides scheduled for prime-time consumption, and as with all of our televised weekly entertainment, the viewing public are invited to share their thoughts on a plethora of social media sites, where sentiment ranges from empathy to violent hostility towards the subject of their favourite reality shows.

Not only do the social media platforms that crave our ongoing commitment, connection and data use this surveillance capitalism model to maximise profits, but so do most other consumer-based industries. Principles of freedom of speech have quickly been replaced with the corporate principle of 'freedom of reach' (Islam, 2002). Each facet of our lives has become digitally documented and has become one of capitalism's most valuable commodities. Every internet search, transaction and interaction is documented and available on the ever-expanding global data ecosystems. Each ground-breaking technological device that society covets records and transmits every detail that it picks up. Privacy is a luxury many cannot afford, with the best deals only available to those who freely give their information to the raft of corporate benefactors through price comparison and reward schemes.

These reward cards themselves have been at the centre of much controversy, with stories emerging that through analysing the consumption habits of their consumers, retailers could essentially 'data mine' their way into the reproductive systems of their customers. A story published in Forbes reported that American retailer Target had used a scoring system by looking at previous purchases and started to send out vouchers to customers for baby and pregnancy-related products based on their previous spending habits. Speaking to *The New York Times*, Target statistician Andrew Pole described how, like other stores, Target collects spending habits and demographic information for all its customers. The only conclusion that can be reached is that each purchase we make becomes a further puzzle piece in the jigsaw of our online identities that are often traded among companies hoping to tempt us into parting with cash for personally targeted goods and services.

How do we turn back the tide of surveillance capitalism when each technological advance offers the corporate giants more keys to society's hopes, dreams and spending habits? Discussing Facebook, Frenkel and Kang (2021) succinctly recognise that there is no way back and that the technology that these corporations have 'unleashed' on society is now firmly embedded in the fabric of our social realities. They state that 'the platform is built upon a fundamental, possibly irreconcilable dichotomy: its purported mission to advance society by connecting people while also profiting off them' (p 300).

Time and time again, we see the attempt to force social media moguls to revoke their hold over our data and atone for their less-than-transparent surveillance practices, yet through toothless legislation and relentless lobbying, their reach keeps expanding with no crimes to answer to. Zuboff (2020) poignantly states that we are now at a tipping point, and society has, unbeknown to them, entered a titanic struggle with the corporations that seek to capture our intimate personal details in their ruthless pursuit of capital. Without reading the terms and conditions, we stumble ever closer to digital servitude, with our avatars languishing in the thoughtfully crafted prisons of our own consumption.

The rise of the technocrat

Capitalism, almost Darwinian in its nature, is the chameleon of economic structures, morphing and contorting throughout the epochs of history, ensuring its dominion over its global subordinates. As we stand on the precipice of the next stage of human history, capitalism once again must adapt. So far, much of this chapter has discussed how technology has resulted in a societal shift from the physical world to the fast, interactive virtual world. A world where identities are meticulously crafted and anyone can be a philosopher in 280 characters. As more of us work, rest and play in online spaces, the kings and queens of these new virtual kingdoms have built their own despotic empires and live by their own set of rules. Governments cannot contain them; international law often does not apply to them, and as they sit on their virtual thrones, great swathes have begun to worship them like new gods. However, the harms of these new gods, including Elon Musk, Jeff Bezos and Mark Zuckerberg, are not confined to the reaches of the internet, as their empires encroach upon all aspects of the human condition.

In the early days of the internet, technocrats such as Steve Jobs could be hailed as revolutionaries who were opening doors to a new epoch in human history. Can the same be said of the new technocrats who are exploiting and capitalising on these early advancements, using technology to further deregulate industries and ensure that those with a capital deficit are relegated to the meagre existence of the precariat? Let's take, for instance, Uber, an American ride-hailing company that transformed the taxi industry almost overnight. Many have indeed hailed the Uber app for its ease of use, driver rating system and the fact that you can use it in approximately 70 countries and 10,500 cities worldwide (Uber, 2023). However, the meteoric rise of the app has resulted in the company becoming the virtual 'middleman' between drivers and customers and, for this service, it demands a steep price. For instance, not only does the company take 25 per cent from drivers for each ride (Hu and Ley, 2023), but it also provides its drivers, classed as independent contractors, with minimal employment benefits, a lack of job security – which can include unwarranted account deactivations – and an inability to negotiate prices (Sainato, 2023). Drivers also have to cover vehicle-related expenses, face significant challenges in unionising and are susceptible to wage fluctuations due to Uber setting prices, which has seen drivers having to increase their hours during the, at the time of writing, cost of living crisis (Collins, 2022).

We have also seen companies such as Amazon, who have faced criticism regarding the harm caused to both employees and the environment, turning to newer forms of media to quell and counter such concerns. Amazon initially launched their warehouse tours in 2014, in which they stated that members of the public can now visit such facilities, which the company deemed 'safer than a department store' (Cook, 2014). The number of tours grew to approximately 21 locations in both the US (for example, Robbinsville in New Jersey and Tracy in California) and Canada (for example, Brampton in Ontario), while, in Europe, there are 23 locations (for example, Rugeley in England, Frankenthal in Germany and Turin in Italy). Amazon has since taken their tours online, allowing customers-turned-tourists to take part virtually, along with a number of recorded tours uploaded onto the Amazon YouTube channel. As Cook (2014) notes, the launch of such tours was likely a response to the rising levels of criticism the company was facing in relation to labour practices and environmental impact. Lynes and Wragg (2023; see also West, 2022) reaffirm such notions, suggesting that such tours are PR efforts designed to qualm concerns related to the company's relationship with the climate and waste, as well as attempting to ensure that the consumer does not reflect on the labour and infrastructure required to deliver their items. Amazon is not alone here, though, with the likes of Sports Direct (Goodley, 2020), Shein (Jones, 2021), Boohoo (Tingle, 2022), JD Sports and Asos (Chapman, 2019) having all been scrutinised for working conditions in warehouses as they transition into online e-commerce. Alongside this, such companies have also begun to emulate Amazon's approach to adopting similar forms of virtual tourism, with companies such as Boohoo launching in-person and virtual tours in 2021 (Rodgers, 2021) and Shein using pre-recorded videos of warehouses on TikTok (Shein_Official, 2022).

Although often exempt from the rules that govern the material world, the technocrats create their own and often enforce them with vigour. The giants of social media, such as Zuckerburg's Facebook, have opted to police their netizens without impunity, drawing criticism that their overzealous use of account banning is an affront to free speech. This dichotomy of these deregulated spaces and their intense policing of speech prompted billionaire Elon Musk to buy Twitter for US$40 million (Clayton and Hoskins, 2022). Sealing the deal in 2022, Musk celebrated with a tweet: 'The bird is free.' Musk, who describes himself as a 'free speech absolutist', set about reversing Twitter bans of controversial suspended users such as the former president of the US, Donald Trump, who was suspended after the Capital Hill riot of 2021. Musk, who has amassed a great deal of criticism for his actions and handling of his new social media empire, responded with the following tweet: 'There is a large graveyard filled with my enemies. I do not wish to add to it, but will if given no choice. Those who pick fights with me do so at their own peril, but maybe this is their lucky day' (Musk, 2023 cited in Goggin and Ingram, 2023).

However, although speech may be free in his virtual world, it comes with a high price in the material world, and many who have exercised this new freedom of speech have felt the real-world ramifications. This has left Twitter (now X) the Wild West of the virtual world where trolls can bask in freedom from the injurious consequences of their actions. Anyone who is brave enough to share an ill-thought opinion faces the wrath of the offended, and, not unlike Bentham's panopticon, many self-regulate their opinions to ensure survival in this harsh new frontier.

Technology giants not only own prime real estate in cyberspace, but they are also the gatekeepers of this virtual world. Like Asbjørnsen's fabled troll that devours anyone who must cross his bridge, these cyber-gods demand a high price for entry into their world. The internet is the life-support machine that keeps the capitalist heart beating, and as such, all its agents must bend the knee. Every corporation depends on the technocrats for survival, every government depends on them to circulate its propaganda and the majority of global citizens can no longer perform the simplest of daily tasks without them. With each technological advancement, their stranglehold on humanity tightens, and we are left with little doubt that they have ushered in a new era – the era of technocracy.

Within the previous chapters, much emphasis has been placed on the nefarious activities of the corporate giants that cast a large shadow across global democracy. However, in this, our penultimate chapter, we start to address how our consciousness is shaped to unquestionably and unequivocally accept the cards that are dealt to the rest of us. Not only do we recognise that governments are the legal arm of the corporate elite that ensures that society bends to their will, but we also recognise that the media has its part to play. Like the marketing department for capitalism and all of its subsidiaries, it keeps society placated and often in a constant state of confusion as to the true nature of the corporations that hold the fabric of global society.

We have flitted from the iniquitous practices of media from the East to the West, demonstrating that the protagonist and the antagonist in any story are as subjective as our own consciousnesses. Moreover, the overtly authoritarian regime shares much in common with the more supposedly democratic nations. We have covered all aspects of media, ranging from traditional journalist practices to the glamour and sway of the social media influencer, thus encompassing consumerism and prosumerism. What unites all of these forms of media is their projection of the capitalist project, ensuring conformity and malleability of global citizens and their ongoing allegiance to the Democratic Republic of Capitalism.

Gramsci (1996) identified that this form of ubiquitous conformity to a regime that is often in direct juxtaposition with the survival of humanity does not start and end with just the entertainment that gets broadcast into our homes via an ever-expanding range of media devices. Instead, this is a multifaceted process that is replicated throughout all of our social institutions, and no more so than that of the education sector. It is at the doors of the education sector that we now firmly knock and demand an explanation as to how knowledge became a commodity.

8

Knowledge, Education and Power

Throughout this book, we have taken the institutions that are the cornerstones of contemporary capitalism that constitute today's power elite, considering politicians, the media, corporations and more. At this point, we turn and face our own employing institutions: the academy or higher education. It is perhaps unsurprising to suggest that elite education in terms of private and selective schooling and highly selective higher education is often a marker of social success and social power. If we are going to consider the means and mechanisms socially privileged elite groups use to reproduce their social position and the degree of social closure or openness of these channels to other groups, then it seems vital to consider the role of the education sector as broadly understood.

While the mass availability of education is a recent phenomenon, the most visible feature of being elite has long been education. Private education has long been a mechanism by which social advancement can be possible, particularly where elite education is predicated on physical closure and small cohort size. The two elements were essential characteristics of boarding schools and of the most exclusive colleges in the UK and the US historically, a collective institutional identity forged by a cohesion that has also been fostered and maintained over time in elite institutions by sophisticated rites and ritual that are then carried by alums for life. Making a man Gordonstoun, Eton, St Paul's, Tonbridge, Harrow or Dulwich, for those who can afford the fees, not only likely secures the best academic results, but learning and social activities meant to develop a strong 'bonding' relationship among members and especially between 'established' students and new entrants, as well as between institutions and their alumni. These organisational forms are often durable and have been strongly influenced by army and religious traditions and are frequently referred to through idiosyncratic terms that serve as social markers of membership. The distinctive and exclusive character of the social culture prevailing in these institutions, notably on the prominent place occupied by sports and games, some of which are practised only in elite boarding schools, and on the crucial socialisation role played by fraternities, sororities, clubs and associations, stay with members conferring continual advantage and a durable network of likely powerful and influential friends, explaining why it has been estimated that as many as one in seven of those who hold the most powerful positions in British society went to top ten independent schools.

That background of advantage and privilege hardly ends when it comes to higher education. As Bhopal and Myers (2023) suggest, following schooling, established advantage continues to play out along a well-trodden path where frequently, elite universities serve to further maintain an imbalance of power and class privilege in favour of social elites, particularly within Western, liberal advanced capitalist economies in the US and UK. With a backdrop of global neoliberalism, they chart the easier path into elite institutions for students from more privileged, affluent backgrounds compared with their historically excluded and marginalised peers. They suggest that while the elite institutions have notionally broadened recruitment and 'widened participation' of a demographic of students from traditionally excluded backgrounds, that has not created full institutional inclusion, and that 'elite universities produce their own hierarchies of "eliteness" within their institutional practices that allow for the recruitment of students of colour while ensuring they sit at the lower end of such hierarchies' (Bhopal and Myers, 2023, p 74).

The tell-tale sign that inclusion is still far out of reach for elite institutions is not measured by who is let in but by who controls the institutions, and those in senior leadership positions across elite institutions in higher education remain a relatively homogenous group. All too often, as academics, we hold others to account but, with less regularity, look introspectively. From the marketisation to the collective amnesia of the academy towards corruption and scandal, each sordid secret of the education sector succinctly demonstrates how, like all other global industries, they are not beyond reproach. Suppose corruption, nepotism and malfeasance are apparent in politics, business and media. In that case, they are also at universities, and yet, rather staggeringly, universities, particularly the higher management of them as societal elites, are very infrequently the focus of criminologists. It has been acknowledged in criminology for well over two decades that structure and culture shape the managerial mind and influence behaviour in ways that foster deviance and cause harm (Punch, 2000, p 243). We have already suggested the notion of partnership pacts, which stress the formation of partnerships between corporations and the government can be problematic, and the state-corporate nexus can be a shield for the malpractices of both. As Bakan argues in *The Corporation*, implicit in the state-corporate nexus is that if corporations and governments are indeed partners, we should be concerned about the state of democracy, as the government seemingly may have already effectively abdicated its sovereignty over the corporation (Bakan, 2006).

Democratic governments, of course, should have a role as the institution in our society, powerful enough to bring corporations to heel and force them to do the right thing through legislation and regulation. Yet increasingly, partnership arrangements negate this as the government's proper role is in the public interest. Of course, while there has been a state-corporate nexus, university and higher education institutions' corporate partnerships and their connection through policy to government make them unique institutions. Of course, universities are not merely drivers of knowledge for knowledge's sake and have increasingly come to be corporate and business-like themselves. They are regarded as vital contributors to economic growth and development, and the oft-alleged benefits of the universities' relationships with corporations, business partners and government are tangible enough: society benefits from a skilled and educated workforce. The government and industry provide funding for research, and universities no doubt are involved in the development of potentially beneficial and, in some instances, lifesaving products. Corporate and commercial partners and industry partnerships with universities can ensure student training and job placement. There is ample evidence that universities do much good, not merely as engines of economic growth, but in fostering values of debate and commitment to lifelong learning.

Education up until the Industrial Revolution was exclusively for the elite. Those who laboured the land had little need for any standardised education. However, once the new worker class started to leave the fields and head towards the expanding towns and cities with the promise of regular employment, an education system for the masses started to take shape. This education was rudimentary, allowing the workforce enough basic knowledge to work the new industrial machinery effectively. In time, as the demands on the workforce grew, so did the expectations of the school system. Until very recently, universities had always been predominantly for the rich and the elite, and later, they were joined by emerging middle classes who had also begun to rank and file into the 'red brick' institutions that still hold elite status today. Then, in 1992, an educational revolution happened.

Although marketisation had slowly begun to creep into the educational sector since the commencement of Thatcher's premiership, it was the erosion of the 'binary line' between the polytechnics and universities that many theorists note as the epicentre of the neoliberal takedown of higher education. The next step in this process was the introduction of 'top-up' tuition fees by Tony Blair's New Labour government in 1998 (for a more in-depth account, see Brown and Carasso, 2013). In 2006, this same government introduced variable fees. In a few short years, this decision would mobilise students across England and Wales to participate in a year of action that created a powerful social movement that erupted with vim and met with violence. Students were enraged at the prospect of tripled tuition fees, and the country witnessed a scale of unparalleled protest since Tony Blair decided to take Britain into war in Iraq (Myers, 2017). Undeterred, Cameron and Clegg's coalition government's stance on fees became ironclad, meaning that for £9,250 pounds per academic year, the working classes were also expected to buy their place in the academy. The marketisation of the British university system had begun in earnest, and along with it, the lie of widened participation.

As universities joined the ranks of other neoliberal institutions, the impetus shifted towards revenue streams and Times Higher Education league tables. Comprehensive schools started to shift from funnelling working-class students into apprenticeships to poorly preparing them to study for a degree at the many post-1992 ex-polytechnical colleges. The deafening chant of 'get a degree, get a better job' was ringing firmly in society's ears. However, these working-class students, unlike their middle- and upper-class contemporaries, were more often than not the first of their families welcomed into higher education, and due to prevailing societal attitudes, which perceived students as layabouts who spend taxpayer money to fight the 'system', many working-class students did not grow up in a family that pushed them toward a university education. Moreover, those students whose families rejoiced that they had entered the academy had little understanding of what this meant for them.

It can be of little doubt that universities are corporate entities, selling degrees to anyone who is willing to pay, and post-1992s have become swept up in this marketisation. They chase students and appeal to them in the same way any business does – bold marketing campaigns, playful hashtags and the promise of a good degree, whether deserved or not. In a world where league tables are used as a benchmark, all are welcome, and none must fail. Inflated grades, progressively easier assessments, and managerial pressure on academics to ensure that all who participate must leave with a first-class honour's degree and a sense of customer satisfaction have become commonplace. Critical thought has been replaced with employability skills, and rather than being handed the tools to emancipate themselves, they are assimilated into it. For many, this does not mean that their newly purchased degrees will open the doors that had been promised to them. Instead, many end up swapping the part-time jobs that got them through university to full-time jobs in the same industry. The only difference is they now have a framed certificate and £46,884 debt (before interest). However, this creeping marketisation of the sector can be heralded by the rise of the entrepreneurial academic, who offer an 'accredited' certificate in a whole manner of subjects, especially when these subjects appeal to the Netflix generations, eager to expand their knowledge into areas such as childhood psychology, serial killers and the occult. Like *Plasmodium falciparum*, they capitalise on the brains of those who have thus far been denied entry to their discipline; they repackage their scholastic endeavours into an 'accessible' course for an affordable $99. Education has, at this point, been reduced to yet another product of rampant consumerism with 'Black Friday' offers and high-profile academics using their media presence to recruit the next consumer.

Of course, higher education can play a vast and undoubtedly significant role in promoting social mobility in modern society, just as it can be at the heart of all manner of progressive and socially beneficial changes. Nevertheless, the most elite universities globally are often at the root of maintaining the status of privileged groups while maintaining a carefully curated visage of educational meritocracy at total odds with much reality. The elite status and branding of these global institutions serve both the interests of the globally and politically privileged and their dominance in the existing global system. In contrast, the higher education sector can most serve to benefit the interests of a minority privileged elite. Universities and colleges have often been the way that a global 'elite' progress along pathways of private education where money, familial connections and political power are far more tied to success than intellectual ability or work effort. Within a system that favours the elite, it is of little wonder that those who are given the top jobs in the British establishment are five times more likely to have been privately educated than the rest of the general population. A study by the Sutton Trust and Social Mobility Commission (2019) highlights how a small number of privately educated people, many of whom went to Oxbridge, continue to dominate high-ranking jobs, where 39 per cent had an independent education, compared with 7 per cent of the general population. The report further broke down the ratio of those that had secured the most coveted positions in the institutions that hold together the fabric of British society, with the most damning figures pointing out that over half of the House of Lords herald from fee-paying schools (Weale, 2019). Before entering higher education, the idea that meritocracy favours diligent effort, with the most industrious and intelligent individuals earning rewards, is based on uncertain foundations. Therefore, the belief that hardworking students with top grades will secure the best jobs may be questionable. The highlighting of Oxbridge is a useful reminder that, while increasingly supposedly meritocratic, most education is socially stratified at the point of delivery, and the best predictor of societal success has long been a parent's bank balance. However, higher education is an important marker of social status. When English universities are ranked on their contributions to social mobility, the least selective post-1992 universities come out on top. However, if we look at the places that produce the highest number of powerful and well-paid people, a minority of rich ultra-elite institutions come out on top. This is clearly significant when we ask, 'Who today are the powerful?'

In an industry that pays their vice chancellors in excess of £250,000 a year and spends more than £87 million in super injunctions, it is easy to see how savings can be made to support these figures in the way of cheap early-stage career academic teaching provisions. In a 2012 survey conducted by the National Union of Students (2013), some worrying trends emerged. Many PhD students, irrespective of their ability or interest, were expected to teach, often without the proper financial remuneration. Like all profit-driven corporations, exploitation of their workforce becomes a necessary component to maximise profits, and although these profits are yet to be distributed to vampiric shareholders, the drive for surplus is there, nonetheless. As identified by Jones (2019), academics, both fledgling and seasoned, are expected to provide a commodified service rather than facilitate and guide student learning. Teaching is reduced to a value-for-money exchange, with institutions expecting a production-line approach to both research and teaching. Academics are also expected to be navigating the choppy waters of social media, and they are required to not only have an online presence but to ensure that their thesis in 120 characters reaches the widest of audiences, bringing the institutions that employ them the greatest adulation, while causing the least amount of offence. Their identity as academics depends on their conformity to the neoliberal agenda and their compliance that they will not damage the 'brand' that their institutional marketing team has carefully constructed. In an industry where there is no competition in price, then 'brand' becomes the deciding factor when customers choose where to buy their education.

Globally, academics are starting to turn away from their careers. In the US, it has been heralded as the 'Great Resignation', with many citing burnout and disillusionment as rationale for their departure. This trend is echoed across universities in the UK, with many disheartened by current pay scales and the ever-increasing demands placed upon them. Academics are routinely measured by the attainment gap. This gap considers race, sex, gender and, to some extent, socio-economic backgrounds of students, but just how a lecturer plugs the gaps that privilege and money have created within the education industry is unclear. Private education and personal tuition form the basis for attainment at one end of the scale, whereas at the other, never quite reaching full potential and relative poverty are the markers. Then, once settled into their studentships, some have little more to concern themselves with than varsity events and deadlines. In contrast, others will have no choice but to face the gig economy and pressures, such as substandard housing, while attempting to break the generational cycle of poverty and debt. This playing field is not level. In fact, it is not a playing field, for some; it is a battlefield that many working-class students will fall upon, as well as the academics that had no choice but to crawl from the trenches to 'go over the top' to attempt to drag them to safety.

Freedom of speech, just watch what you say

The most discerning of these customers control the narrative, usually those with middle-class parents who have given them the space to explore their human condition and an understanding of what that is. They are the students who join the unions, become academic reps and keep an eye on Twitter, ensuring that their lecturers do not engage in problematic discourse. These are the students that the neoliberal university craves as they are media savvy and, when they assume the role of the satisfied customer, will run their own social media marketing campaigns along with institutionally endorsed hashtags. However, these are the students that have universities running scared. One problematic tweet, misconstrued paper, and then the offending academic can watch as their whole career unravels before their eyes.

Cancel culture within the higher education system is often heralded as a misnomer, a rhetorical myth that has been fabricated by the right wing to suggest that the left violently shouts down their ideological positions. However, when you scratch beneath this widely accepted veneer, it becomes possible to see the caveats of this argument. Pippa Norris (2023) conducted a study, and her evidence suggests that cancel culture is not a myth and that scholars are less willing to speak out if colleagues do not share their moral beliefs. Drawing from Noelle-Neumann's (1974) spiral of silence thesis, minority voices become silenced against the amplified voices of the acceptable majority. The majority of ideological standpoints vocalised within academia tend to be left-liberal, and those that foster more conservative or less liberal beliefs tend to be within the minority. Thus, these minority voices silence themselves in fear of, at best, being shunned and, at worst, being labelled a bigot whose academic work is construed as a direct affront to societal progress. Those who fall into this latter camp face ad hominem attacks, student demonstrations and forced resignation. At this point, it is worth noting that as society progresses, change is implemented, resulting in certain problematic ideological voices being less palatable and eventually extinct. However, who decides which voices are problematic is where it starts becoming utterly problematic. From the voices that have voluntarily silenced themselves to those that find themselves subject to a university-implemented 'non-disclosure agreement', a worrying trend of censorship becomes evident within the sector of social society that places itself at the forefront of informed good practice. Moreover, this has wider and much more nefarious implications that are not confined to the lecture theatres. Academia has long since provided the intelligentsia that challenge the oppressive structures within society. Cancel culture is not just a weapon to be wielded by those who claim to protect society from unsettling voices; it can be used to suppress the voices that underpin societal change and, more importantly, those voices that challenge the dominant order that much of this book seeks to challenge. Once this happens, rather than institutions that create knowledge, they become training grounds for young enquiring minds to be fully assimilated within the hierarchal structures of capitalism who, without question, embrace their subsequent commodification. With academics being forced to bend the knee to university executives whose main concern is market forces, the lines of defence against rampant marketisation and academic integrity are slowly deteriorating. With each new crop of fledgling lecturers that have chosen to forego reading the philosophies of their contemporaries in favour of target-driven league tables, it is difficult to see this tide of neoliberalism turning.

Nowhere has this cancel culture been more starkly apparent than in criminology, which on several occasions has found itself at the forefront of gender identity wars, particularly around the issue of trans rights. In particular, Professor Jo Phoenix, a criminologist formerly of the Open University, became one of the figures at the forefront of debates around cancellation. Phoenix was due to give a talk at the University of Essex in December 2019 about 'trans rights, imprisonment and the criminal justice system'. It was cancelled by the university, partly due to security concerns.

As the university's vice chancellor suggested, universities have statutory responsibilities under the law, which include upholding academic freedom and the freedom of speech within the parameters of the legal system and ensuring that equality, diversity and inclusion quotas are met.

The relationship between these responsibilities, of course, can 'come[s] to the fore in moments of contestation'. Additionally, 'universities have a vital role in convening difficult and sometimes uncomfortable conversations, and in curating the spaces in which ideas that some may find challenging or unpopular can be expressed and debated' (Forster, 2021).

Phoenix's invitation came at a point where there was (and arguably still is) little common ground between those who believe that trans women are women and regard themselves as trans-inclusive and those who, like Phoenix, hold gender-critical views, including the immutability of biological sex and the inherent problem of conflating biological sex with socially constructed gender. Phoenix has set her views out in some detail and length, including in written evidence to Parliament, and they are much more nuanced and complex than simply the suggestion that she is transphobic or trans-exclusive. However, her positioning and questioning of gender-inclusive ideology made her a target for some students and campaigners who view her as transphobic.

On the day of the planned seminar, complaints were made that Professor Phoenix held transphobic views, and these views were tantamount to hate speech. Furthermore, after a flyer circulated around the university that displayed violent imagery and the text 'shut the fuck up, TERF', the university decided that there were a series of credible threats from students to disrupt the seminar and cancelled due to security concerns, intending for it to be rescheduled. However, a later meeting of the Department of Sociology decided by way of a vote to rescind the invitation and to disinvite Professor Phoenix to a future seminar. An apology was then issued for the hurt caused to the trans community.

The Reindorf Review (Akua Reindorf, 2021), commissioned by the university, suggested that while 'in isolation, the decision to cancel the seminar was unavoidable in the circumstances', the situation could have been avoided by proper understanding and timely use of the university's external speaker notification procedure. It also stated that in the context of the systemic and decision-making failures that led to it, the cancellation amounted to a breach of Professor Phoenix's right to freedom of expression and the associated legal duties to which the university was subject.

Moreover, the university's decision to block Professor Phoenix and disinvite her was unlawful. Barrister Akua Reindorf, the report's author, categorically stated that there was no reasonable basis to suggest that Professor Phoenix would pose any threat or engage in any unlawful speech. Moreover, the decision to exclude her was unnecessary and completely disproportionate. It stated that Professor Phoenix should be offered an open apology and an opportunity to give a seminar at the Centre for Criminology.

It was far from the end of the matter. After her treatment at Essex, Phoenix resigned from her position at the Open University, suggesting her views resulted in treatment that had made her position untenable and launched an employment tribunal against her former employer. Phoenix alleges that a senior manager told her that she was "like the racist uncle at the Christmas dinner table". She states that when she started to cry, it suggested that if she could not cope with it, she could be put in touch with counselling services.

It was at this point that she was instructed not to speak about her research in departmental meetings; this included her research on transgender debates within the criminal justice system (Ricciardelli et al, 2020). Then, over 360 of her colleagues signed a public letter condemning the Gender Critical Research Network that she had established in the wake of the experience at Essex, going as far as to call for the Open University not only to remove all funding but all support from the Gender Critical Research Network, citing that gender-critical feminism was 'fundamentally hostile to the rights of trans people' (Phoenix, 2021).

In a statement written by Professor Phoenix discussing the contents of this open letter, she refers to 'demonstrably false and extremely damaging accusations' pertaining to what she had discussed during a podcast in which she had participated. In the same statement, Professor Phoenix goes on to discuss several derogatory tweets that called her gender-critical beliefs into question, making reference to her alleged 'transphobia' along with the slur 'TERF' originating from the then equality, diversity and inclusion representative for her faculty. This has resulted in Professor Phoenix crowdfunding an employment tribunal to hold the Open University to account for what she describes as a 'public campaign of harassment' that has rendered her 'working life unbearable'.

Alarmingly, Phoenix's treatment, along with other calls for cancellation, came shortly after confidence in many of the social sciences had been dented by what has become known as the Grievance Studies Hoax. This project resulted from a collaboration by a team of three authors – Peter Boghossian, James Lindsay and Helen Puckrose – who sought to highlight poor academic practice and the erosion of exemplary scholarship in a plethora of academic fields, particularly within the social sciences.

Their research entailed submitting artificial and often nonsensical academic research papers to leading academic journals in areas such as culture, race, and gender and sexuality studies within the field of social sciences. This was done to determine whether they would pass academic peer review, and more alarmingly, several were deemed acceptable for academic publication. Causing much in the way of controversy and widespread media attention, the project spanned the years 2017/2018 until journalists uncovered their hoax research when it had been discovered that 'Helen Wilson', the pseudonym used in an article published in *Gender, Place & Culture*, did not exist.

Lindsay et al (2018) exposed glaring issues within an area of the social sciences, which they call 'grievance studies'. They elaborate that a culture had developed within certain academic areas where only certain conclusions were tolerated and social grievances were weighted ahead of objective truths. The trio, identifying themselves as leftist and liberal politically, described their project as an attempt to raise awareness in the academic community about the detrimental effect of identity politics and activist-based scholarship on leftist political projects and the social sciences in general.

By the conclusion of their study, only six of the 20 hoax papers had been rejected. Of the four that had been published, there were arguments stating that dogs engage in rape culture and that by anally penetrating themselves with sex toys, men could reduce their transphobia. They had also written published articles that referenced chaining and gagging white students in academic classes as a useful pedagogical tool for helping them recognise their white privilege over their black counterparts, as well as the re-writing of Adolf Hitler's biography *Mein Kampf* as a feminist piece published in a feminist academic journal.

The times they aren't a-changin'

For decades of inattention to higher education, the development community now recognises that universities provide the human capital necessary for technological catch-up and faster growth. Amid the rapid liberalisation of the sector, higher education enrolments have increased across the developing world. However, corruption and fraud in higher education have become a growing problem with grave implications for education systems, institutions and broader society.

Nevertheless, conversations about campus crime often revolve around limited perspectives rooted in established administrative criminological traditions. These discussions typically focus on conventional and one-dimensional understandings, such as the assessment of rates for both violent and property crimes, and the examination of victimisation demographics and risk factors for students, while rarely challenging the conventional definitions in place. The marketisation of higher education in the UK has created greater consumerism across higher education and more significant opportunities for crime and criminality. Simply try googling 'buy UK university fake degree' and a plethora of sites will be returned. While buying a fake degree may cast aspersions on the value of higher education more broadly, less extreme forms of academic misconduct and contract cheating have grown extensively.

In August 2018, research published by Swansea University indicated that as many as one in seven recent graduates internationally may have paid someone to undertake their assignment for them, potentially representing 31 million students across the globe, and institutions were only successfully identifying a small number of these. The COVID-19 pandemic compelled higher education providers to swiftly transition to remote teaching and assessment as an emergency response. This required an adjustment of teaching, learning and assessment methods to accommodate digital delivery for students spread across different locations. Additionally, there was a need to adapt the support structures for student communities and prioritise the unique health and mental well-being circumstances during these challenging times. At the heart of the mission of universities today is not providing education for education's sake but a rather narrow education that is consumerist and highly targeted at satisfying the purchaser. Evidence of this has been provided aptly by the now higher education regulator, the Office for Students, established by the Higher Education and Research Act (2017) and coming into existence on 1 January 2018. The Office for Students inherited The Higher Education Funding Council for England's funding responsibilities (aside from those for research which passed to UK Research and Innovation) and the Office for Fair Access was given responsibility for promoting fair access to higher education. They state that the articulation of their role is as follows:

> Students have consumer rights and are protected by consumer protection law. However, many are young and inexperienced consumers, making important choices about what and where to study with limited personal knowledge to guide them. In addition, choosing a university and course is likely to be a one-off decision and can be difficult to change once a student has started. It also leads to a significant

investment of their time and money. While the idea of students as 'consumers' of their higher education is by no means uncontested, consumer protection legislation generally means that students should receive clear, accurate and timely information about their course and university or college; that student contracts should contain fair terms and conditions; and that there should be fair mechanisms for dealing with complaints. (Office for Students, 2023)

While this seems unarguably fair on one level, the shift to a neoliberal model of higher education based on education that meets consumer demands is very different to the traditional values of the university, particularly from the period of the European Renaissance. The collective establishments of education in universities in medieval Western Europe reflected a trend of guild organisation to protect themselves from local laws, high prices and prejudices. More comprehensive needs within medieval society for people with skills and learning saw universities grow to meet the demand. The Byzantine Empire had higher education provided by scholars sponsored by the emperor himself, mostly organised in a school associated with the palace in Constantinople. In China, where rigorous education in the classics was the vital prerequisite for official positions, there was a system of official schools (as well as, of course, lots of private tutoring). In the Muslim world, where Islam was a central organising principle, schools were associated with mosques. In Western Europe, scholars had to organise themselves into guilds like other skilled professionals. Over time, these guilds developed into the kinds of universities we know today. However, perhaps we ought to note the influence of an ideology of social and scientific advancement and progress tied to the new scientific pursuit of truth and the expansion of human knowledge that also featured. The danger is that marketisation is an antithesis or paradox of such pursuits. While a few voices have raised their heads above the parapet, critical criminologists such as Simon Winlow (2022) have expressed some concern about marketisation in higher education.

Each year, institutions compete for a slice of the billions spent on tuition fees, with elite institutions accruing mass fortunes of generational wealth with the likes of Oxford and Cambridge hoarding wealth into the billions. Within an industry with a steady stream of customers and state funding, the wealth-creation potential starts to look very attractive to not only those with the intention to exploit this lucrative sector legally but also those looking for the next nefarious get-rich-quick scheme. An easy target for this exploitation is the international student. From scam emails and phone calls from 'bogus' officials from the Home Office demanding money for visa issues, to the students that become wittingly/unwittingly embroiled in money laundering schemes, there is much that the academic 'fonejacker' can attempt to turn a profit from. With phishing scams increasing exponentially in 2022, a report commissioned by cloud security firm Zscaler found that education was the most targeted industry.

However, the institutions themselves are not beyond this level of corruption. In 2008, the London School of Economics awarded a PhD to Saif al-Islam Gaddafi, the son of the then leader of the Libyan government, Muammar Gaddafi. Allegations that his thesis had escaped the usual academic rigour placed upon PhD students soon started to circulate, with accusations of ghost-writing and plagiarism. With reports of vast amounts of money donated or promised from the Libyan regime, the relationship between the London School of Economics and Gaddafi was catapulted into international speculation, culminating in the resignation of director Sir Howard Davies. The appeal of the elite universities is quite apparent when we understand, for example, how former Pakistan Prime Minister Imran Khan, Emperor Naruhito of Japan, now jailed Burmese former leader Aung San Suu Kyi and President of Ghana Nana Akufo-Addoall are alumni of the University of Oxford. Oxford, Cambridge and Sandhurst Royal Military Academy have arguably been formative in the education of numerous rich and influential political figures, and Britain's fee-paying private boarding schools are a magnet for the privileged elite. Arguably, Oxford has never been a university solely for the British elite. In the mid-2000s, 5 per cent of the world's foreign ministers had studied at St Anthony's College, Oxford's postgraduate college for political studies. In 2012, Oxford opened the Blavatnik School of Government, funded by a donation from an oligarch from Putin's Russia, who now lives in London, who secured the honour of having his name on the gate when he gave a reported £75 million to Oxford. The institute's opening web page (Homepage, ND) (at the time of writing) proudly proclaims, 'A WORLD BETTER LED, BETTER SERVED AND BETTER GOVERNED' and proudly announces:

> We seek students from across the globe and in 2021 we welcomed a cohort hailing from 48 different countries. Our alumni tell us that the diversity in our classrooms – not just nationality but also age, experiences, and background – enriches our cohorts in ways that set the school apart from others.

This is all for annual course fees of £49,080 irrespective of where in the globe students hail from. Of course, those fees do not cover accommodation or other living costs. Despots have deep pockets when assuring that their legacy would not only be the continuation of their regimes but also that through nepotism and cunning, international relationships would be forged in the student union bars of Oxford et al. Therefore, it is perhaps unsurprising that those more advantaged families are also now inclined to use their economic, cultural and social edge to ensure their children stay at the top of the social class ladder. Moreover, the wealthy parents embroiled in the US admissions scandal are testimony that these donations for degrees are not confined to the political palaces of the Global South.

In 2019, the fallout from a US federal investigation into a sham charity run by a 'college-prep' professional, William 'Rick' Singer, and the wealthy parents that had spent millions to circumnavigate the admissions procedures of prestigious colleges such as Stanford and Yale, was akin to a Hollywood blockbuster. Investigations led to prosecutions, which resulted in hefty fines and prison sentences. *Desperate Housewives* actor Felicity Huffman was one of the many that were reprimanded. After admitting to paying to have her daughter's college exam answers corrected, Huffman was sentenced to 14 days in federal prison along with fines and community service.

In the US, like the UK, there are problems with federal student loan fraud, which happens when falsified information is used on a student loan application in order to obtain funds through the US Department of Education.

As in the UK, individuals may target the federal student loan system because these loans are often low-interest and have a long grace period. In the UK in 2023, the Student Loans Company (SLC) will pay more than £2 billion to 2 million students in the run-up to the 2023/4 academic year and reminds people to be vigilant at core funding periods, which are dispersed three times yearly but normally commence at the start of an academic year around September. As payments make their way to students, the company often warns new and returning students not to be fooled into disclosing personal details or clicking on links in emails or text messages, as they could be installing malware. The marketisation and loan agreements clearly create conditions for fraud. In the last three years, the government has claimed that the SLC's dedicated customer compliance teams have stopped £1.2 million from being lost to fraudsters from students' bank accounts (GOV.UK, 2022). However, it is difficult to verify or test these figures, and the sphere is very little researched. Of course, students can be victims of loan fraud. In 2013, Olajide Onikoyi was jailed, having sent fake student loan company emails to potential victims inviting them to click on a link to update their student loan details. Onikoyi used the personal details he phished from the hoax website to gain access to their bank accounts and withdraw large amounts of money, adding up to a staggering £393,000 from 238 victims. After being found guilty of conspiracy to defraud and money laundering, it was revealed that Onikoyi had conspired with associates from Lithuania, Russia and the UK in an effort to compromise the victims' bank accounts.

There are, of course, sometimes blurry lines between the criminals and the education providers and students' status as offenders and victims. In 2017, the BBC's flagship current affairs programme *Panorama* secretly filmed agents offering to get bogus students admitted into a government-approved private college for a £200 fee to allow the bogus students to claim student loans fraudulently. For £1,500 a year, the agent offered to fake attendance records and to provide all their coursework. *Panorama* spent ten months investigating dishonest education agents and bogus students who were committing frauds that targeted private colleges – also known as alternative providers – that offered courses approved for student loans. Agents were secretly filmed supplying fake documents, including a qualification certificate, to a BBC undercover researcher posing as a bogus student who wanted to cheat their way onto courses and apply for student loans. The private college at the centre of the scandal was, at the time, just one of the 112 private colleges through the student loan system that paid some £400 million per year, and students involved in the scam became eligible for up to £11,000 in maintenance loans to cover living expenses and up to £6,000 in tuition fee loans, paid directly to colleges that were awarded each year. Furthermore, while the college might be private, the one highlighted by *Panorama* had recently partnered with the Open University, which has recently started to offer degree courses in partnership with Grafton, the private college involved.

However, not unlike the subprime mortgage bubble that brought on the financial crash of 2008, student loans are an unfathomable debt generator, and society collectively fails to recognise its shaky foundations as a never-ending debt cycle. In the UK, the student loan system has caused much in the way of controversy, with students and financial watchdogs calling the repayment process unclear and confusing:

> Each year, at the Student Loans Company, we process around 2 million student finance applications worth some £22 billion in loans and grants. We dedicate ourselves to supporting 9.4 million customers and administering a loan book valued at £227.5 billion. For our customers, the nation's students, we enable them to invest in their futures by funding further and higher education. (Home, 2023)

This neglects, of course, questions about whether the use of student debt and the student loan company is largely predatory and unethical. In the UK, the SLC is an executive non-departmental public body company in the UK that provides student loans. It is owned by the UK Government Department for Education (85 per cent), along with the Scottish and Welsh governments and the Northern Ireland Executive, each of whom holds a 5 per cent stake. The SLC is funded entirely by the UK government and the devolved administrations. It is responsible for both providing loans to students and collecting loan repayments alongside His Majesty's Revenue and Customs (HMRC).

The SLC was established in 1989 to provide grants and loans to students studying in the UK from 1990 to 1998. These essentially were mortgage-style fixed loans, which were aimed at helping students with the cost of living, and were originally to be repaid directly to the SLC for a set term at fixed rates. From 1998, with the introduction of increased higher education university tuition fees, the SLC instead began providing loans under a different Income-Contingent Repayment (ICR) rate that was controversial from the outset because of the way it was regarded as benefitting higher earners who repaid more rapidly. From 2006, loans covered the cost of tuition fees in addition to living costs. Repayments for these loans were collected by HMRC via the pay-as-you-earn tax system. The ICR loan scheme was replaced with a new ICR scheme in 2012 to include a longer repayment period following a further governmental increase in tuition fees, which was adopted almost universally across the higher education sector. In the late 1990s, the government sold off the early mortgage-style student loans to investors. In 1998, Greenwich NatWest raised £1 billion; in 1999, Deutsche Bank and the Nationwide Building Society also raised £1 billion. The SLC's remaining mortgage-style loans, for which payments mainly were in arrears, were sold to a consortium in 2013 for £160 million, and in 2014, the government indicated that it would start selling the SLC's £12 billion book of 1998–2012 ICR loans to improve the UK public finances. The loans were sold to Income Contingent Student Loans (2002–2006) Plc, a group of silent investors. The SLC would remain responsible for the day-to-day administration of all duties related to the repayment of these loans, which were now paid on to the investors. There has been minimal exploration of the ethical and moral aspects surrounding these sales, particularly regarding the immediate gains for the government, which may come at the expense of potentially higher long-term returns. This is especially relevant when considering that the infrastructure to oversee the programme remains a persistent public responsibility.

A report by the National Audit Office in July 2018 concluded that the first sale had achieved value for money; however, other commentators have said that the sales show that the government 'prefers cash today over larger sums of cash tomorrow' (Hubble and Bolton, 2020). Indeed, a government review of the sales programme was published alongside Budget 2020 and concluded that 'following the ONS' recent change in the accounting treatment of student loans, sales would now have new impacts on borrowing and net investment. … As such, the review announces that the government will not make further sales of student loans' (Hubble and Bolton, 2020). Of course, a further issue might be that with the expansion of student loans with higher fees, sales might not be so attractive to investors. While early loans seem to have been capable of yielding profit, student loans today look like something of a bubble fit to burst. Currently, in the UK, student loans are complex, and the ability of most 18-year-olds to fully understand or comprehend the terms that they are signing up to perhaps should be questioned. On graduation, the average English student now has a student debt of around £45,000. While interest quickly rises, fewer than 20 per cent of graduates are forecast to repay their loans fully. A calculation made through the student loan calculator shows that alums with an average student debt of £45,000 with a median graduate starting salary of £25,000 would see their loan swell to over £100,000 by the time it was eventually cancelled after a 30-year period. During that time, the repayments of the loan would peak at over £4,000 per year.

Students who commence their studies in September of 2023 will see the cost of student finance rise, with the payback terms increasing to 40 years before this debt is cancelled. This means that many graduates have the prospect of paying back their student loans well into the latter part of their working lives and will end up having to pay back over double the amount of their original loan.

Student finance is incredibly complex to understand, but in essence, only a fraction of today's students will pay their full loans back. The key way a student loan differs from standard loans is that they do not appear on an individual's credit history: the debt students take on while at university will not impact their ability to take out other forms of credit like personal loans or credit cards, and lenders will not know how much students have paid or need to pay off. This generation that goes to higher education is taking on a debt that will be with them throughout most of their working lives. The same is true in the US, where the Biden administration is, at the time of writing, considering the cancellation of student debts. In the US, more than 42 million people, roughly one in six adults in the population, hold student debt, which averages roughly US$30,000 for a four-year undergraduate degree. Recent graduates are typically saddled with monthly bills of around US$400, and the financial stress arising from this commitment can arguably be attributed to an entire generation of college graduates being financially held back. The Biden administration proposed US$39 billion of student loan forgiveness for some 804,000 low-earner borrowers after the Supreme Court ruled against a separate, more sweeping loan forgiveness plan the government had endorsed.

Value for money

As with all other public institutions, education is heavily politicised, with each global administration pulling the strings to their country's learning institutions. In the US, debates rage over the proposed forgiveness of student debt, and in the UK, multiple overhauls of their student loan system have been implemented by a string of different governments, with students starting their courses in September 2023 facing a reduced repayment threshold of £25,000. Although higher education has become a big business, it is not only at the whim of market forces but also political point scoring. Like Schrodinger's cat, higher education is both public and privatised. In the UK, widened participation is encouraged unless, of course, the subject of choice is deemed to be 'low quality'. In 2023, the Conservative government cited that they must save students from 'rip off' courses, with Rishi Sunak stating: "They're being taken advantage of with low-quality courses that don't lead to a job that makes it worth it, leaving them financially worse off. That's what we're clamping down on today" (GOV.UK, 2023). The Labour opposition called their plan to cap 'low-quality' courses a 'cap on aspirations'.

If a human capital model is applied to education, and we then only engage with education and training that is value for money that will yield a profitable return on our efforts, many disciplines could be lost forever to those of us who only have access to a national curriculum and post-1992 universities. The essence of the Conservative party's argument that they are 'saving' students from unnecessary debt comes after sustaining and exacerbating the neoliberal culture of student indebtedness introduced by the New Labour government. Looking beyond criticisms of university administrations as bureaucratic and self-serving entities, it becomes evident that their interests are increasingly divergent from the academic mission of the university. This shift is fuelled by factors such as political naïvety, poor leadership, short-term thinking and overemphasis on metrics. Moreover, more overt forms of corruption and even 'crime' have also emerged within some institutions. As Philip Altbach (2015, p 7) has argued, despite the plethora of indicators for measuring and ranking universities by the quality of their research and teaching, credit ratings, reputation and other market factors such as impact, innovation, graduate employability and the student experience, 'no one has developed a worldwide academic corruption index', and the issue of corruption and criminality in universities, and the leadership of them, is often overlooked. Corruption in universities is not a new phenomenon and clearly has a different global character, but what is new, according to Chapman and Lindner (2016, p 247), is a 'unique convergence of pressures that are creating a heightened threat to the integrity of the higher education enterprise worldwide'. Transparency International (2013) identifies various factors contributing to academic corruption. These include reduced public funding for higher education and diminishing salaries, leading universities to rely on their own revenue sources, often through increased tuition fees. There is growing pressure on academics to secure external grants, commercialize research findings, or establish for-profit ventures. Additionally, academics face heightened expectations to publish in prestigious journals, driven by universities' aspirations to enhance their national and international standing in global university rankings. The overarching demand is for universities to generate their own financial resources. Yet the introduction of student loans and finance models, at least in the UK, was predicated at least on the need to create better working conditions and pay for academic staff. This clearly has not happened, and what has happened for the most part is that executive pay has swelled significantly, and conditions for most staff have worsened significantly. The message from on high in universities should be to communicate an aspiration to create critical thinkers who think about improving society. That environment is one that academics – at all levels – can aspire to create. There is not much evidence it has happened. In 2014, in the Russell Group, basic pay for bosses jumped by an average of over £20,000 to nearly £293,000, and with added-in pension contributions, the figure went up to £318,500. At the same time, vice chancellors insisted their staff accept a 1 per cent pay rise – which, after inflation, meant a pay cut – as any more would be 'unaffordable'. Young researchers were being placed on temporary, low-paying contracts. University cleaners and support staff are bundled off to outsourcing companies that do not even give sick pay. The situation has changed little in 10 years, but there have been glimpses at the quality being assured in vice chancellors hired under such a regimen that does not suggest it is the brightest and best rising to the top.

In January 2019, Dominic Shellard, a prominent vice chancellor at De Montfort University in the UK, faced significant public scrutiny due to a 22.3 per cent increase in his remuneration compared with the previous year, which coincided with De Montfort University being awarded Teaching Excellence Framework Gold status. For the academic year 2017–18, Shellard's remuneration comprised a £350,000 salary (up from £286,000 in 2016–17), £1,000 in health benefits and £6,000 in pension contributions. Additionally, he enjoyed perks like an Ivy Club membership. It was later revealed that Shellard had business ties with the chair of the Remuneration Committee of the Board of Governors, who had approved his £64,000 pay rise. Amid a storm of controversy and allegations of malpractice, Shellard resigned from the university in 2019 and received an extra £270,000, equivalent to nine months' pay. After the resignation of Dominic Shellard, De Montfort University came under scrutiny, leading to a formal investigation by the Office for Students. The investigation report highlighted significant governance failures at De Montfort University, particularly in relation to the oversight of the vice chancellor. In a rare example from 2014, Robert Smedley, the former pro-vice chancellor of Edge Hill University, and his partner were sentenced to five years each in prison for defrauding the institution of £500,000. However, it is rare for cases to end in the criminal courts, and we perhaps ought to ask, could such criminality represent the tip of the iceberg?

In 2021, news outlets indicated that approximately 50 UK universities had received over £52 million in direct cash payments for tuition and fees from students originating from countries known to pose a 'high risk' for money laundering, with notable mentions of West African nations like Ghana and

Nigeria. The University of Essex took £5.4 million in cash, followed by the University of Manchester at £5 million, and the Chinese were noted as the nationality paying most cash, with universities taking £7.7 million. This is before we move to now emerging concerns about bought influence for Chinese state actors undermining British national interests and security that are beginning to emerge in 2023. As of 2023, UK universities do not face the same AML regulations as other sectors, leaving them particularly susceptible to kleptocrats and criminals seeking to invest 'unexplained wealth' and buy prestige for themselves and their families. Given this elevated risk and the universities' inclination to turn a blind eye and avoid probing, the moral responsibility of higher education, especially its well-paid executives, should be a more significant point of emphasis.

As Simon Winlow has argued, the very essence of the university as historically understood has become merely a haunting memory:

> Despite appearing regularly in the public proclamations of government ministers and university leaders – the core ideals of the university no longer play a significant role in Britain's higher education sector and rarely intrude upon the working lives of British academics. The university's traditional telos was tied to the pursuit of truth and the expansion of human knowledge. However, only vague traces of the university's grand ideals can now be found throughout large expanses of Britain's university system. … [T]races of the university's grand ideals can now be found throughout large expanses of Britain's university system. These traces take a ghostly form. (Winlow, 2022, p 479)

Winlow suggests the commercialised and marketised nature of knowledge production in higher education establishments is currently so resolutely inaugurated as a guiding principle in our universities that it is taken for granted in academic circles and it often seems pointless to challenge it or even acknowledge the possibility of a different system. With each gratuitous display of corruption, it is not difficult to assess that a system that favours the wealthy will attract those with money willing to do anything to shape the futures of their children. Moreover, an industry that generates billions in revenue will attract the morally depraved in search of lucrative Ponzi schemes. This cynical pyramid scheme deludes with notions of widened participation, whereas in all earnest, it is just the bottom of this pyramid that swells yearly with the expectations and student debt of the working-class masses desperate to claw their way to its summit with the elite that has comfortably exploited the system since its creation. Disillusioned academics slowly watch their souls wither at the realisation that the quality of their craft languishes in second place to the ability to assimilate into the neoliberal framework that has encroached upon the academy. Freethinkers are quickly replaced with marketable personalities, academic integrity is replaced with marketing slogans, and each facet of academic worth is reduced to popularity and monetary value. Courses that are deemed unprofitable and not 'value for money' are cut. Thus, disciplines that were once the cornerstone of academia become lost to all but the privileged. As with all contemptible industries, the conditions are created that nurture corruption, and much can be exploited; however, the blame always lies at the feet of the 'few rotten apples' that upset the academic apple cart rather than the ongoing corporate failings that show contemporary marketised and consumerist higher education might not entirely be lining up to the highest of principles.

Epilogue

The day the music died

As the late Bill Hicks once stated, "Don't worry; don't be afraid, ever, because this is just a ride", and in this instance, this ride through the bleak hellscape of late capitalism in the epoch of the corporate giants as we enter the heated up and sped up stage of the Anthropocene. However, before we get to neatly draw this book to its conclusions, there's still so much more to say: the commodification of charity and social causes, sports washing, governmental glaucoma toward global emissions, the commodification of youth and human flesh, 'legal' human trafficking and modern-day slavery, predatory housing markets and the billionaires destined to outlive the youth that it consumes, and maybe, just maybe, if anyone can survive the end of days, it'll be those hauled up in their underground bunkers.

The elites' coup d'état over its global population and the global precariat is the ability to assimilate the concerns, wants, desires and beliefs of the many into their cultures of value. The empty promise of entirely ethical capitalism might be hollow, but global corporations seem to show a willingness to change their practices and representation, not only trying to tap into the articulate, socially aware consumer base that patrols social media, but to weaponise their identity. This faux ethical corporate consciousness provides a useful human shield around their massively unethical and often exploitative practices. Voices of descent are not only quashed through an intricate web of legalities and more and less overt forms of oppression. The power of nation states has eroded, and the most powerful actors now are state-corporate nexus. How can you fight the powerful when you don't even know who the powerful actually are?

The traditional notions of power have been all but replaced with highly contestable bickering on the notions of privilege. Akin to the work of Raymen (2022), who argues that the term 'harm' has been splintered into countless facets, so too has the notion of privilege, a term that is now so contested that merely alluding to it will ignite fervour and emotively charged arguments (be it on social media, academic articles or books). A term, in essence, lacking so much ontological cohesion that society spends more energy attempting to define it than searching for a route to emancipation.

As C. Wright Mills pointed out, the interwoven interests of politics, media, military and corporations have rendered ordinary citizens powerless. However, he was composing his work during an era characterised by well-defined nation states, a time when the divisions of the Cold War were evident, and the nation state, particularly in the Western context, was separate from the corporation. The divisions between capitalism and communism held. Then, as Fukuyama (1992) noted, history ended, and one ideology won. Perhaps since, the global citizenry has largely been the loser. Today, much of Western society is still led to believe that they are not just passive and that politics is not just done to them, but that they are complicit in their own choices and, through democratic practices, help shape the global political landscape. The illusion of choice is reinforced by rampant capitalism; those lucky enough to be born in the privileged West can choose from an almost unlimited array of possibilities when deciding what to squander, diminishing supplies of disposable incomes on what to eat, what to wear, these choices only limited to the money in our pockets (Klein, 2000). However, when choosing who to vote for, the options dramatically narrow, and making an informed choice seems almost impossible when most of the information received comes from a media oligopoly owned by a handful of monolithic conglomerates that not only favour the laissez-faire economics of the ruling elite but profit from them directly (Herman and Chomsky, 2008).

From the oppressive pedagogy employed to keep the disadvantaged in a state of rigid conformity (Freire, 1996) to the use of the mass media to manufacture consent (Herman and Chomsky, 1988), after the triumph of free-market capitalism, we are moving further away from any hope of egalitarianism to totalitarianism. Born from the US hegemonic project to assure American self-interest, these neoliberal economic policies have ensured the 'land of the free' has enjoyed long-term global dominance (Chossudovsky, 2003). That may not hold forever. Moreover, the will of their financial institutions has been exercised almost ubiquitously around the globe since World War II and has been replicated by elites from all corners of the globe. Each superpower wields a similar modus operandi to ensure that its own particular flavour of neocolonialism spreads across the globe in a flurry of international loans, investments and land grabs (Rapanyane, 2021). Giant global corporations have increased their investment in countries such as China, and while a narrative of China as a global purchasing power is emerging, global firms are deep inside the Chinese political infrastructure, pushing hard for greater powers without restraints (Nolan, 2012).

From the withering of the nation state to the corporate interference in the world's political stage, the neoliberal agenda has unequivocally assured greater freedoms for the world's oligarchs, with the freedom to generate more capital, regardless of human, environmental or ethical costs. Their crimes often go unnoticed, and those that do fall under the scrutiny of the public eye are attributed to the lone wolves who unscrupulously play the system. The global system itself remains unblemished. Through lobbying, cronyism and nepotism, nation-state governments have become mere subsidiaries of the corporate elite that yank on the strings of global economies. The age of corporatocracy is in full swing.

So, where do we go from here? Perhaps if the game is so rigged, we need to upturn the board and start again. We certainly need new forms of pluralism that are currently not fashionable with the divisive and individualistic identity theories that dominate in the West today. Yet dismantling the entire ideology of the West and all it proclaims to stand for in terms of morality, rights and human value similarly feels like a fool's errand. Nation states have done little to slow the ever growth of big finance, big pharma and big tech. The social democratic consensus of the immediate post-war years has given way to a new phase of neoliberal capitalism that is leaving workers further behind and reshaping the global structure. Yet a precariat, a mass class defined by instability, lack of identity and erosion of rights, is emerging across the globe. As their needs cannot be met within the current system, the now global precariat and everyone who is not elite arguably carry a transformative potential, and that might constitute a huge threat, a threat elites would do well to remember. If the global elite fails to heed the warnings, the day may come when the many demand that the few pay for their crimes.

References

'1992–2018: The U.S. Financial Crisis' (ND) *Council on Foreign Relations*, [online], Available from: https://www.cfr.org/timeline/us-financial-crisis

'A day in the life of an Amazon delivery driver' (2016) *BBC News*, [online] 11 November, Available from: https://www.bbc.co.uk/news/uk-engl and-37912858

Abdul, A. (2009) 'The effects of global financial crisis on Nigerian economy', *International Journal of Investment and Finance*, 1(1&2): 11–21.

'Actress Felicity Huffman begins 14-day jail term for cheating scam' (2019) *BBC News*, [online] 15 October, Available from: https://www.bbc.co.uk/news/world-us-canada-50061120

Alejandro, J. (2010) 'Journalism in the age of social media', *Reuters Institute for the Study of Journalism*, [online], Available from: https://reutersinstit ute.politics.ox.ac.uk/sites/default/files/research/files/Journalism%252 0in%2520the%2520Age%2520of%2520Social%2520Media.pdf

Alimahomed-Wilson, J. and Reese, E. (2020) *The Cost of Free Shipping*, London: Pluto books.

Alimahomed-Wilson, J. and Reese, E. (2021) 'Surveilling Amazon's warehouse workers: racism, retaliation and worker resistance amid the pandemic'. *Work in the Global Economy*, 1(1–2): 55–73.

Altbach, P.G. (2015) 'What counts for academic productivity in research universities?', *International Higher Education*, (79): 6–7.

Alzola, M. (2013) 'Corporate dystopia: the ethics of corporate political spending', *Business & Society*, 52: 388–426.

'Amazon Prime' (ND) *Amazon*, [online], Available from: https://www.ama zon.co.uk/amazonprime

'Amazon.com Announces First Quarter Results' (2023) *Amazon Investor Relations*, [online] 27 April, Available from: https://ir.aboutamazon.com/news-release/news-release-details/2023/Amazon.com-Announces-First-Quarter-Results/default.aspx#:~:text=SEATTLE%2D%2D(BUSIN ESS%20WIRE)%2D%2D,billion%20in%20first%20quarter%202022

Amundsen, I. (2019) *Political Corruption in Africa: Extraction and Power Preservation*, Cheltenham: Edward Elgar Publishing.

REFERENCES

Anderson, J.L. (2012) 'Charles Taylor and the Killing Tree', *The New Yorker*, [online] 26 April, Available from: https://www.newyorker.com/news/news-desk/charles-taylor-and-the-killing-tree

Anderton, C.H. and Brauer, J. (2016) *Economic Aspects of Genocides, Other Mass Atrocities, and Their Prevention*, Oxford: Oxford University Press.

Andrejevic, M. (2002) 'The kinder, gentler gaze of Big Brother: reality TV in the era of digital capitalism'. *New Media & Society*, 4(2): 251–70.

'Annual Performance Report 2022/23' (2023) *Thames Water*, [online], Available from: https://www.thameswater.co.uk/media-library/home/about-us/investors/our-results/2023-reports/annual-performance-report-2022-23.pdf

Arendt, H. (1963) *Eichmann in Jerusalem: A Report on the Banality of Evil*, London: Penguin Books.

Arendt, H. (1970) *On Violence*, New York: MarinerBKS.

Arendt, H. (1971) 'Thinking and moral considerations', *Social Research*, 38(3): 417–46.

Arguedas, A.R., Robertson, C.T., Fletcher, R. and Nielsen, R.K. (2022) 'Echo chambers, filter bubbles, and polarisation: a literature review', *Reuters Institute for the Study of Journalism*, [online], Available from: https://ora.ox.ac.uk/objects/uuid:6e357e97-7b16-450a-a827-a92c93729a08/download_file?safe_filename=Arguedas_et_al_2022_echo_chambers_filter.pdf&file_format=pdf&type_of_work=Report

'Arms Trade' (ND) *United Nations: Office for Disarmament Affairs*, [online], Available from: https://www.un.org/disarmament/convarms/att/

Aspinall, A. (2014) 'THIRD shopper finds "sweatshop cry for help" label sewn into £10 Primark dress', *Mirror*, [online] 25 June, Available from: https://www.mirror.co.uk/news/uk-news/third-shopper-finds-sweatshop-cry-3762570

Atkinson, R. (2020) *Alpha City How London Was Captured by the Super-Rich*, London: Verso.

Bacon, T.R. (2011) *Elements of Influence: The Art of Getting Others to Follow Your Lead*, New York: AMACOM.

Bahadoran, Z., Mirmiran, P. and Azizi, F. (2015) 'Fast food pattern and cardiometabolic disorders: a review of current studies', *Health Promotion Perspectives*, 5(4): 231–40.

Bakan, J. (2006) 'The Corporation: the pathological pursuit of profit and power', *Society and Business Review*, 1(3): 281–2.

Banks, K. (2023) 'BP found guilty after worker died in offshore fall in 2014', *BBC News*, [online] 14 July, Available from: https://www.bbc.co.uk/news/uk-scotland-north-east-orkney-shetland-66190373

Barlow, D.E. and Barlow, M.H. (2010) 'Corporate crime news as ideology: news magazine coverage of the Enron case', *The Journal of Criminal Justice Research*, 1(1): 1–36.

Basu, D. (2018) *Dictionary of Pure and Applied Physics*, Boca Raton: CRC Press.

'BBC Director General Tim Davie quizzed on Lineker row' (2023) *BBC News*, [online] 10 March, Available from: https://www.bbc.co.uk/news/av/uk-64922157

Beioley, K. (2022) 'UK judge halts trial of two defendants in Saudi bribery case', *Financial Times*, [online] 14 July, Available from: https://www.ft.com/content/15219d46-58f1-4d3b-918d-ee198d7a6f81

Bell-Metereau R. (2006) 'Reality TV: Remaking Television Culture edited by Laurie Ouellette and Susan Murray (New York University Press, 2004)', *Quarterly Review of Film and Video*, 23(5): 443–8.

Bentham, J. (1995) *The Panopticon Writings*, London: Verso.

Bernays, E.L. (1928) *Propaganda*, New York: Horace Liveright.

Bernays, E.L. (2004) *Propaganda*, New York: Ig Publishing.

Bhopal, K. and Myers, M. (2023) *Elite Universities and the Making of Privilege: Exploring Race and Class in Global Educational Economies*, Abingdon: Taylor & Francis.

'Big brands have mistreated their workers throughout the COVID-19 crisis' (2020) *Clean Clothes Campaign*, [online], Available from: https://cleanclothes.org/blog/big-brands-have-mistreated-their-workers-throughout-the-covid-19-crisis

Bischoff, P. (2023) 'Internet Censorship 2023: a global map of internet restrictions', *Comparitech*, [online] 26 January, Available from: https://www.comparitech.com/blog/vpn-privacy/internet-censorship-map/

Block, A.A. and Weaver, C.A. (2004) *All Is Clouded by Desire: Global Banking, Money Laundering, and International Organized Crime*, London: Praeger.

Boggan, S. (1996) 'Arming Africa: who is the second-largest supplier of weapons in the world? China? France? Russia? No, it's Britain', *Independent*, [online] 19 November, Available from: https://www.independent.co.uk/news/world/arming-africa-who-is-the-secondlargest-supplier-of-weapons-in-the-wor-ld-china-france-russia-no-it-s-britain-1353101.html

Bonds, E. (2015) 'Challenging climate change's new "security threat" status', *Peace Review: A Journal of Social Justice*, 27: 209–16.

Bonds, E. (2016) 'Upending climate violence research: fossil fuel corporations and the structural violence of climate change', *Human Ecology Review*, 22(1): 1–22.

Botsman, R. (2017) 'Big data meets Big Brother as China moves to rate its citizens', *Wired*, [online] 21 October, Available from: https://www.wired.co.uk/article/chinese-government-social-credit-score-privacy-invasion

Boyce, G. and Ville, S. (2002) *The Development of Modern Business*, Hampshire: Palgrave.

'Brand Audit Report 2021' (2021) *Break Free from Plastic*, [online], Available from: https://www.breakfreefromplastic.org/wp-content/uploads/2021/10/BRAND-AUDIT-REPORT-2021.pdf

Braverman-Bronstein, A., Camacho-García-Formentí, D., Zepeda-Tello, R., Cudhea, F., Singh, G.M., Mozaffarian, D. and Barrientos-Gutierrez, T. (2020) 'Mortality attributable to sugar sweetened beverages consumption in Mexico', *International Journal of Obesity*, 44(6): 1341–9.

Breithaupt, J. (2001) *Physics*, Cheltenham: Nelson Thornes.

Briggs, D., Telford, L., Lloyd, A., Ellis, A. and Kotzé, J. (2021) *Lockdown: Social Harm in the Covid-19 Era*, London: Palgrave.

'Britain's ten richest Instagram influencers – and how you can give up the day job and join them' (2021) *Evening Standard*, [online] 1 April, Available from: https://www.standard.co.uk/business/how-become-millionaire-soc ial-media-influencer-uk-ten-wealthiest-b926856.html

Broersma, M. and Graham, T. (2012) 'SOCIAL MEDIA AS BEAT: Tweets as a news source during the 2010 British and Dutch elections', *Journalism Practice*, 6(3): 403–19.

Brookman, F. (2005) *Understanding Homicide: A Critical Introduction*, London: Sage.

Brown, R. and Carasso, H. (2013) *Everything for Sale? The Marketisation of UK Higher Education*, London: Taylor and Francis.

Bruner, R.F. (2020) 'The first modern financial crises: the South Sea and Mississippi bubbles in historical perspective', *Journal of Applied Corporate Finance*, 32(4): 17–33.

Brown W. (2015) *Undoing the Demos: Neoliberalism's Stealth Revolution*, Brooklyn, NY: Zone Books.

Brussee, V. (2021) 'China's social credit system is actually quite boring', *Foreign Policy Magazine*, [online] 15 September, Available from: https://foreignpolicy.com/2021/09/15/china-social-credit-system-authoritarian/

Bufacchi, V. (2005) 'Two concepts of violence', *Political Studies Association*, 3: 193–204.

Bunz, M. (2010) 'Most journalists use social media such as Twitter and Facebook as a source', *The Guardian*, [online] 15 February, Available from: https://www.theguardian.com/media/pda/2010/feb/15/journalists-social-music-twitter-facebook

Burgess, M. (2023) 'The bizarre reality of getting online in North Korea', *Wired*, [online] 8 June, Available from: https://www.wired.com/story/internet-reality-north-korea/

Burgis, T. (2020) *Kleptopia: How Dirty Money is Conquering the World*, London: William Collins.

Burton, F., and Carlen, P. (1979) *Official Discourse: On Discourse Analysis, Government Publications, Ideology, and the State* (1st edn), London: Routledge & Kegan Paul.

Button, M. and Tunley, M. (2014) 'Criminal activity in the financial sector', in M. Gill (ed) *The Handbook of Security*, London: Palgrave Macmillan, pp 427–49.

Cahill, H. (2023) 'The £14bn debt that could sink Thames Water', *The Times*, [online] 29 June, Available from: https://www.thetimes.co.uk/article/the-14bn-debt-that-could-sink-thames-water-bvtrphw90

Campbell, C. (1989) *The Romantic Ethic and the Spirit of Modern Consumerism*, Oxford: Blackwell Publishers.

Campbell, S. (2023) 'Amazon users: how many people use Amazon In 2023?', *The Small Business Blog*, [online] 18 June, Available from: https://thesmallbusinessblog.net/amazon-users/

Canales, K. and Mok, A. (2022) 'China's "social credit" system ranks citizens and punishes them with throttled internet speeds and flight bans if the Communist Party deems them untrustworthy', *Insider*, [online] 28 November, Available from: https://www.businessinsider.com/china-social-credit-system-punishments-and-rewards-explained-2018-4?r=US&IR=T

Canning, V. and Tombs, S. (2021) *From Social Harm to Zemiology: A Critical Introduction*, Oxfordshire: Routledge.

'Carbon emissions of richest 1 percent more than double the emissions of the poorest half of humanity' (2020) *Oxfam*, [online] 21 September, Available from: https://www.oxfam.org/en/press-releases/carbon-emissions-richest-1-percent-more-double-emissions-poorest-half-humanity#:~:text=The%20richest%2010%20percent,of%20humanity%20(7%20percent

Carrier, J.G. (2022) *A Handbook of Economic Anthropology*, Cheltenham: Edward Elgar Publishing Limited.

Carson, W.G. (1982*) Other Price of Britain's Oil: Safety and Control in the North Sea*, New Jersey: Rutgers University Press.

Carswell, J. (2001) *The South Sea Bubble*, Stroud: Sutton Publishing Ltd.

Cash, D. (2019) 'A New Era for Chinese Credit Rating Provision', *Journal of Business Law (Forthcoming)*, Available from SSRN: https://ssrn.com/abstract=3411675

Castillo, C., El-Haddad, M., Pfeffer, J. and Stempeck, M. (2014) 'Characterizing the life cycle of online news stories using social media reactions', in *Proceedings of the 17th ACM Conference on Computer Supported Cooperative Work & Social Computing (CSCW '14)*, Association for Computing Machinery, New York, NY, USA, pp 211–23. https://doi.org/10.1145/2531602.2531623

Chambliss, W.J. (1978) *On the Take: From Petty Crooks to Presidents*, Indiana: Indiana University Press.

Chancel, L., Piketty, T., Saez, E. and Zucman, G. (2022) 'World Inequality Report 2022', *World Inequality Lab*, [online], Available from: https://wir2022.wid.world/www-site/uploads/2023/03/D_FINAL_WIL_RIM_RAPPORT_2303.pdf

REFERENCES

Chang, D. (2022) 'State Troopers now patrolling high-crime areas in Philly', *NBC Philadelphia*, [online] 16 June, Available from: https://www.nbcphila delphia.com/news/local/seeking-peace-in-philly/state-police-and-philly-police-to-increase-presence-in-high-crime-areas/3273415/

Chapman, B. (2019) 'JD Sports and Asos warehouses compared to "dark satanic mills" amid concerns over working conditions', *The Independent*, [online] 7 May, Available from: https://www.independent.co.uk/news/business/news/jd-sports-asos-warehouses-working-conditions-unite-trade-union-a8902566.html

Chapman, D.W. and Lindner, S. (2016) 'Degrees of integrity: the threat of corruption in higher education', *Studies in Higher Education*, 41(2): 247–68.

Chatain, P.L., McDowell, J., Mousset, C., Schott, P.A. and De Willebois. (2009) *Preventing Money Laundering and Terrorist Financing*, Washington: The World Bank.

Chen, M. and Grossklags, J. (2022) 'Social control in the digital transformation of society: a case study of the Chinese social credit system', *Social Sciences*, 11(6): 229.

Chen, Y. (2020) 'From bitter to better: a collective effort to improve workers' rights in the coffee industry', *University of Pennsylvania Journal of International Law*, 42(1): 1–49.

Chisholm, J., Sharma, S. and Sharp, R. (2022) 'Brittney Griner: WNBA star arrives at US hospital after being released by Russia in prisoner swap', *The Independent*, [online] 10 December, Available from: https://www.independent.co.uk/news/world/americas/brittney-griner-russia-trade-viktor-bout-exchange-b2242405.html

Chomsky, N. (2003) *Power and Terror: Post 9–11 Talks and Interviews*, New York: Seven Stories Press.

Chossudovsky, M. (2003) *The Globalization of Poverty and the New World Order*, Stockton: Global Research.

Christophers, B. (2023) *Our Lives in Their Portfolios: Why Asset Managers Own the World*, London: Verso Books.

Cissel, M. (2012) 'Media framing: a comparative content analysis on mainstream and alternative news coverage of Occupy Wall Street', *The Elon Journal of Undergraduate Research in Communications*, 3: 67–77.

Clayton, P. and Hoskins, J. (2022) 'Elon Musk takes control of Twitter in $44bn deal', *BBC News*, [online] 28 October, Available from: https://www.bbc.co.uk/news/technology-63402338

Clifford, T. (2020) 'Jim Cramer: the pandemic led to "one of the greatest wealth transfers in history"', *CNBC*, [online] 4 June, Available from: https://www.cnbc.com/2020/06/04/cramer-the-pandemic-led-to-a-great-wealth-transfer.html

CNN (2016) 'Michael Moore: Flint water crisis "a racial crime"', *YouTube*, [online] 28 January, Available from: https://www.youtube.com/watch?v=3bciXJdz2YE

'Cobalt' (2020) *U.S. Geological Survey*, [online], Available from: https://pubs.usgs.gov/periodicals/mcs2022/mcs2022-cobalt.pdf

'Collective Action in banking: the Wolfsberg Group's role in a fast-evolving industry' (2022) *Basel Institute on Governance*, [online] 22 March, Available from: https://baselgovernance.org/blog/collective-action-banking-wolfsberg-groups-role-fast-evolving-industry

Collins, R. (2022) 'Cost of living: Deliveroo and Uber couriers face uphill struggle', *BBC News*, [online] 28 December, Available from: https://www.bbc.co.uk/news/newsbeat-63914936

Collins, V.E. and Pujol, M. (2016) 'Secrets exposed? Selective state concern and the prosecution of notorious arms trafficker Viktor Bout', *Critical Criminology*, 24: 93–109.

'Colorado miners strike and Columbine mine massacre, 1927 - Sam Lowry' (2006) *Libcom.org*, [online] 10 November, Available from: https://libcom.org/history/1927-colorado-miners-strike-and-columbine-mine-massacre

Conboy, K.J. and Morrison, J. (2002) *The CIA's Secret War in Tibet*, Kansas: University of Kansas Press.

Cook, J. (2014) 'Yes, you can now take a tour of one of Amazon's massive warehouse facilities', *GeekWire*, [online] 26 April, Available from: https://www.geekwire.com/2014/yes-can-now-take-tour-massive-amazon-warehouse-facility/

Cooper, J. (2012) *Margaret Thatcher and Ronald Reagan: A Very Political Special Relationship*. Hampshire: Palgrave.

Cooper, V. and Whyte, D. (2017) *The Violence of Austerity*. London: Pluto Press.

Cooper, V. and Whyte, D. (2022) 'Grenfell, austerity, and institutional violence', *Sociological Research Online*, 27(1): 207–16.

Copson, L. (2018) 'Beyond 'Criminology vs. Zemiology': reconciling crime with social harm', in Boukli, Avi (Paraskevi) and Kotze, Justin (eds) *Zemiology: Reconnecting Crime and Social Harm*, Palgrave Macmillan, pp 33–56.

'Core principles of effective banking supervision' (1997) *Bank for International Settlements*, [online] September, Available from: https://www.bis.org/publ/bcbsc102.pdf

'Corruption Perceptions Index' (2021) *Transparency International: The Global Coalition Against Corruption*, [online], Available from: https://www.transparency.org/en/cpi/2021?gclid=CjwKCAjws--ZBhAXEiwAv-RNL6InSjeOgC_RmM8zxGlBE21cfpKZZZINxfZR9mXXwyMze64US5_a6BoClLwQAvD_BwE

REFERENCES

'Countries of special concern' (2021) *Genocide Watch*, [online], Available from: https://www.genocidewatch.com/_files/ugd/137a5c_46ae98784 ceb4064b4e5d94291155a68.pdf

'Crackdown on rip-off university degrees' (ND) *GOV.UK*, Available from: https://www.gov.uk/government/news/crackdown-on-rip-off-university-degrees

Crank, J. and Jacoby, L. (2014) *Crime, Violence, and Global Warming*, Abingdon: Routledge.

Crawford, K. (2023) 'Study: when public hospitals go private, low-income patients lose', *Stanford Institute for Economic Policy Research*, [online] 9 January, Available from: https://siepr.stanford.edu/news/study-when-public-hospit als-go-private-low-income-patients-lose

Croall, H. (2001) *Understanding White Collar Crime*, Buckingham: Open University.

'Crocodile' (2017) *Black Mirror*.

Crouch, C. (2004) *Post-democracy*, Cambridge: Polity Press.

Currie, E. (1997) 'Market, crime and community', *Theoretical Criminology*, 1(2): 147–72.

'Customer due diligence for banks' (2001) *Bank for International Settlements*, [online] October, Available from: https://www.bis.org/publ/bcbs85.pdf

Daems, T. and Beken, T.V. (2018) *Privatising Punishment in Europe?* Abingdon: Routledge.

Dahl, R.A. (1957) 'The concept of power', *Behavioural Science*, 2(3): 201–15.

Damji, M. (2022) 'Prison privatisation: a failure of the British penal system', *St Andrews Law Review*, [online] 20 March, Available from: https://www. standrewslawreview.com/post/prison-privatisation-a-failure-of-the-brit ish-penal-system

'Danske Bank pleads guilty to fraud on U.S. banks in multi-billion dollar scheme to access the U.S. financial system' (2022) *Office of Public Affairs*, [online] 13 December, Available from: https://www.justice.gov/opa/pr/ danske-bank-pleads-guilty-fraud-us-banks-multi-billion-dollar-scheme-access-us-financial

'Darfur: new weapons from China and Russia fuelling conflict'(2012) *Amnesty International*, [online] 9 February, Available from: https://www. amnesty.org/en/latest/press-release/2012/02/darfur-new-weapons-china-and-russia-fuelling-conflict/

Davey, C. (2023) 'The environmental impacts of cobalt mining in Congo', *EARTH.ORG*, [online] 28 March, Available from: https://earth.org/ cobalt-mining-in-congo/#:~:text=Cobalt%20is%20fast%20turning%20f rom,are%20vital%20for%20soil%20fertility.

Davidson, H. (2022) 'China using influencers to whitewash human rights abuses, report finds', *The Guardian*, [online] 20 October, Available from: https://www.theguardian.com/world/2022/oct/20/china-using-infl uencers-to-whitewash-human-rights-abuses-report-finds

Davies, J. (2019) 'From severe to routine labour exploitation: the case of migrant workers in the UK food industry', *Criminology & Criminal Justice*, 19(3): 294–310.

Davies, P., Francis, P. and Jupp, V. (1999) *Invisible Crimes: Their Victims and their Regulation*, London: Palgrave McMillan.

Davis, J. and Tallis, R. (2013) *NHS SOS: How the NHS Was Betrayed and How We Can Save It*, London: Oneworld Publications.

Dayaram, S. (2022) 'The metals inside your iPhone are more precious than you thought', *CNET*, [online] 23 November, Available from: https://www.cnet.com/tech/mobile/the-metals-inside-your-iphone-are-more-precious-than-you-thought-heres-why/

Debord, G. (2005) *Society of the Spectacle*, Chico, California: AK Press.

'Democratic Republic of Congo: "This is what we die for": human rights abuses in the Democratic Republic of the Congo power the global trade in cobalt' (2016) *Amnesty International*, [online] 19 January, Available from: https://www.amnesty.org/en/documents/afr62/3183/2016/en/

Deng, I. and Feng, C. (2022) 'Foxconn raises hourly rate in Shenzhen to US$3.30 after Zhengzhou Covid-19 lockdown dents iPhone production', *South China Morning Post*, [online] 8 November, Available from: https://www.scmp.com/tech/big-tech/article/3198868/foxconn-raises-hourly-rate-shenzhen-us330-after-zhengzhou-covid-19-lockdown-dents-iph one-production

Doerr, S. and Hofmann, B. (2020) 'Recessions and mortality: a global perspective', BIS Working Papers No. 910: Monetry and Economic Department, *Bank for International Settlements*, [online], Available from: https://www.bis.org/publ/work910.pdf

Doig, A. (1984) *Corruption and Misconduct in Contemporary British Politics*, London: Penguin.

Dong, J. (2022) 'China's internet censors try a new trick: revealing users' locations', *The New York Times*, [online] 18 May, Available from: https://www.nytimes.com/2022/05/18/business/china-internet-censors-ip-addr ess.html

Donnelly, D. (2023) 'China social credit system explained – what is it and how does it work?', *Horizons*, [online] 6 April, Available from: https://nhglobalpartners.com/china-social-credit-system-explained/

Doyal, L. and Gough, I. (1991) *A Theory of Human Need*, New York: Springer.

REFERENCES

Drinhausen, K and Brussee, V. (2022) 'China's social credit system in 2021: from fragmentation towards integration', *Mercator Institute for China Studies*, [online] 9 May, Available from: https://merics.org/en/report/chinas-social-credit-system-2021-fragmentation-towards-integration

'Drug overdose death rates' (ND) *National Institute on Drug Abuse*, [online], Available from: https://nida.nih.gov/research-topics/trends-statistics/overdose-death-rates

Duggan, M., Gupta, A., Jackson, E. and Templeton, Z.S. (2023) 'The impact of privatization: evidence from the hospital sector', *National Bureau of Economic Research*, January. https://doi.org/10.3386/w30824

Duncan, P., Blood, D., McIntyre, N. and Davies, R. (2022) 'Jets linked to Russian oligarchs appear to have kept flying despite sanctions', *The Guardian*, [online] 31 March, Available from: https://www.theguardian.com/world/2022/mar/31/jets-linked-to-russian-oligarchs-appear-to-have-kept-flying-despite-sanctions

Dupuy, A. (2014) *Haiti: From Revolutionary Slaves to Powerless Citizens: Essays on the Politics and Economics of Underdevelopment, 1804–2013*, London: Routledge.

Dye, T.R. (2002) *Who's Running America? The Bush Restoration*, Prentice Hall, New Jersey.

'Earth Day 2022 Investing in Our Planet by Investing in Water Optimism' (2022) Earthday.org, [online], Available from: Earth Day 2022 Brochure (dupont.com)

Edwards, R. (2021) 'Revealed: the 43 peers entangled in big oil', *The Ferret*, [online] 27 October, Available from: https://theferret.scot/oil-industry-43-peers-shares-directors/

Ekdale, B. and Tully, M. (2020) 'Cambridge Analytica in Africa – what do we know?' *Democracy in Africa*, [online] 10 January, Available from: http://democracyinafrica.org/cambridge-analytica-africa-know/

Elbagir, N., Abdelaziz, S. and Spark, S.L. (2018) 'Made in America', *CNN*, [online], Available from: https://edition.cnn.com/interactive/2018/09/world/yemen-airstrikes-intl/

Elgin, B. (2021) 'McDonald's struggles to fix its massive methane problem', *Bloomberg*, [online] 1 December, Available from: https://www.bloomberg.com/news/articles/2021-12-01/the-carbon-footprint-of-mcdonald-s-menu-very-big?leadSource=uverify%20wall

Elias, N. (1994) *Civilizing Process*, New Jersey: Wiley–Blackwell.

Eligon, J. (2021) 'Jacob Zuma, former South African President, is arrested', *The New York Times*, [online] 7 July, Available from: https://www.nytimes.com/2021/07/07/world/africa/jacob-zuma-arrested-south-africa.html

'Elite' (ND) *Cambridge Dictionary*, [online], Available from: https://dictionary.cambridge.org/dictionary/english/elite#google_vignette

Ellis, A. (2019) A de-civilizing reversal or system normal? Rising lethal violence in post-recession austerity United Kingdom, *British Journal of Criminology*, 59(4): 862–78. https://doi.org/10.1093/bjc/azz001

Ellis, R. (2017) *Men, Masculinities and Violence: An Ethnographic Study*, London: Routledge.

Eloise, M. (2019) 'Jade Goody was exploited by the media – and Britain's hatred of "chavs" meant it was somehow OK', *The Independent*, [online] 8 August, Available from: https://www.independent.co.uk/voices/jade-goody-documentary-channel-4-reality-tv-big-brother-chav-class-a9046551.html

Embrick, D.G. (2015) 'Two nations, revisited: the lynching of Black and Brown bodies, police brutality, and racial control in "post-racial" Amerikkka', *Critical Sociology*, 41(6): 835–43.

Enrich, D. (2017) *The Spider Network: The Wild Story of a Math Genius, a Gang of Backstabbing Bankers, and One of the Greatest Scams in Financial History*, New York: Custom House.

Erman, M. (2022) 'Pfizer expects to hike U.S. COVID vaccine price to $110-$130 per dose', *Reuters*, [online] 21 October, Available from: https://www.reuters.com/business/healthcare-pharmaceuticals/pfizer-expects-price-covid-vaccine-110-130-per-dose-2022-10-20/

'Estimating illicit financial flows resulting from drug trafficking and other transnational organized crimes' (2011) *United Nations Office on Drugs and Crime*, [online] October, Available from: https://www.unodc.org/docume nts/data-and-analysis/Studies/Illicit_financial_flows_2011_web.pdf

Evans, R. and Pegg, D. (2022) 'UK used "deniable fiddle" to hide £60m of payments to Saudis, court told', *The Guardian*, [online] 9 May, Available from: https://www.theguardian.com/uk-news/2022/may/09/uk-denia ble-fiddle-hide-60m-payments-saudis-court-told

'Exposed: the dirty dozen filling up the ocean with plastic pollution' (2022) *Surfers Against Sewage*, [online], Available from: https://www.sas.org.uk/upda tes/exposed-the-dirty-dozen-filling-up-the-ocean-with-plastic-pollution/

'Fact sheet: plastics in the ocean' (2022) *Earth Day*, [online] 5 March, Available from: https://www.earthday.org/fact-sheet-plastics-in-the-ocean/#:~:text=There%20is%20more%20microplastic%20in,by%20 22%2Dfold%20by%20plastics.

Fahel, D. (2017) 'Chronic lead exposure: a non-traumatic brain injury', *Brain Injury Association of America*, [online] 3 May, Available from: https://www.biausa.org/public-affairs/public-awareness/news/chronic-lead-expos ure-a-non-traumatic-brain-injury

'Fashion Transparency Index 2023' (2023) *Fashion Revolution*, [online], Available from: https://www.fashionrevolution.org/about/transparency/

'Fearing Covid, workers flee from Foxconn's vast Chinese iPhone plant' (2022) *CNBC*, [online] 31 October, Available from: https://www.cnbc.com/2022/10/31/fearing-covid-workers-flee-from-foxconns-vast-chinese-iphone-plant.html

Feinstein, A. and Smidman, A. (2021) 'Britain's "robust" arms export controls are a fiction', *Declassified UK*, [online] 14 September, Available from: https://declassifieduk.org/britains-robust-arms-export-controls-are-a-fiction/

Felson, R.B. (2009) 'Violence, crime and violent crime', *International Journal of Conflict and Violence*, 3(1): 23–39.

Ferrell, J. (1999) 'Cultural criminology', *Annual Review of Sociology*, 25: 395–418.

Fisher, M. (2009) *Capitalist Realism: Is There No Alternative?* Alresford: Zero Books.

Fisher, M. (2015) 'Yes, North Korea has the internet. Here's what it looks like', *Vox*, [online] 19 March, Available from: https://www.vox.com/2014/12/22/7435625/north-korea-internet

Forst, B. and Manning, P.K. (1999) *The Privatization of Policing: Two Views (Controversies in Public Policy)*, Georgetown: Georgetown University Press.

Forster, A. (2021) 'Review of two events involving external speakers', *University of Essex*, [online] 17 May, Available from: https://www.essex.ac.uk/blog/posts/2021/05/17/review-of-two-events-with-external-speakers

Foucault, M. (1977) *Discipline and Punish: The Birth of the Prison* (A. Sheridan, Transl.), New York: Random House Vintage Books.

Foucault, M. (1991) *Discipline and Punish: The Birth of a Prison*, London: Penguin.

Foucault, M. (1998) *The History of Sexuality: The Will to Knowledge*, London: Penguin.

Foucault, M. (2011) *The Courage of the Truth*, Hampshire: Palgrave Macmillan.

Foucault, M. (Edited by Rabinow, P) (1991) *The Foucault Reader: An Introduction to Foucault's Thought*, London: Penguin.

'Foxconn factory workers in Zhengzhou raised the alarm "amid the fire and water"' (2022) *China Labour Bulletin*, [online] 8 November, Available from: https://clb.org.hk/en/content/foxconn-factory-workers-zhengzhou-raised-alarm-%E2%80%9Camid-fire-and-water%E2%80%9D

Foy, H., Srivastava, M., White, E. and Dempsey, H. (2021) 'Davos highlights: Putin warns of "all against all" fight if global development is neglected', *Financial Times*, [online] 27 January, Available from: https://www.ft.com/content/3c352034-fa6e-4b41-b10b-cfb5666d6a75

Frehen, R.G.P., Goetzmann, W.N. and Rouwenhorst, K.G. (2012) 'New evidence on the first financial bubble', *Yale International Center for Finance*, [online], Available from: http://depot.som.yale.edu/icf/papers/fileuploads/2542/original/2008_ICF_WPS_09-04_Goetzmann_Bubble.pdf

Freire, P. (1996) *Pedagogy of the Oppressed* (revised), New York: Continuum.

Frenkel, S. and Feuer, A. (2021) ' "A total failure": The Proud Boys now mock Trump', *New York Times*, [online] 20 January, Available from: https://feedback.no-art.info/en/!documents/2021_A%20Total%20Failure_nytimes.pdf

Frenkel, S. and Kang, C. (2021) *An Ugly Truth: Inside Facebook's Battle for Domination*, New York: HarperCollins.

Fukuyama, F. (1992) *The End of History and the Last Man*, New York: Free Press.

Gallo, C. (2015) 'How the Apple store creates irresistible customer experiences', *Forbes*, [online] 10 April, Available from: https://www.forbes.com/sites/carminegallo/2015/04/10/how-the-apple-store-creates-irresistible-customer-experiences/?sh=520bee2c17a8

Galtung, J. (1969) 'Violence, peace and peace research', *Journal of Peace Research*, 6(3): 167–91.

Galtung, J. (1990) 'Cultural violence', *Journal of Peace Research*, 27(3): 291–305.

Gill, O. and Millard, R. (2022) 'Water supplies will be turned off "for weeks" amid summer heatwaves', *The Telegraph*, [online] 17 December, Available from: https://www.telegraph.co.uk/business/2022/12/17/water-supplies-will-turned-weeks-amid-summer-heatwaves/

Giuliani, E.M. (2015) 'Strangers in the Village? Colonial policing in rural Bengal, 1861 to 1892', *Modern Asian Studies*, 49(5): 1378–27.

Glasser, M. (1998), 'On violence: a preliminary communication', *The International Journal of Psychoanalysis*, 79: 887–902.

Global Corruption Report: Education – Publications (2013) Transparency.org, Available from: https://www.transparency.org/en/publications/global-corruption-report-education

'Global GDP – Statistics & Facts' (2023) *Statista*, [online], Available from: https://www.statista.com/topics/7747/gross-domestic-product-gdp-worldwide/#topicOverview

'Global Growth Tracker: world economies by GDP' (2022) *Council for Foreign Relations*, [online] 20 July, Available from: Global Growth Tracker: World Economies by GDP (cfr.org)

Goertzel, T. (1994) 'Belief in conspiracy theories', *Political Psychology*, 15(4): 731–42.

Goggin, B. and Ingram, D. (2023) 'With X under fire, Elon Musk digs in and finds support from conservatives', *NBC News*, [online] 22 November, Available from: With X under fire, Elon Musk digs in and finds support from conservatives (nbcnews.com)

Goldacre, B. (2012) *Bad Pharma: How Drug Companies Mislead Doctors and Harm Patients*, London: Fourth Estate.

Goodair, B. and Reeves, A. (2022) 'Outsourcing health-care services to the private sector and treatable mortality rates in England, 2013-20: an observational study of NHS privatisation', *Lancet Public Health*, 7(7): 638–46.

Goodley, S. (2020) 'Have working conditions improved at the Sports Direct warehouse?', *The Guardian*, [online] 23 July, Available from: https://www.theguardian.com/business/2020/jul/23/have-working-conditions-improved-at-the-sports-direct-warehouse

Gottschalk, P. (2019) 'BP Deepwater Horizon oil spill claims investigated by Special Master Freeh: a case for application of convenience theory to white-collar misconduct', *Pakistan Journal of Criminology*, 11(1): 1–15.

Grabar, H. (2017) 'Apple is building "town squares" now, because somebody has to', *SLATE*, [online] 12 September, Available from: https://slate.com/business/2017/09/apple-stores-are-called-town-squares-now.html

Gramsci, A. (1996) *Prison Notebooks*, vol 2. Trans. and ed. J. Buttigieg, New York: Columbia University Press.

Gramsci, A., Hoare, Q. and Nowell-Smith, G. (1971) *Selections from the Prison Notebooks of Antonio Gramsci*, London: Lawrence and Wishart.

Gray, G.C. (2009) 'The responsibilization strategy of health and safety: neo-liberalism and the reconfiguration of individual responsibility for risk', *The British Journal of Criminology*, 49(3): 326–42.

Graz, J.C. (2010) 'How powerful are transnational elite clubs? The social myth of the world economic forum', *New Political Economy*, 8(3): 321–40.

Greene, R. (2010) *The Art of Seduction*, London: Profile Books.

Greenfield, P. (2022) 'Nothing will change on climate until death toll rises in west, says Gabonese minister', *The Guardian*, [online] 31 October, Available from: Nothing will change on climate until death toll rises in west, says Gabonese minister | Cop27 | The Guardian

'Greensill: What is the David Cameron lobbying row about?', *BBC News*, [online] 9 August, Available from: https://www.bbc.co.uk/news/uk-politics-56578838

Greenwald, G. (2013) 'XKeyscore: NSA tool collects "nearly everything a user does on the internet"', *The Guardian*, [online] 31 July, Available from: https://www.theguardian.com/world/2013/jul/31/nsa-top-secret-program-online-data

Gricius, G. (2018) 'The Danske Bank scandal is the tip of the iceberg', *Foreign Policy*, [online] 8 October, Available from: https://foreignpolicy.com/2018/10/08/the-danske-bank-scandal-is-the-tip-of-the-iceberg-money-laundering-estonia-denmark-regulation-financial-crime/

Griffiths, J. (2019) 'World marks 30 years since Tiananmen massacre as China censors all mention', *CNN*, [online] 4 June, Available from: https://edition.cnn.com/2019/06/03/asia/tiananmen-june-4-china-censorship-intl/index.html

Gross, E. (1980) 'Organizational structure and organizational crime', in G. Geis and E. Stotland (eds) *White-Collar Crime: Theory and Research*, Beverly Hills: Sage, pp 53–76.

'Gun deaths by country 2019' (2020) *World Population Review*, [online], Available from: https://worldpopulationreview.com/country-rankings/gun-deaths-by-country

Hall, S. (2007) 'The emergence and breakdown of the pseudo-pacification process', in K. Watson (ed) *Assaulting the Past*, Newcastle upon Tyne: Cambridge Scholars Press.

Hall, S. (2012a) *Theorising Crime and Deviance: A New Approach*, London: Sage.

Hall, S. (2012b) 'The solicitation of the trap: on transcendence and transcendental materialism in advanced consumer-capitalism'. *Human Studies*, 35: 365–81.

Hall, S. and Wilson, D. (2014) 'New foundations: pseudo-pacification and special liberty as potential cornerstones for a multi-level theory of homicide and serial murder', *European Journal of Criminology*, 11(5): 635–55.

Hall, S. and Winlow, S. (2015) *Revitalizing Criminological Theory: Towards a New Ultra-Realism*, London: Routledge.

Hall, S. and Winlow, S. (2018) 'Ultra-realism', in W.S. DeKeseredy and M. Dragiewicz (eds) *Routledge Handbook of Critical Criminology* (2nd edn), London: Routledge, pp 43–57.

Hall, S., Winlow, S. and Ancrum, C. (2008) *Criminal Identities and Consumer Culture: Crime, Exclusion and the New Culture of Narcism*, Devon: Willan Publishing.

Han, R., and Shao, L. (2022) 'Scaling authoritarian information control: how China adjusts the level of online censorship', *Political Research Quarterly*, 75(4): 1345–59.

Hanrahan, J. (2022) 'Ground floor at the Amazon warehouse' [Podcast]. Wilmington: Megacorp, Available from: https:// www.youtube.com/watch?v=pbvmye0GD6Q

Harding, S. (2020) 'Getting to the point? Reframing narratives on knife crime', *Youth Justice*, 20(1–2): 31–49.

Harris, R. (1994) 'The Bubble Act: its passage and its effects on business organization', *The Journal of Economic History*, 54(3): 610–27.

Hart, M. (2018) *The Awaiting World Through Popular Culture: The Future of Our Technology Driven Capitalist Society – An Ultra-realist Analysis of Black Mirror's Nosedive*, Dissertation (MA), Birmingham City University.

Hartley, R.D. (2008) *Corporate Crime: A Reference Handbook*, California: ABC-CLIO.

Harvey, D. (2007) *A Brief History of Neoliberalism*, Oxford: Oxford University Press.

'Hated in the Nation' (2016) *Black Mirror*.

Hayward, C.R. (2000) *De-Facing Power*, Cambridge: Cambridge University Press.

Hayward, K. and Smith, O. (2017) 'Crime and consumer culture' in A. Liebling, S. Maruna and L. McAra (eds) *The Oxford Handbook of Criminology* (6th edn), Oxford: Oxford University Press, pp 306–20.

Hellier, D. (1995) 'How one arms scandal led to another', *Independent*, [online] 8 November, Available from: https://www.independent.co.uk/news/how-one-arms-scandal-led-to-another-1580850.html

Helm, D. (2017) *Burn Out: The Endgame for Fossil Fuels*, London: Yale University Press.

Henry, S. and Milovanovic, D. (1996) *Constitutive Criminology: Beyond Postmodernism*, London: Sage.

Herforth A., Bai, Y., Venkat, A., Mahrt, K., Ebel, A. and Masters, W.A. (2020) *Cost and Affordability of Healthy Diets across and within Countries*, Rome: Food and Agriculture Organization of the United Nations.

Herman, E.S. and Chomsky, N. (2008) *Manufacturing Consent: The Political Economy of the Mass Media*, Random House.

Hickel, J. (2017) 'Aid in reverse: how poor countries develop rich countries', *The Guardian*, [online] 14 January, Available from: https://www.theguardian.com/global-development-professionals-network/2017/jan/14/aid-in-reverse-how-poor-countries-develop-rich-countries

Hickel, J. (2020) 'Apartheid in the World Bank and the IMF', *Aljazeera*, [online] 26 November, Available from: https://www.aljazeera.com/opinions/2020/11/26/it-is-time-to-decolonise-the-world-bank-and-the-imf

Hickey, S. and Grierson, J. (2015) 'Former City trader Tom Hayes given 14-year sentence for Libor rigging', *The Guardian*, [online] 3 August, Available from: https://www.theguardian.com/uk-news/2015/aug/03/former-city-trader-tom-hayes-convicted-of-libor-rigging

Hillary: The Movie (2008) [Film] Directed by Alan Peterson. United States: Citizens United.

Hillman, A., Keim, G. and Schuler, D. (2004) 'Corporate political activity: a review and research agenda', *Journal of Management*, 30: 837–58.

Hillyard, P. and Tombs, S. (2008) 'Beyond criminology?', in D. Dorling, D. Gordon, P. Hillyard, C. Pantazis, S. Pemberton and S. Tombs (eds) *Criminal Obsessions: Why Harm Matters More Than Crime*, London: Centre for Crime and Justice Studies, pp 6–24.

Hillyard, P. and Tombs, S. (2017) 'Social harm and Zemiology', in A. Liebling, S. Maruna and L. McAra (eds) *The Oxford Handbook of Criminology*, 6th edn, Oxford: Oxford University Press, pp 284–305.

Hillyard, P., Pantazis, C., Tombs, S. and Gordon, D. (2004) *Beyond Criminology: Taking Harm Seriously*, London: Pluto Press.

Hirschman, A.O. (1977) *The Passions and the Interests: Political Arguments for Capitalism before Its Triumph*, Princeton: Princeton University Press.

Hiscott, G. (2023) 'Water firms face staggering £60 BILLION debts amid Thames Water collapse threat', *Mirror*, [online] 29 June, Available from: https://www.mirror.co.uk/money/water-firms-face-staggering-60-30352212

'History of the BBC: Chairmen of the BBC' (ND) *BBC News*, [online], Available from: https://www.bbc.co.uk/historyofthebbc/research/chairmen-of-the-bbc

Hobbes, T. (1651) *Leviathan*, Oxford: Oxford University Press.

Hodkinson, S. (2018) 'Grenfell foretold: a very neoliberal tragedy' in C. Needham, E. Heins and J. Rees (eds) *Social Policy Review 30*, Bristol: Bristol University Press, pp 5–26.

Hoffman, S. (2017) 'Managing the state: social credit, surveillance and the CCP's plan for China', *China Brief*, 17(11), Available from: https://www.refworld.org/docid/59bb92874.html

Home (2023) *Student Loans Company*, Available from: https://careers.slc.co.uk/

Homepage (ND) Homepage | Blavatnik School of Government, Available from: https://www.bsg.ox.ac.uk/

Homer, S. (2004) *Jacques Lacan*, Abingdon: Routledge.

'Homicide in England and Wales: year ending March 2019' (2020) *Office for National Statistics*, [online] 13 February, Available from: https://www.ons.gov.uk/peoplepopulationandcommunity/crimeandjustice/articles/homicideinenglandandwales/yearendingmarch2019

'Homicide in England and Wales: year ending March 2021' (2022) *Office for National Statistics*, [online] 10 February, Available from: https://www.ons.gov.uk/peoplepopulationandcommunity/crimeandjustice/articles/homicideinenglandandwales/yearendingmarch2021

Hopgood, S. (2013) *The Endtimes of Human Rights*, New York: Cornell University Press.

Hopkins, A.G. (2002) *Globalisation in World History*, London: Pimlico Publishing.

Horowitz, J. (2023) 'What happens when $2 trillion is sucked out of the global economy? It may not be pretty', *CNN Business*, [online] 19 May, Available from: https://edition.cnn.com/2023/05/19/economy/quantitative-tightening-global-impact/index.html

Horton, H. (2022) 'Calls to cut bonuses for UK water bosses until reservoirs built and leaks fixed', *The Guardian*, [online] 15 August, Available from: https://www.theguardian.com/environment/2022/aug/15/uk-water-boss-bonuses-reservoirs-built-leaks-fixed

Howarth, R.W. and Jacobson, M.Z. (2021) 'How green is blue hydrogen?', *Energy Science & Engineering*, 9(10): 1676–87.

Hu, W. and Ley, A. (2023) 'Uber drivers say they are struggling: "this is not sustainable"', *The New York Times*, [online] 12 January, Available from: https://www.nytimes.com/2023/01/12/nyregion/cab-uber-lyft-drivers.html

REFERENCES

Hubble, S. and Bolton, P. (2020) 'Update on the sale of student loans', *House of Commons Library*, [online], Available from: https://commonslibrary.parliament.uk/research-briefings/cbp-8348/

Hutton, G., Shalchi, A. and Ward, M. (2022) 'Financial services: contribution to the UK economy'. *House of Commons Library*, [online] 1 September, Available from: https://commonslibrary.parliament.uk/research-briefings/sn06193/

'Identifying the separatists linked to the downing of MH17' (2019) *Bellingcat*, [online] 19 June, Available from: https://www.bellingcat.com/news/uk-and-europe/2019/06/19/identifying-the-separatists-linked-to-the-downing-of-mh17/

'Is Coca-Cola's latest promise really a step forward?' (2022) *Plastic Soup*, [online], 18 February, Available from: https://www.plasticsoupfoundation.org/en/2022/02/is-coca-colas-latest-promise-really-a-step-forward/

'Is your lobbyist failing on climate?' (2023) *F Minus*, [online], Available from: https://fminus.org/#database

Isaacson, W. (2011) *Steve Jobs*, London: Simon & Schuster.

Islam, R. (2002) 'Into the looking glass: what the media tell and why - an overview', in R. Islam (ed) *The Right to Tell: The Role of Mass Media in Economic Development*, World Bank Publications, pp 1–23.

Jenkins, S. (2021) 'Cameron predicted lobbying would be the next big scandal – now he's part of it', *The Guardian*, [online] 22 March, Available from: https://www.theguardian.com/commentisfree/2021/mar/22/david-cameron-lobbying-inquiry-covid-contracts-cronyism-allegations

Jensen, W.J. (2018) *A Peculiar Transition: Healing the Trauma of Mormon Faith Crisis* [Kindle Edition], Transworld Media.

Jewkes, Y. (2004) *Media and Crime*, London: Sage Publications.

Johnson, D. (2022) 'Russia must be held accountable for committing genocide in Ukraine', *Atlantic Council*, [online] 31 August, Available from: https://www.atlanticcouncil.org/blogs/ukrainealert/russia-must-be-held-accountable-for-committing-genocide-in-ukraine/

Johnson-Cartee, K.S. and Copeland, G. (2004) *Strategic Political Communication: Rethinking Social Influence, Persuasion, and Propaganda*, Oxford: Rowman & Littlefield Publishers, Inc.

Johnston, A. (2008) *Zizek's Ontology: A Transcendental Materialist Theory of Subjectivity*, Evanston: North-Western University Press.

Jones, L. (2019) *Lee Jones – The Seven Deadly Sins of Marketisation in British Higher Education, Brave New Europe*, Available from: https://braveneweurope.com/lee-jones-the-seven-deadly-sins-of-marketisation-in-british-higher-education

Jones, L. (2021) 'Shein suppliers' workers doing 75-hour week, finds probe', *BBC News*, [online] 12 November, Available from: https://www.bbc.co.uk/news/business-59245708

Jones, M. (2022) 'UK paid more than £300m by Saudi military for weapons systems training', *Action on Armed Violence*, [online] 1 September, Available from: https://aoav.org.uk/2022/uk-paid-more-than-300m-by-saudi-milit ary-for-weapons-systems-training/

Jordan D. and Conway Z. (2023) 'Amazon strikes: workers claim their toilet breaks are timed'. *BBC News*, [online] 25 January, Available from: https:// www.bbc.co.uk/news/business-64384287

'Josephine Hamilton and Others vs Post Office Limited' (2021) *The Court of Appeal*, 23 April, Royal Courts of Justice: London. Case No. 202001558 B3, [online], Available from: https://www.judiciary.uk/judgments/ hamilton-others-v-post-office-limited/

Julien, P. (1995) *Jacques Lacan's Return to Freud: The Real, the Symbolic, and the Imaginary*, London: New York University Press.

Kara, S. (2022) *Cobalt Red: How the Blood of the Congo Powers Our Lives*, New York: Saint Martin's Griffin.

Keefe, P.R. (2017) 'Why corrupt bankers avoid jail', *The New Yorker*, [online] 24 July, Available from: https://www.newyorker.com/magazine/2017/07/ 31/why-corrupt-bankers-avoid-jail

Kelly, A. (2019) 'Apple and Google named in US lawsuit over Congolese child cobalt mining deaths', *The Guardian*, [online] 16 December, Available from: https://www.theguardian.com/global-development/2019/dec/16/apple- and-google-named-in-us-lawsuit-over-congolese-child-cobalt-mining-deaths

Kelly, C., Lynes, A. and Dean-Hart, M. (2022) ' "Graze culture" and serial murder: brushing up against "familiar monsters" in the wake of 9/11' in C. O'Callaghan and S. Fanning (eds) *Serial Killers on Screen*, London: Palgrave Macmillan, pp 295–321.

Kennedy, S. (2021) 'Revealed: fossil fuel companies lobby UK government for gas "compromise" ahead of COP26', *4 News*, [online] 7 July, Available from: https://www.channel4.com/news/revealed-fossil-fuel-companies- lobby-uk-government-for-gas-compromise-ahead-of-cop26

King J. (2018) 'How Black Lives Matter has changed US politics', *New Internationalist*, [online] 5 March, Available from: https://newint.org/featu res/2018/03/01/black-lives-matter-changed-politics

Kirby, P. (2022) 'Brittney Griner: Russia frees US basketball star in swap with arms dealer Viktor Bout', *BBC News*, [online] 9 December, Available from: https://www.bbc.co.uk/news/world-europe-63905112

Kirk, T. (2013) *The Longman Companion to Nazi Germany*, London: Routledge.

Kirk-Wade, E. (2023) 'UK arms exports: statistics', *House of Commons Library*, [online] 16 January, Available from: https://commonslibrary.parliament. uk/research-briefings/cbp-8310/#:~:text=The%20most%20common%20t ype%20of,in%20real%20terms%202022%20prices)

Klein, N. (2014) *This Changes Everything: Capitalism vs. the Climate*, New York: Simon & Schuster.

REFERENCES

Klein, N. (2020) *No Logo*, Hammersmith: Flamingo.

Kollewe, J. and Wearden, G. (2023) 'Contingency plans being drawn up for Thames Water collapse', *The Guardian*, [online], 28 June, Available from: https://www.theguardian.com/business/2023/jun/28/contingency-plans-reportedly-being-drawn-up-for-thames-water-collapse

Kristen K.M. and Monazzam, N. (2023) 'Private prisons in the United States', *The Sentencing Project*, [online], 15 June, Available from: https://www.sentencingproject.org/reports/private-prisons-in-the-united-states/

Kuldova, T., Østbø, J. and Raymen, T. (2024) *Luxury and Corruption: Challenging the Anti-Corruption Consensus*, Bristol: Policy Press.

Kumar, N. (2022) 'An army of faceless suits is taking over the $4 Trillion hedge fund world', *Bloomberg*, [online] 20 January, Available from: https://www.bloomberg.com/news/features/2022-01-30/top-hedge-funds-citadel-millennium-shift-4-trillion-sector-from-rock-stars?leadSource=uverify%20wall

Kumar, R. (2021) 'How China uses the news media as a weapon in its propaganda war against the West', *Reuters Institute*, [online] 2 November, Available from: https://reutersinstitute.politics.ox.ac.uk/news/how-china-uses-news-media-weapon-its-propaganda-war-against-west

Kuo, L. (2019) 'China bans 23m from buying travel tickets as part of "social credit" system', *The Guardian*, [online] 1 March, Available from: https://www.theguardian.com/world/2019/mar/01/china-bans-23m-discredited-citizens-from-buying-travel-tickets-social-credit-system

Kynaston, D. (2020) *Till Time's Last Sand: A History of the Bank of England 1694–2013*, London: Bloomsbury Publishing.

Lacan, J. (1973) *Four Fundamental Concepts of Psycho-Analysis*, London: Penguin.

Lacan, J. (1997) *Ecrits: A Selection*, Abingdon: Routledge.

Lacey, N. and Zedner, L. (2012) 'Legal constructions of crime', in M. Maguire, R. Morgan and R. Reiner (eds) *The Oxford Handbook of Criminology*, 5th edn, Oxford: Oxford University Press, pp 159–81.

Lanier, J. (2019) *Ten Arguments for Deleting Your Social Media Accounts Right Now*, London: Vintage.

Lankov, A. (2022) 'What's in it for the working man? Why North Koreans show up for low-wage jobs', *NK News*, [online] 16 February, Available from: https://www.nknews.org/2022/02/whats-in-it-for-the-working-man-why-north-koreans-show-up-for-low-wage-jobs/

Lapira, T.M. and Thomas, H.F. (2017) *Revolving Door Lobbying: Public Service, Private Influence, and the Unequal Representation of Interests*, Kansas: University Press of Kansas.

'Largest companies by market cap' (2023) *CompaniesMarketCap*, [online], Available from: https://companiesmarketcap.com/

Latzer, B. (2021) *The Roots of Violent Crime in America: From the Gilded Age through the Great Depression*, Baton Rouge: LSU Press

Laville, S. and Carrington, D. (2023) 'Thames Water pipe leaks at highest level in five years, FoI reveals', *The Guardian*, [online] 22 June, Available from: https://www.theguardian.com/environment/2023/jun/22/thames-water-pipe-leaks-at-highest-level-in-five-years-foi-reveals

Laville, S. and Horton, H. (2023) 'Water firms discharged raw sewage 300,000 times last year, court hears', *The Guardian*, [online] 4 July, Available from: https://www.theguardian.com/environment/2023/jul/04/thames-water-fined-33m-for-pumping-sewage-into-rivers

Laville, S. (2022) 'Jail water firm bosses over "appalling" pollution, says Environment Agency', *The Guardian*, [online] 14 July, Available from: https://www.theguardian.com/environment/2022/jul/14/jail-water-firm-bosses-over-appalling-pollution-says-environment-agency#:~:text=The%20agency%20said%20water%20firms,fines%20for%20breaching%20environmental%20laws

Lavoipierre, A., Smiley, S. and Evlin, L. (2018) 'Children mining cobalt in slave-like conditions as global demand for battery material surges', *Australian Broadcasting Corporation*, [online] 24 July, Available from: https://www.abc.net.au/news/2018-07-25/cobalt-child-labour-smartphone-batteries-congo/10031330

Lawrence, E.O. (2016) 'The missing links: towards the effective management and control of corruption in Nigeria, Africa and the Global South', *International Journal of Criminology and Sociology*, 5: 25–40.

'Lawsuit settled over heart valve implicated in about 300 deaths' (1992) *The New York Times*, [online] 25 January, Available from: https://www.nytimes.com/1992/01/25/us/lawsuit-settled-over-heart-valve-implicated-in-about-300-deaths.html

Lea, J. and Young, J. (1984) *What Is to Be Done About Law and Order?* New York: Penguin.

Leigh, D. and Evans, R. (2010) 'BAE admits guilt over corrupt arms deals', *The Guardian*, [online] 6 February, Available from: https://www.theguardian.com/world/2010/feb/05/bae-systems-arms-deal-corruption

Lenzer, J. (2006) 'Secret report surfaces showing that Pfizer was at fault in Nigerian drug tests', *BMJ*, 332(7552): 1233.

Lepiarz, J. (2020) 'The German company that enabled the Holocaust', *DW News*, [online] 23 January, Available from: https://www.dw.com/en/the-german-company-that-enabled-the-holocaust/a-52128223

Lerner, M. (2018) '10 years later: how the housing market has changed since the crash', *The Washington Post*, [online] 4 October, Available from: https://www.washingtonpost.com/news/business/wp/2018/10/04/feature/10-years-later-how-the-housing-market-has-changed-since-the-crash/

Lessig, L. (2012) *Republic, Lost: How Money Corrupts Congress – and a Plan to Stop It*, New York: Twelve.

Lessig, L. (2018) *America, Compromised*, Chicago: University of Chicago Press.

REFERENCES

Levi, M (2022) 'Lawyers as money laundering enablers? An evolving and contentious relationship', *Global Crime*, 23(2): 126–47.

Levi, M. (2006) 'The media construction of financial white-collar crimes', *The British Journal of Criminology*, 46(6): 1037–57.

Lewis, J. (2004) *Too Close for Comfort? The Role of Embedded Reporting During the 2003 Iraq War: Summary Report.* Cardiff University.

Lewis, M., Herron, L., Chatfield, M.D., Tan, R.C., Dale, A., Nash, S. and Lee, A.J. (2023) 'Healthy food prices increased more than the prices of unhealthy options during the COVID-19 pandemic and concurrent challenges to the food system', *International Journal of Environmental Research and Public Health*, 20(4): 3146.

Leyton, E. (1986) *Hunting Humans: The Rise of the Modern Multiple Murderer*, Toronto: McClelland and Stewart.

Li, Z., Friedman, E. and Ren, H. (2016) *China on Strike: Narratives of Worker's Resistance*, Chicago: Haymarket Books.

Lim, J. (2015) *Leader Symbols and Personality Cult in North Korea*, London: Routledge.

Lin, L.Y. and Milhaupt, C.J. (2021) 'China's Corporate Social Credit System: The Dawn of Surveillance State Capitalism?' *European Corporate Governance Institute*, Law Working Paper No. 610/2021.

Lindsay, J.A., Boghossian, P. and Pluckrose, H. (2018) 'Academic grievance studies and the corruption of scholarship', *Areo Magazine*, 2 October, p 2018.

Lineker, G. (2023a) 'Good heavens, this is beyond awful. https://t.co/f0f tgwxbwp', *Twitter*, Available from: https://twitter.com/GaryLineker/sta tus/1633094764865126400?ref_src=twsrc%5Etfw%7Ctwcamp%5Etwe etembed%7Ctwterm%5E1633094764865126400%7Ctwgr%5E%7Ctw con%5Es1_&ref_url=https%3A%2F%2Fwww.goodto.com%2Fentert ainment%2Fwhat-did-gary-lineker-say

Lineker, G. (2023b) 'There is no huge influx. we take far fewer refugees than other major European countries. this is just an immeasurably cruel policy directed at the most vulnerable people in language that is not dissimilar to that used by Germany in the 30s, and I'm out of order?', *Twitter*, Available from: https://twitter.com/GaryLineker/status/1633111662352891 908?ref_src=twsrc%5Etfw%7Ctwcamp%5Etweetembed%7Ctwt erm%5E1633111662352891908%7Ctwgr%5E89a13b11fbb83812951eb3d0e 90c5f7c08bf710a%7Ctwcon%5Es1_&ref_url=https%3A%2F%2Fwww. sportingnews.com%2Fsg%2Ffootball%2Fnews%2Fgary-lineker-bbc-motd-controversy-tweet-explained%2Fbmfqfh5gwrlst1hhedwcxtrz

Liu, C. (2019) 'Multiple social credit systems in China', *Economic Sociology: The European Electronic Newsletter*, 21(1): 22–32.

Liu, J. (2022) 'China's Zhengzhou, home to world's largest iPhone factory, ends Covid lockdown. Other cities do the same', *CNN Business*, [online] 30 November, Available from: https://edition.cnn.com/2022/11/30/tech/china-apple-foxconn-zhengzhou-lifts-lockdown-hnk-intl/index.html

'Living Planet Report 2020' (2020) *WWF*, [online] 10 September, Available from: https://www.worldwildlife.org/publications/living-planet-report-2020

Loader, I. and Sparks, R. (2011) *Public Criminology?*, London: Routledge.

Lopez-Claros, A., Dahl, A.L. and Groff, M. (2020) *Global Governance and the Emergence of Global Institutions for the 21st Century*, Cambridge: Cambridge University Press.

Lord of War (2005) [Film] Directed by Andrew Niccol. United States: Entertainment Manufacturing Company.

Lynch, M. (2011) 'Crack pipes and policing: a case study of institutional racism and remedial action in Cleveland', *Law & Policy*, 33(2): 179–214.

Lynch, M.J. (2020) 'Green criminology and environmental crime: criminology that matters in the age of global ecological collapse', *Journal of White Collar and Corporate Crime*, 1(1): 50–61.

Lynes, A., Yardley, E. and Ntanos, L. (2021) *Making Sense of Homicide: A Student Textbook*, Hampshire: Waterside Press.

Lynes, A. and Wragg, E. (2023) '"Smile for the camera": online warehouse tours as a form of dark tourism within the era of late capitalism', *Tourism and Hospitality Research*, https://doi.org/10.1177/14673584231173507

Ma, A. (2018) 'China has started ranking citizens with a creepy "social credit" system – here's what you can do wrong and the embarrassing ways you can be punished', *Insider*, [online] 8 April, Available from: https://www.insider.com/china-social-credit-system-punishments-and-rewards-explained-2018-4

Machin, D. and Mayr, A. (2012) 'Corporate crime and the discursive deletion of responsibility: a case study of the Paddington rail crash', *Crime, Media, Culture*, 9(1): 63–82.

Magdy, S. (2023) 'Report: arms supplied by UK, US killed civilians in Yemen', *AP News*, [online] 11 January, Available from: https://apnews.com/article/politics-united-kingdom-yemen-government-saudi-arabia-a8dd0a5e5d2f42f1ae4b0e6d309f96cb

Maizland, L. (2022) 'China's repression of Uyghurs in Xinjiang', *Council on Foreign Relations*, [online] 22 September, Available from: https://www.cfr.org/backgrounder/china-xinjiang-uyghurs-muslims-repression-genocide-human-rights

Mares, D.M. (2009) 'Civilization, economic change, and trends in interpersonal violence in western societies', *Theoretical Criminology*, 13(4): 1362–4806.

Marples, A. (2020) 'The South Sea Bubble of 1720', The National Archives, [online] 18 September, Available from: https://blog.nationalarchives.gov.uk/the-south-sea-bubble-of-1720/

Martine, L. (2007) 'The banality of evil', *SciencePo*, [online] 3 November, Available from: https://www.sciencespo.fr/mass-violence-war-massa cre-resistance/en/document/banality-evil.html#:~:text=Arendt's%20t erm%2C%20the%20expression%20%E2%80%9Cbanality,evil)%20w ere%20committed%20and%20the

Marx, K. (1867) *Capital, Volume One, Part One: Commodities and Money*, Available from: http://www.marxists.org/archive/marx/works/1867-c1/ ch01.htm

Marx, K. and Engels, F. (1967) *The Communist Manifesto*, London: Penguin.

'Mass shootings in 2023' (2023) *Gun Violence Archive*, [online], Available from: https://www.gunviolencearchive.org/reports/mass-shooting

Matilal, S. and Höpfl, H. (2009) 'Accounting for the Bhopal disaster: footnotes and photographs', *Accounting, Auditing & Accountability Journal*, 22(6): 953–72.

Matsakis, L. (2019) 'How the West got China's social credit system wrong', *Wired*, [online] 29 July, Available from: https://www.wired.com/story/ china-social-credit-score-system/

Mattei, U. and Nader, L. (2008) *Plunder: When the Rule of Law is Illegal*, Oxford: Wiley-Blackwell.

Mayer, D., Cava, A. and Baird, C. (2014) 'Crime and punishment (or the lack thereof) for financial fraud in the subprime mortgage meltdown: reasons and remedies for legal and ethical lapses', *American Business Law Journal*, 51(3): 515–97.

McCarthy N. (2018) 'Report: Amazon workers skip toilet breaks to keep their jobs', *Statista*, [online] 17 April, Available from: https://www.statista.com/chart/ 13554/report_- amazon-workers-skip-toilet-breaks-to-keep-their-jobs/

McClanahan, B., Brisman, A. and South, N. (2015) 'Privatization, pollution and power: a green criminological analysis of present and future global water crises', in G. Barak (ed) *The Routledge International Handbook of the Crimes of the Powerful*, Abingdon: Routledge, pp 223–35.

McCully, E. (2014) *Ida M. Tarbell: the woman who challenged big business—and won!* (1st edn), Boston: Clarion Books.

McDonald, H. (2014) 'Primark denies purchasing clothes made in forced labour camps or prisons', *The Guardian*, [online] 25 June, Available from: https://www.theguardian.com/business/2014/jun/25/primark-den ies-purchasing-clothes-made-forced-labour-camps-prisons

'McDonald's workers speak out over sexual abuse claims' (2023) *BBC News*, [online] 18 July, Available from: https://www.bbc.co.uk/news/business-65388445

McGann, J.G. (2016) *The Fifth Estate: Think Tanks, Public Policy, and Governance*, Washington: Brookings Institution Press.

McGreal, C. (2007) 'Arms deal investigators probe BAE payments to South African', *The Guardian*, [online] 6 January, Available from: https://www. theguardian.com/world/2007/jan/06/bae.armstrade

McLynn, F. (1989) *Crime and Punishment in Eighteenth Century England*, London: Routledge.

McMillen, A. (2017) '"His death still hurts": the Pfizer anti-smoking drug ruled to have contributed to suicide', *The Guardian*, [online] 15 September, Available from: https://www.theguardian.com/business/2017/sep/15/his-death-still-hurts-the-pfizer-anti-smoking-drug-ruled-to-have-contributed-to-suicide#:~:text=In%20the%20US%2C%20Pfizer%20made,raised%20the%20risk%20of%20suicide

Meek, J. (2014) *Private Island: Why Britain Now Belongs to Someone Else*, London: Verso.

Merchant, B. (2017) 'Life and death in Apple's forbidden city', *The Guardian*, [online] 18 June, Available from: https://www.theguardian.com/technology/2017/jun/18/foxconn-life-death-forbidden-city-longhua-suicide-apple-iphone-brian-merchant-one-device-extract

'Mexico's long war: drugs, crime, and the cartels' (2022) *Council on Foreign Relations*, [online] 7 September, Available from: https://www.cfr.org/backgrounder/mexicos-long-war-drugs-crime-and-cartels

Micha, R., Peñalvo, J.L., Cudhea, F., Imamura, F., Rehm, C.D. and Mozaffarian, D. (2017) 'Association between dietary factors and mortality from heart disease, stroke, and Type 2 Diabetes in the United States', *JAMA*, 317(9): 912–24.

Michalowksi, R. and Kramer, R. (2006) *State-Corporate Crime: Wrongdoing at the Intersection of Business and Government*, New Brunswick: Rutgers University Press.

Mills, C.W. (1956) *The Power Elite*, Oxford: Oxford University Press.

Mills, T. (2016) *The BBC: Myth of a Public Service*, London: Verso.

Milmo, C. (2023) 'Russia-Ukraine war: how Putin's oligarchs are supplied with luxury Western goods despite sanctions', *iNews*, [online] 26 May, Available from: https://inews.co.uk/news/russia-ukraine-war-putins-oligarchs-supplied-luxury-western-goods-despite-sanctions-2365727

Milne, R. and Winter, D. (2018) 'Danske: anatomy of a money laundering scandal', *Financial Times*, [online] 19 December, Available from: https://www.ft.com/content/519ad6ae-bcd8-11e8-94b2-17176fbf93f5

Mirowski, P. and Plehwe, D. (2015) *The Road from Mont Pèlerin: The Making of the Neoliberal Thought Collective* (2nd edn), Harvard: Harvard University Press.

Molina, B. (2014) 'iPhone 13: yes, people still wait in line to get the new iPhone', *USA Today Tech*, [online], Available from: https://eu.usatoday.com/story/tech/2021/09/24/iphone-13-here-consumers-line-up-get-apples-new-smartphone/5841673001/

Monbiot, G. (2016) 'Neoliberalism: the ideology at the root of all our problems', *The Guardian*, [online] 15 April, Available from: https://www.theguardian.com/books/2016/apr/15/neoliberalism-ideology-problem-george-monbiot

REFERENCES

'Money laundering and illicit finance' (ND) *National Crime Agency*, [online], Available from: https://www.nationalcrimeagency.gov.uk/what-we-do/crime-threats/money-laundering-and-illicit-finance

'Money laundering cases registered at Agency doubled in last six years according to Eurojust's new report' (2022) *European Union Agency for Criminal Justice Cooperation*, [online] 20 October, Available from: https://www.eurojust.europa.eu/news/money-laundering-cases-registered-agency-doubled-last-6-years-according-eurojusts-new-report#:~:text=Due%20to%20its%20clandestine%20nature,Euros%20%2D%20is%20laundered%20each%20year

Moore, J.M. (2015) 'The "New Punitiveness" in the context of British imperial history', *Criminal Justice Matters*, 101(1): 10–13.

Morrell, L. (2016) 'Amazon comes under fire for stress placed on its delivery drivers', *eDelivery*, [online] 11 November, Available from: https://edelivery.net/2016/11/amazon-comes-fire-stress-placed-delivery-drivers/

Muncie, J. (2013) 'Social harm', in E. McLaughlin and J. Muncie (eds) *The Sage Dictionary of Criminology*, 3rd edn, London: Sage, pp 430–32.

Murphy, R. (2023) *Cut the Crap: Accounting for Clean Water*, Cambridgeshire: Corporate Accountability Network Ltd.

Murray, A. (2022) 'Cobalt mining: the dark side of the renewable energy transition', *EARTH.ORG*, [online] 27 September, Available from: https://earth.org/cobalt-mining/

'Myanmar: UN expert urges Security Council resolution to stop weapons fuelling spike in military attacks on civilians' (2022) *United Nations*, [online] 22 February, Available from: https://www.ohchr.org/en/press-releases/2022/02/myanmar-un-expert-urges-security-council-resolution-stop-weapons-fueling?LangID=E&NewsID=28142

Myers, M. (2017) *Student Revolt; Voices of the Austerity Generation*, London: Pluto.

National Institute on Drug Abuse (ND), [online], Available from: https://nida.nih.gov/

National Union of Students (2013) 'Postgraduates who teach', *National Union of Students*, [online], Available from: https://www.nusconnect.org.uk/resources/postgraduates-who-teach-2013

Neate, R. (2016) 'Welcome to Jail Inc: how private companies make money off US prisons', *The Guardian*, [online] 16 June, Available from: https://www.theguardian.com/us-news/2016/jun/16/us-prisons-jail-private-healthcare-companies-profit

Neate, R. (2022) '"Extra level of power": billionaires who have bought up the media', *The Guardian*, [online] 3 May, Available from: https://www.theguardian.com/news/2022/may/03/billionaires-extra-power-media-ownership-elon-musk

Neate, R. and Rankin, J. (2018) 'Danske Bank money laundering "is biggest scandal in Europe"', *The Guardian*, [online] 20 September, Available from: https://www.theguardian.com/business/2018/sep/20/danske-bank-money-laundering-is-biggest-scandal-in-europe-european-commission

Newburn, T. (2016) 'Social disadvantage, crime, and punishment', in H. Dean and L. Platt (eds) *Social Advantage and Disadvantage*, Oxford: Oxford University Press, pp 322–40.

Newton C. (2020) 'Amazon's poor treatment of workers is catching up to it during the coronavirus crisis', *The Verge*, [online], Available from: https://www.theverge.com/interface/2020/4/1/21201162/amazon-delivery-delays-coronavirus-worker-strikes

'Nigeria: Shell complicit in the arbitrary executions of Ogoni Nine as writ served in Dutch court' (2017) *Amnesty International*, [online] 29 June, Available from: https://www.amnesty.org/en/latest/press-release/2017/06/shell-complicit-arbitrary-executions-ogoni-nine-writ-dutch-court/

Nkulu, C.B.L., Casas, L., Haufroid, V., De Putter, T., Saenen, N.D. Kayembe-Kitenge, T. et al (2018) 'Sustainability of artisanal mining of cobalt in DR Congo', *Nature Sustainability*, 1: 495–504.

Noelle-Neumann, E. (1974) 'The spiral of silence a theory of public opinion', *Journal of Communication*, 24(2): 43–51.

Nolan, P. (2012) 'Is China buying the world?', *Challenge*, 55(2): 108–18.

Norris, P. (2023) 'Cancel culture: Myth or reality?', *Political Studies*, 71(1): 145–74.

'North Korea' (ND) *Reporters without Borders*, [online], Available from: https://rsf.org/en/country/north-korea

'North Korea sentences two South Korean journalists to death in absentia' (2017) *Committee to Protect Journalists*, [online] 1 September, Available from: https://cpj.org/2017/09/north-korea-sentences-two-south-korean-journalists/

Norton-Taylor, R. (2012) 'Iraq arms prosecutions led to string of miscarriages of justice', *The Guardian*, [online] 9 November, Available from: https://www.theguardian.com/world/defence-and-security-blog/2012/nov/09/arms-iraq-saddam-hussein

'Nosedive' (2016) *Black Mirror*.

Nurse, A. (2020) 'Masculinities and animal harm', *Men and Masculinities*, 23(5): 908–26.

O'Connor, S. (2013) 'Amazon unpacked', *Financial Times*, [online] 8 February, Available from: http://wtf.tw/ref/oconnor.pdf

'OHCHR assessment of human rights concerns in the Xinjiang Uyghur Autonomous Region, People's Republic of China' (2022) *United Nations Human Rights Office of the High Commissioner*, [online] 31 August, Available from: https://www.ohchr.org/sites/default/files/documents/countries/2022-08-31/22-08-31-final-assesment.pdf

Oksala, J. (2011) 'Violence and neoliberal governmentality', *Constellations*, 18(3): 474–86, Oxford: Blackwell Publishing Ltd.

Omoto, C. and Lurquin, P. (2015) *Genetics & Society*, Morrisville: Lulu Publishing.

Oreskes, N. and Conway, E.M. (2011) *Merchants of Doubt: How a Handful of Scientists Obscured the Truth on Issues from Tobacco Smoke to Global Warming*, London: Bloomsbury.

Otamonga, J. and Poté, J.W. (2020) 'Abandoned mines and artisanal and small-scale mining in Democratic Republic of the Congo (DRC): survey and agenda for future research', *Journal of Geochemical Exploration*, 208: 106394.

Pallister, D. (2006) 'The arms deal they called the dove: how Britain grasped the biggest prize', *The Guardian*, [online] 15 December, Available from: https://www.theguardian.com/world/2006/dec/15/bae.saudiarabia

Parlapiano, A., Playford, A. and Kelly, K. (2022) 'These 97 members of Congress reported trades in companies influenced by their committees', *The New York Times*, [online] 13 September, Available from: https://www.nytimes.com/interactive/2022/09/13/us/politics/congress-memb ers-stock-trading-list.html

Parr, A. (2014) *The Wrath of Capital: Neoliberalism and Climate Change Politics*, New York: Columbia University Press.

Parsons, T. (1967) *Sociological Theory and Modern Society*, New York: The Free Press.

Pastor, J.F. (2003) *The Privatization of Police in America: An Analysis and Case Study*, Jefferson: McFarland.

Paul, H. (2010) *The South Sea Bubble an Economic History of Its Origins and Consequences*, London: Routledge.

Pauli, B.J. (2020) 'The Flint water crisis', *WIREs Water*, 7(3): e1420.

Pearce, F. (1976) *Crimes of the Powerful*, London: Pluto.

Pearce, F. and Tombs, S. (1989) 'Bhopal: union carbide and the hubris of the capitalist technocracy', *Social Justice*, 16(2): 116–45.

Pearce, F. and Tombs, S. (2012) *Bhopal: Flowers at the Altar of Profit and Power*, North Somercotes: CrimeTalk Books.

Peat, J. (2023) 'New BBC chairman donated to organisations advocating for privatisation of BBC – reports', *The London Economic*, [online] 27 February, Available from: https://www.thelondoneconomic.com/news/new-bbc-chairman-donated-to-organisations-advocating-for-privatisat ion-of-bbc-reports-344206/

Pecci, K.L., Blair, P.W. and Budris, K.P. (2022) 'The big beverage playbook for avoiding responsibility', *Conservation Law Foundation*, [online], Available from: https://www.clf.org/wp-content/uploads/2022/02/2022-02-09-CLF-Beverage-Playbook-Report.pdf

Pegg, D., Makortoff, K., Chulov, M., Lewis, P. and Harding, L. (2022) 'Revealed: Credit Suisse leak unmasks criminals, fraudsters and corrupt politicians', *The Guardian*, [online] 20 February, Available from: https://www.theguardian.com/news/2022/feb/20/credit-suisse-secrets-leak-unmasks-criminals-fraudsters-corrupt-politicians

Pemberton, S. (2008) 'Where next? The future of the social harm perspective', in D. Dorling, D. Gordon, P. Hillyard, C. Pantazis, S. Pemberton and S. Tombs (eds) *Criminal Obsessions: Why Harm Matters More than Crime*, 2nd edn, London: Centre for Crime and Justice Studies, pp 70–91.

Pemberton, S.A. (2015) *Harmful Societies Understanding Social Harm*, Bristol: Policy Press.

Penney, J. and Dadas, C. (2014) '(Re)Tweeting in the service of protest: digital composition and circulation in the Occupy Wall Street movement', *New Media & Society*, 16(1): 74–90.

Perkel, C. (2011) 'Occupy Canada protesters say much already accomplished but much still to do', *Global News*, [online] 23 October, Available from: https://globalnews.ca/news/169026/occupy-canada-protesters-say-much-already-accomplished-but-much-still-to-do-3/

Perlmutter, L. (2022) '"It's plunder": Mexico desperate for water while drinks companies use billions of litres', *The Guardian*, [online] 28 July, Available from: https://www.theguardian.com/global-development/2022/jul/28/water-is-the-real-thing-but-millions-of-mexicans-are-str uggling-without-it

Peterson, C.H., Rice, S.D., Short, J.W., Esler, D., Bodkin, J.L., Ballachey, B.E. and Irons, D.B. (2003) 'Long-term ecosystem response to Exxon Valdez oil spill', *Science*, 302(5653): 2082–6.

Peterson-Withorn, C. (2023) 'Forbes' 37th Annual World's Billionaires List: facts and figures 2023', *Forbes*, [online] 4 April, Available from: https://www.forbes.com/sites/chasewithorn/2023/04/04/forbes-37th-annual-worlds-billionaires-list-facts-and-figures-2023/?sh=715c0ac477d7

Pfaff, J. (2017) *Locked In: The True Causes of Mass Incarceration—and How to Achieve Real Reform*, New York: Basic Books.

'Pfizer, BioNTech and Moderna making $1,000 profit every second while world's poorest countries remain largely unvaccinated' (2021) *Oxfam International*, [online] 16 November, Available from: https://www.oxfam.org/en/press-releases/pfizer-biontech-and-moderna-making-1000-pro fit-every-second-while-worlds-poorest

'Pharma lobbying held deep influence over opioid policies' (2016) *The Center for Public Integrity*, [online] 18 September, Available from: https://publ icintegrity.org/politics/state-politics/pharma-lobbying-held-deep-influe nce-over-opioid-policies/

'Phishing attacks up 50%, education sector most targeted: report' (2023) *The Economic Times*, [online] 18 April, Available from: https://economictimes.indiatimes.com/tech/technology/phishing-attacks-up-50-education-sector-most-targeted-report/articleshow/99584819.cms

Phoenix, J. (2021) 'Harassed, silenced & compared to a racist for my gender critical views', *CrowdJustice*, Available from: https://www.crowdjustice.com/case/harassed-silenced-for-my-gender-critical-views/

Pinker, S. (2011) *The Better Angels of our Nature*, London: Penguin.

Pomranz, M. (2022) 'Fast food chains are being sued over "forever chemicals" in their packaging', *Food & Wine*, [online] 18 April, Available from: https://www.foodandwine.com/news/mcdonalds-burger-king-forever-chemicals-packaging-lawsuit

Pretorius, D. (2022) *The Shepherds of Inequality and the Futility of Our Efforts to Stop Them*, Bloomington: Xlibris.

'Prevention of criminal use of the banking system for the purpose of money-laundering' (1988) *Bank for International Settlements*, [online] 28 December, Available from: https://www.bis.org/publ/bcbsc137.htm

'Proceedings and Debates of the 91st Congress Second Session: Volume 116 – Part 4' (1970) *Congressional Record*, Washington: United States Government Printing Office.

'Proven reoffending statistics: October to December 2019' (2021) Ministry of Justice, [online], 28 October, Available from: https://www.gov.uk/government/statistics/proven-reoffending-statistics-october-to-december-2019

Public Health England (2019) Annual Report and Accounts 2019–2020 (publishing.service.gov.uk)

Punch, M. (2000) 'Suite violence: why managers murder and corporations kill', *Crime, Law and Social Change*, 33: 243–80.

Rapanyane, M.B. (2021) 'Neocolonialism and new imperialism: unpacking the real story of China's Africa engagement in Angola, Kenya, and Zambia', *Journal of African Foreign Affairs*, 8(3): 89.

Raymen, T. (2018) 'Living in the end times through popular culture: an ultra-realist analysis of The Walking Dead as popular criminology', *Crime, Media, Culture*, 14(3): 429–47.

Ray, L. (2011) *Violence and Society*, London: Sage.

Raymen, T. (2019) 'The enigma of social harm and the barrier of liberalism: why Zemiology needs a theory of the good', *Justice, Power and Resistance*, 3(1): 133–63.

Raymen, T. (2022) *The Enigma of Social Harm: The Problem with Liberalism*, London: Routledge.

Raymen, T. and Smith, O. (2016) 'What's deviance got to do with it? Black Friday sales, violence and hyper-conformity', *British Journal of Criminology*, 56(2): 389–405.

Raymen, T. and Smith, O. (2019a) 'Deviant leisure: a critical criminological perspective for the twenty-first century', *Critical Criminology*, 27: 115–30.

Raymen, T. and Smith, O. (eds) (2019b) *Deviant Leisure: Criminological Perspectives on Leisure and Harm*, London: Palgrave Macmillan.

Raymen, T. and Kuldova, T.Ø. (2020) 'Clarifying ultra-realism: a response to Wood et al.', *Continental Thought & Theory*, 3(2): 244–63.

Recuero, R. (2015) 'Social media and symbolic violence', *Social Media & Society*, 1(1): 1–3.

Reiman, J. (1984) *The Rich Get Richer and the Poor Get Prison: Ideology, Class, and Criminal Justice* (10th edn), London: Routledge.

Reiman, J. and Leighton, P. (2013) *The Rich Get Richer and the Poor Get Prison: Thinking Critically About Class and Criminal Justice* (13th edn), London: Pearson Publishing.

Reindorf, Akua (2021) 'Review of the circumstances resulting in and arising from the cancellation of the Centre for Criminology seminar on Trans Rights, Imprisonment and the Criminal Justice System, scheduled to take place on 5 December 2019, and the arrangements for speaker invitations to the Holocaust Memorial Week event on the State of Antisemitism Today, scheduled for 30 January 2020 REPORT', 21 December 2020. Included as PDF in 'Review of two events involving external speakers'. 17 May 2021. Essex Blog, University of Essex, [online], Available from: https://www.essex.ac.uk/blog/posts/2021/05/17/review-of-two-events-with-externalspeaker

Ricciardelli, R., Phoenix, J. and Gacek, J. (2020) '"It's complicated": Canadian correctional officer recruits' interpretations of issues relating to the presence of transgender prisoners', *The Howard Journal of Criminal Justice*, 59(1): 86–104.

'Richard Sharp: who is the former BBC chairman?' (2023) *BBC News*, [online] 28 April, Available from: https://www.bbc.co.uk/news/uk-64368677

Riley, R. (2018) 'Sh-h-h. Snyder state update left out 75% drop in reading proficiency in Flint', *Detroit Free Press*, [online], Available from: https://eu.freep.com/story/news/columnists/rochelle-riley/2018/02/06/sh-h-h-snyder-state-update-left-out-75-drop-reading-proficiency-flint/1074057001/

Robinson, E. and Robbins, R.C. (ND) '1968: sources, abundance, and the fate of atmospheric pollutants', *Smoke & Fumes*, [online], Available from: https://www.smokeandfumes.org/documents/document16

Rodgers, D. (2021) 'Boohoo is now giving walking tours of its allegedly exploitative factories', *Dazed*, [online] 9 August, Available from: https://www.dazeddigital.com/fashion/article/53783/1/boohoo-tours-factories-fast-fashion-exploitation-leicester-supply-chain-plt

Roose, K. (2021) 'What is QAnon, the viral pro-Trump conspiracy theory', *The New York Times,* [online] 3 September, Available from: https://www.nytimes.com/article/what-is-qanon.html

Rosenfeld, J. (2019) 'US labor studies in the twenty-first century: understanding laborism without labor', *The Annual Review of Sociology*, 45: 449–65.

Ross, R. (2006) *Slaves to Fashion*, Michigan: University of Michigan Press.

Roth, C. (2021) *The War on Small Business: How the Government Used the Pandemic to Crush the Backbone of America*, New York: HarperCollins.

Roth, M.P. (2014) *An Eye for an Eye: A Global History of Crime and Punishment*, London: Reaktion Books Ltd.

Rothe, D. and Kauzlarich, D. (2016) *Crimes of the Powerful White-Collar Crime and Beyond* (2nd edn), London: Routledge.

Rothstein, R. (2017) *The Colour of Law: A Forgotten History of How Our Government Segregated America*, New York: Boni & Liveright.

Rousseau, J.J. (1990) *Rousseau, Judge of Jean-Jacques*, Hanover: Dartmouth College Press.

Ruggiero, V. and South, N. (2013) 'Green criminology and crimes of the economy: theory, research and praxis', *Critical Criminology*, 21: 359–73.

Ryan, F., Impiombato, D. and Pai, H.-T. (2022) 'Frontier influencers: the new face of China's propaganda', *Australian Strategic Policy Institute*, [online] 20 October, Available from: https://www.aspi.org.au/report/frontier-infl uencers

Sabbagh, D. (2023) 'Yemen: 87 civilians killed by UK and US weapons in just over a year', *The Guardian*, [online] 11 January, Available from: https://www.theguardian.com/world/2023/jan/11/yemen-87-civilians-killed-by-uk-and-us-weapons-in-just-over-a-year

Sainato, M. (2019) "Go back to work" outcry over deaths on Amazon's warehouse floor', *The Guardian*, [online], Available from: https://www.theg uardian.com/technology/2019/oct/17/amazon-warehouse-worker-deaths

Sainato, M. (2023) "It was traumatic": Uber, Lyft drivers decry low pay and unfair deactivations', *The Guardian*, [online] 10 March, Available from: https://www.theguardian.com/business/2023/mar/10/uber-lyft-dri ver-suspension-deactivation-pay

Sauer, P. (2022a) 'Putin grants Russian citizenship to US whistleblower Edward Snowden', *The Guardian*, [online] 26 September, Available from: https://www.theguardian.com/us-news/2022/sep/26/putin-gra nts-russian-citizenship-to-us-whistleblower-edward-snowden

Sauer, P. (2022b) 'Viktor Bout: the 'Lord of War' at centre of Brittney Griner prisoner swap', *The Guardian,* [online] 8 December, Available from: https://www.theguardian.com/world/2022/dec/08/viktor-bout-the-lord-of-war-at-centre-of-brittney-griner-prisoner-swap

Savini, D. (2018) 'Drivers delivering Amazon packages accused of devastating and deadly accidents', *CBS Chicago*, [online] 15 May, Available from: https://chicago.cbslocal.com/2018/05/15/amazon-drivers-accu sed-deadly-accidents/

Sayki, I. (2023) 'Despite record federal lobbying spending, the pharmaceutical and health product industry lost their biggest legislative bet in 2022', *Open Secrets*, [online] 2 February, Available from: https://www.opensecr ets.org/news/2023/02/despite-record-federal-lobbying-spending-the-pharmaceutical-and-health-product-industry-lost-their-biggest-legislat ive-bet-in-2022/

Schlosberg, J. (2016) 'Should he stay or should he go? Television and online news coverage of the Labour party in crisis', Media Reform Coalition, London: Birkbeck University of London.

Schmitt, C. (2013) *Dictatorship: From the Origin of the Modern Concept of Sovereignty to Proletarian Class Struggle*, Cambridge: Polity Press.

Schneider, N. (2014) *Brazilian Propaganda: Legitimising an Authoritarian Regime*, Florida: University Press of Florida.

Schubert, A. (1991) *The Credit-Anstalt Crisis of 1931*, Cambridge: Cambridge University Press.

Schüle, A. and Sowade, T. (2018) *Between Persecution and Participation Biography of a Bookkeeper at J. A. Topf & Söhne*, New York: Syracuse University Press.

Schwendinger, H. and Schwendinger, J. (1970) 'Defenders of order or guardians of human rights', *Issues in Criminology*, 5(2): 123–57.

Seltzer, M. (1998) *Serial Killers: Death and Life in America's 'Wound Culture'*, Abingdon: Routledge.

Shackel, P.A. (2019) 'How a 1897 massacre of Pennsylvania coal miners morphed from a galvanizing crisis to forgotten history', *Smithsonian Magazine*, [online] 13 March, Available from: https://www.smithsonian mag.com/history/how-1897-massacre-pennsylvania-coal-miners-morp hed-galvanizing-crisis-forgotten-history-180971695/

Shalchi, A. (2022) 'Research briefing: unexplained wealth orders', *House of Commons Library*, [online] 14 April, Available from: https://commonslibr ary.parliament.uk/research-briefings/cbp-9098/

Sharwood, S. (2022) 'China orders web operators to spring clean its entire internet', *The Register*, [online] 27 January, Available from: https://www. theregister.com/2022/01/27/china_internet_spring_clean/

Shein_Official (2022) 'TikTok of Shien Warehouse Centre', [online], Available from: https://www.tiktok.com/@shein_official/video/7182 745739720756481?lang=en

Shimo, A. (2018) 'While Nestlé extracts millions of litres from their land, residents have no drinking water', *The Guardian*, [online] 4 October, Available from: https://www.theguardian.com/global/2018/oct/04/onta rio-six-nations-nestle-running-water

Shirbon, E. (2009) 'French power brokers convicted over arms to Angola', *Reuters*, [online] 27 October, Available from: https://www.reuters.com/ article/idUSLR440868

Sikka, P. (2023) 'Water privatisation is a scandal', *Tribune*, [online] 11 July, Available from: https://tribunemag.co.uk/2023/07/water-privatisation-is-a-scandal#:~:text=The%20government%20sold%20water%20entities,classic%20private%20equity%20business%20model

Silva, F.R.D. (2016) 'Trans-imperial and cross -cultural networks for the slave trade, 1580s–1800s', in C. Antunes and A. Polonia (eds) *Beyond Empires: Global, Self-Organizing, Cross-Imperial Networks, 1500–1800*, Boston: Brill, pp 41–69.

Skeggs, B., Wood, H. and Thumim, N. (2008) 'Oh goodness I am watching reality TV: how methods make class in audience research'. *European Journal of Cultural Studies* 11(1): 5–24.

Slapper, G. and Tombs, S. (1999) *Corporate Crime*, Harlow: Longman.

Smith, I., Smith, R., Parker, G. and Smyth, J. (2021) 'Lex Greensill cited David Cameron in bungled Australian lobbying', *Financial Times*, [online] 9 April, Available from: https://www.ft.com/content/0cffbfed-d7c3-44d0-bf1b-183673a68be4

Smith, O. (2016) 'Deviant leisure: emerging perspectives on leisure, consumerism, and crime', *British Society of Criminology*, [online], Available from: http://www.britsoccrim.org/wp-content/uploads/2016/04/Deviant-Leisure-Oliver-Smith.pdf

Smith, P. (2023) 'Net worth of Primark in the United Kingdom (UK) 2010–2022', *Statista*, [online] 26 September, Available from: https://www.statista.com/statistics/866899/primark-stores-net-worth-united-kingdom-uk/

Smith, R.B. and Perry, M. (2022) 'Legal incentives and constraints on innovation: keeping the balance', *Proceedings of the 17th European Conference on Innovation and Entrepreneurship, ECIE*, 504–11.

'Socialist Constitution of the Democratic People's Republic of Korea' (2014) Pyongyang: Foreign Languages Publishing House.

'Something's not right here: poor working conditions persist at Apple supplier Pegatron' (2015) *China Labour Watch*, [online] 22 October, Available from: https://chinalabor.wpenginepowered.com/wp-content/uploads/2021/04/2015.10-Apple-Pegatron-report-FINAL-compress.pdf

Soron, D. (2007) 'Cruel weather: natural disasters and structural violence', *Transformations*, 14 [online], Available from: https://www.transformationsjournal. org/journal/issue_14/article_01.shtml

Souhami, A. (2011) 'Institutional racism and police reform: an empirical critique', *Policing and Society: An International Journal of Research and Policy*, 24(1): 1–21.

'South Africa arms deal that landed Zuma in court: what you need to know' (2018) *BBC News*, [online] 6 April, Available from: https://www.bbc.co.uk/news/world-africa-43668243

Speck, W.A. and Kilburn, M. (2006) 'Promoters of the South Sea Bubble (act. 1720)', *Oxford Dictionary of National Biography*, [online] 25 May, Available from: https://www.oxforddnb.com/display/10.1093/ref:odnb/9780198614128.001.0001/odnb-9780198614128-e-92793;jsessionid=BEDAA4D828C0ED34800FE2E7DDA3AB20

Spitzer, S. and Scull, A.T. (1977) 'Privatization and capitalist development: the case of the private police', *Social Problems*, 25(1): 18–29.

Squires, P. (2000) *Gun Culture or Gun Control? Firearms, Violence and Society*, London: Routledge.

Squires, P. (2014) 'The curious case of public subsidy for Britain's gun culture elite', *OpenDemocracy*, [online] 25 May, Available from: https://www.opendemocracy.net/en/shine-a-light/curious-case-of-public-subsidy-for-britains-gun-culture-elite/

Standing, G. (2011) *The Precariat: The New Dangerous Class*, London: Bloomsbury.

Stanko, E.A. (2001) 'The day to count: reflections on a methodology to raise awareness about the impact of domestic violence in the UK', *Criminology & Criminal Justice*, 1: 215–26.

'Statement from the Registrar and Secretary' (ND) *University of Essex*, [online], Available from: https://www.essex.ac.uk/student/registrar-and-secretary-statement

Staton, T. (2012) 'Pfizer expects to wrap up Prempro suits for $1.2B total', *Fierce Pharma*, [online] 19 June, Available from: https://www.fiercepharma.com/regulatory/pfizer-expects-to-wrap-up-prempro-suits-for-1-2b-total#:~:text=The%20price%20tag%20Pfizer's%20(%24,replacement%20drugs%20caused%20breast%20cancer

Stern, M. (2016) '"Black Mirror" creator Charlie Brooker on China's 'social credit' system and the rise of Trump', *Daily Beast*, [online] 13 April, Available from: https://www.thedailybeast.com/black-mirror-creator-charlie-brooker-on-chinas-social-credit-system-and-the-rise-of-trump

Stohl, R. and Grillot, S. (2009) *The International Arms Trade*, Cambridge: Polity Press.

Stohl, R., Schroeder, M. and Smith, D. (2007) *The Small Arms Trade*, Oxford: Oneworld Publications.

Stone, B. (2014) *The Everything Store: Jeff Bezos and the Age of Amazon*, London: Penguin.

Stone, J. (2021) 'British arms sales to Saudi Arabian regime three times higher than previously thought, investigation finds', *Independent*, [online] 14 July, Available from: https://www.independent.co.uk/news/uk/politics/saudi-arabia-uk-arms-sale-b1884158.html

Strugar, M. (2023) 'Fascinating Amazon statistics UK edition [2023]', *CyberCrew*, [online] 30 March, Available from: https://cybercrew.uk/blog/amazon-statistics-uk/

Sundberg, U. (2002) 'Durban: the third world conference against racism, racial discrimination, xenophobia and related intolerance', *International Journal of Criminal Law*, 73: 301–17.

Sutherland, E. (1949) *White Collar Crime*, New York: Dryden Press.

Sutter, J.D. (2012) 'Slavery's last stronghold', *CNN*, [online], Available from: https://edition.cnn.com/interactive/2012/03/world/mauritania.slaverys.last.stronghold/index.html#:~:text=It%20wasn't%20until%20five,country%20is%20slavery's%20last%20stronghold

Swift, A. (2013) 'Majority in U.S. still believe JFK killed in a conspiracy', *GALLUP*, [online] 15 November, Available from: https://news.gallup.com/poll/165893/majority-believe-jfk-killed-conspiracy.aspx

Taylor, A. and Gessen, K. (2011) *Occupy: Scenes from Occupied America*, London: Verso.

Taylor, A. and Smucker, J. (2021) 'Occupy Wall Street changed everything ten years later, the legacy of Zuccotti Park has never been clearer', *New York Magazine*, [online] 17 December, Available from: https://nymag.com/intelligencer/2021/09/occupy-wall-street-changed-everything.html

Taylor, I. (1999) *Crime in Context: A Critical Criminology of Market Societies*, New York: Routledge.

Taylor, P. and Cooper, C. (2008) '"It was absolute hell": inside the private prison', *Capital & Class*, 32(3): 3–30.

Terrell, E. (2020) 'The year is 1720 and the South Sea Company has some stock to sell', *Library of Congress Blogs*, [online] 14 December, Available from: https://blogs.loc.gov/inside_adams/2020/12/the-south-sea-bubble/

Teschke, B. (2019) 'The social origins of the 18th Century British Grand Strategy: a historical sociology of the peace of Utrecht', in A.H.A. Soons (ed) *The 1713 Peace of Utrecht and Its Enduring Effects*, Boston: Brill, pp 120–56.

'Thames Water ordered to pay record £20 million for river pollution' (2017) *Environment Agency*, [online] 22 March, Available from: https://www.gov.uk/government/news/thames-water-ordered-to-pay-record-20-million-for-river-pollution

'The contaminated blood scandal' (ND) *The Haemophilia Society*, [online], Available from: https://haemophilia.org.uk/public-inquiry/the-infected-blood-inquiry/the-contaminated-blood-scandal/#:~:text=In%20the%201970s%20and%201980s,unaware%20of%20their%20own%20infection

'The Dirty Dozen' (2019) *National Council for Occupational Safety and Health*, [online], Available from: https://nationalcosh.org/sites/default/files/uploads/2019_Dirty_Dozen.pdf

'The disappearing rainforests' (ND) *Rain-Tree*, [online], Available from: https://rain-tree.com/facts.htm#:~:text=Rainforests%20once%20covered%2014%25%20of,both%20developing%20and%20industrial%20countries

'The Export Control Joint Unit' (ND) *GOV.UK*, [online], Available from: https://www.gov.uk/government/organisations/export-control-joint-unit/about

'The Flint water crisis: systemic racism through the eyes of Flint' (2017) *Michigan Civil Rights Commission*, [online] 17 February, Available from: https://www.michigan.gov/-/media/Project/Websites/mdcr/mcrc/reports/2017/flint-crisis-report-edited.pdf

'The Global Risks Report 2023' (2023) *World Economic Forum*, [online], Available from: https://www3.weforum.org/docs/WEF_Global_Risks_Report_2023.pdf

The Haemophilia Society (ND) [online], Available from: https://haemophilia.org.uk/

'The Long Fuse: Misinformation and the 2020 Election' (2021) *Atlantic Council*, [online] 2 March, Available from: https://www.atlanticcouncil.org/in-depth-research-reports/the-long-fuse-eip-report-read/

'The National Anthem' (2011) *Black Mirror.*

'The rate of exploitation (the case of the iPhone)' (2019) *Tricontinental: Institute for Social Research Notebook Nº2*, [online], Available from: https: 190927_Notebook-2_EN_Final_Print.pdf

'The South African arms deal' (2020) *Corruption Tracker*, [online] 28 November, Available from: https://corruption-tracker.org/case/the-south-african-arms-deal

'The state of the world's forests 2020' (2020) *Food and Agriculture Organization of the United Nations*, Rome: FAO and UNEP.

The Wolf of Wall Street (2013) [Film] Directed by Martin Scorsese. United States: Paramount Pictures.

Tiernan, L. (2021) 'Ambulances called nearly 1,000 times to Amazon's UK warehouses', *WSWS*, [online] 25 November, Available from: https://www.wsws.org/en/articles/2021/11/26/amuk-n26.html

Tifft, L. (1995) 'Social harm definitions of crime', *The Critical Criminologist*, 7(1): 9–13.

Tillman, R.H., Pontell, H.N. and Black, W.K. (2018) *Financial Crime and Crises in the Era of False Profits*, Oxford: Oxford University Press.

Tingle, R. (2022) 'Inside the UK Boohoo warehouse where staff who compare themselves to "slaves" walk 7.5 miles a shift in "32C heat" – as MP compares "disturbing" conditions to a Victorian workhouse', *The Daily Mail*, [online] 23 November, Available from: https://www.dailymail.co.uk/news/article-11460849/Boohoo-faces-fresh-scandal-factory-working-conditions.html

Todd, R. (2017) 'Mil-Tec – a cautionary tale', *Ray Todd.blog*, [online], Available from: https://raytodd.blog/2018/07/12/mil-tec-a-cautionary-tale/

Tombs, S. (2019) 'Grenfell: the unfolding dimensions of social harm', *Justice, Power and Resistance*, 3(1): 61–88.

Tombs, S. (2020) 'Home as a site of state-corporate violence: Grenfell Tower, aetiologies and aftermaths', *The Howard Journal of Criminal Justice*, 59(2): 120–42.

REFERENCES

Tombs, S. (2021) 'Reframing regulation: "privatisation", de-democratisation and the end of social protection?', *OpenEdition Journals*, XXVI-2 [online], Available from: https://journals.openedition.org/rfcb/7826

Tombs, S. and Whyte, D. (2015) *The Corporate Criminal: Why Corporations Must be Abolished*, Abingdon: Routledge.

Tooze, A. (2018a) *Crashed: How a Decade of Financial Crises Changed the World*, London: Penguin.

Tooze, A. (2018b) 'The forgotten history of the financial crisis: what the world should have learned in 2008', *Foreign Affairs*, [online] 13 August, Available from: https://www.foreignaffairs.com/articles/world/2018-08-13/forgotten-history-financial-crisis

Touchberry, R. (2023) 'Fossil fuel lobbyists buoyed by green groups, liberal climate efforts', *The Washington Times*, [online] 5 July, Available from: https://www.washingtontimes.com/news/2023/jul/5/fossil-fuel-lobbyists-buoyed-green-groups-liberal-/

Treadwell, J., Briggs, D., Winlow, S. and Hall, S. (2013) 'Shopocalypse now: consumer culture and the English Riots of 2011', *British Journal of Criminology*, 53(1): 1–17.

Truss, L. (2020) 'The new fight for fairness – Liz Truss' speech at the Centre for Policy Studies', *Centre for Policy Studies*, [online] 17 December, Available from: https://capx.co/the-new-fight-for-fairness-liz-truss-speech-at-the-centre-for-policy-studies/

'Trust, equity and local action' (2022) World Disasters Report. International Federation of Red Cross and Red Crescent Societies: Geneva, [online], Available from: https://www.ifrc.org/sites/default/files/2023-03/2022_IFRC-WDR_EN.0.pdf.pdf

Tucker, P. (2021) 'Climate change is already disrupting the military. It will get worse, officials say', *Defence One*, [online] 10 August, Available from: https://www.defenseone.com/technology/2021/08/climate-change-already-disrupting-military-it-will-get-worse-officials-say/184416/

Tudor, K. (2018) 'Toxic sovereignty: understanding Fraud as the expression of special Liberty within late-capitalism', *Journal of Extreme Anthropology*, 2(2): 7–21.

Tun, M. (2018) 'Colonial cruelty: the expression and perpetuation of violence in Theodor de Bry's America', *Bulletin of Hispanic Studies*, 95(2): 145–62.

Tyler, I. (2013) *Revolting Subjects*, London: Zed Books.

'U.S. vulnerabilities to money laundering, drugs, and terrorist financing: HSBC case history' (2012) *Committee on Homeland Security and Governmental Affairs*, [online] 17 July, Available from: https://www.hsgac.senate.gov/wp-content/uploads/imo/media/doc/PSI%20REPORT-HSBC%20CASE%20HISTORY%20(9.6).pdf

'UK arms exports to Saudi Arabia' (2018) *Action on Armed Violence*, [online] 11 November, Available from: https://aoav.org.uk/2018/uk-arms-export-to-saudi-arabia/

'Ukraine: Putin announces special military operation in TV declaration' (2022) *BBC News*, [online] 24 February, Available from: https://www.bbc.co.uk/news/av/world-60505319

'Understanding the Libor scandal' (2016) *Council on Foreign Relations*, [online] 12 October, Available from: https://www.cfr.org/backgrounder/understanding-libor-scandal

'United Kingdom GDP' (2023) *Trading Economics*, [online], Available from: https://tradingeconomics.com/united-kingdom/gdp#:~:text=GDP%20in%20the%20United%20Kingdom%20is%20expected%20to%20reach%203080.00,macro%20models%20and%20analysts%20expectations

'United Nations Office for Disaster Risk Reduction: Annual Report 2020' (2020) *United Nations*, Geneva: United Nations Office for Disaster Risk Reduction.

United Nations (1948) *Convention on the Prevention and Punishment of the Crime of Genocide*, [online], Available from: https://www.ohchr.org/en/professionalinterest/pages/crimeofgenocide.aspx

'Universities must not allow a "decade of grade inflation to be baked into the system"' (2022) *Office for Students*, [online] 12 May, Available from: https://www.officeforstudents.org.uk/news-blog-and-events/press-and-media/universities-must-not-allow-a-decade-of-grade-inflation-to-be-baked-into-the-system/

'Universities told to end grade inflation' (2019) *GOV.UK*, [online] 24 March, Available from: https://www.gov.uk/government/news/universities-told-to-end-grade-inflation

'US gun control: what is the NRA and why is it so powerful?' (2023) *BBC News*, [online] 13 April, Available from: https://www.bbc.co.uk/news/world-us-canada-35261394

'Use Uber in cities around the world' (ND) *Uber*, [online], Available from: https://www.uber.com/global/en/cities/

Valukas, A.R. (2010) 'White-collar crime and economic recession', *University of Chicago Legal Forum*, Article 2, Available from: http://chicagounbound.uchicago.edu/uclf/vol2010/iss1/2?utm_source=chicagounbound.uchicago.edu%2Fuclf%2Fvol2010%2Fiss1%2F2&utm_medium=PDF&utm_campaign=PDFCoverPages

van Gelder, S. (2011) *This Changes Everything: Occupy Wall Street and the 99% Movement*, San Francisco: Berrett-Koehler Publishers, Inc.

Vanderklippe, N. (2018) 'Chinese blacklist an early glimpse of sweeping new social-credit control', *The Globe and Mail*, [online] 3 January, Available from: https://www.theglobeandmail.com/news/world/chinese-blacklist-an-early-glimpse-of-sweeping-new-social-credit-control/article37493300/

Varoufakis, Y. (2016) *And the Weak Suffer What They Must? Europe, Austerity and the Threat to Global Stability*, London: Vintage.

Verma, P. (2022) 'Raytheon quietly resumed political donations to election deniers, report finds', *The Boston Globe*, [online] 3 January, Available from: https://www.bostonglobe.com/2022/01/03/business/raytheon-quietly-resumed-political-donations-election-deniers-report-finds/

Viswanatha, A. (2021) 'Officer Brian Sicknick: what we know about his death', *The Wall Street Journal*, [online] 21 April, Available from: https://archive.ph/20210421150320/https://www.wsj.com/articles/officer-brian-sicknick-what-we-know-about-his-death-11619010119#selection-3441.5-3441.57

von Blomberg, M. and Yu, H. (2023) 'Shaming the untrustworthy and paths to relief in China's social credit system', *Modern China*, 0(0), https://doi.org/10.1177/00977004231152138

Vulliamy, E. (2011) 'How a big US bank laundered billions from Mexico's murderous drug gangs', *The Guardian*, [online] 3 April, Available from: https://www.theguardian.com/world/2011/apr/03/us-bank-mexico-drug-gangs#:~:text=At%20the%20height%20of%20the,on%20the%20brink%20of%20collapse

Wakeman, S. (2016) 'The moral economy of heroin in "Austerity Britain"' *Critical Criminology*, 24(3): 363–77.

Walcot, C. (2019) 'William Hogarth's "The South Sea Scheme" and the topography of speculative finance', *British Library*, [online] 10 May, Available from: https://www.bl.uk/picturing-places/articles/william-hogarths-the-south-sea-scheme-and-the-topography-of-speculative-finance

Walker, P. (2008) 'Thai police arrest suspected "Merchant of Death" arms dealer', *The Guardian*, [online] 6 March, Available from: https://www.theguardian.com/world/2008/mar/06/thailand.russia

Wall Street (1987) [Film] Directed by Oliver Stone, United States: American Entertainment.

Wang, M. (2017) 'China's chilling "social credit" blacklist', *Human Rights Watch*, [online] 12 December, Available from: https://www.hrw.org/news/2017/12/12/chinas-chilling-social-credit-blacklist

Wang, Y. (2020) 'In China, the "Great Firewall" is changing a generation', *Human Rights Watch*, [online] 1 September, Available from: https://www.hrw.org/news/2020/09/01/china-great-firewall-changing-generation

Ward, J. (2016) '84-year-old grandma killed by Amazon delivery truck in little village', *DNAinfo*, [online] 22 December, Available from: https://www.dnainfo.com/chicago/20161222/little-village/elderly-woman-struck-killed-by-truck-little-village-police-say/

Ward, V. (2010) *The Devil's Casino: Friendship, Betrayal, and the High Stakes Games Played Inside Lehman Brothers*, Hoboken: Wiley.

'Water and sewerage companies in England: environmental performance report 2022' (2023) *Gov.uk*, [online], 12 July, Available from: https://www.gov.uk/government/publications/water-and-sewerage-companies-in-england-environmental-performance-report-2022

Watkins, J., Wulaningsih, W., Da Zhou C., Marshall, D.C., Sylianteng, G.D.C., Rosa, P.G.D. et al (2017) 'Effects of health and social care spending constraints on mortality in England: a time trend analysis', *BMJ Open*, https://doi.org/10.1136/bmjopen-2017-017722

Watson, J.E.M., Shanahan, D.F., Di Marco, M., Allan, J., Laurence, W.F., Sanderson, E.W. et al (2016) 'Catastrophic declines in wilderness areas undermine global environment targets', *Current Biology*, 26(21): 2929–34.

Weale, A. (2019) *The Will of the People: A Modern Myth,* John Wiley & Sons.

'We must stop universities exploiting the unpaid labour of PhD students' (2018) *The Guardian*, [online] 4 May, Available from: https://www.theguardian.com/higher-education-network/2018/may/04/we-must-stop-universities-exploiting-the-unpaid-labour-of-phd-students

Wearmouth, R. (2023) 'Steve Barclay brought a private healthcare lobbyist into government', *The New Statesman*, [online] 13 March, Available from: https://www.newstatesman.com/politics/uk-politics/2023/03/steve-barclay-brought-private-healthcare-lobbyist-into-government

Weaver, M. (2013) 'How Brown Moses exposed Syrian arms trafficking from his front room', *The Guardian*, [online] 21 March, Available from: https://www.theguardian.com/world/2013/mar/21/frontroom-blogger-analyses-weapons-syria-frontline

Weaver, M. (2022) 'Millions cannot afford to heat homes as UK faces Arctic snap', *The Guardian*, [online] 8 December, Available from: https://www.theguardian.com/society/2022/dec/08/uk-weather-millions-households-cannot-afford-heat-homes

Weber, M. (1978) *Economy and Society: An Outline of Interpretive Sociology*, Berkley: University of California Press.

Webster, B. (2023a) 'Gas industry paid lobbyists £200,000 to get MPs' support for blue hydrogen', *Open Democracy*, [online] 18 January, Available from: https://www.opendemocracy.net/en/blue-hydrogen-appg-alexander-stafford-lobbying-shell/

Webster, C. (2023b) *Rich Crime, Poor Crime: Inequality and the Rule of Law*, Bingley: Emerald.

Webster, R.A. (2019) 'World's biggest prison convention comes to world prison capital', *Nola*, [online] 26 January, Available from: https://www.nola.com/news/crime_police/worlds-biggest-prison-convention-comes-to-world-prison-capital-website-reports/article_f699b547-9f61-5366-a5fd-31d6e1d1eeeb.html

Weedon, C. (1987) *Feminist Practice and Poststructuralist Theory*, Oxford: Blackwell.

Weisenthal, J. and Johnson, R. (2011) 'Here's how Occupy Wall Street came to a sudden, unexpected end today', *Insider*, [online] 15 November, Available from: https://www.businessinsider.com/how-police-cleared-occupy-wall-street-2011-11?r=US&IR=T

West, E. (2022) *Buy Now: How Amazon Branded Convenience and Normalised Monopoly*, London: MIT Press.

Westneat, D. (2020) 'Coronavirus survival comes with a $1.1 million, 181-page price tag', *The Seattle Times*, [online] 12 June, Available from: https://www.seattletimes.com/seattle-news/inspiring-story-of-seattle-mans-coronavirus-survival-comes-with-a-1-1-million-dollar-hospital-bill/

Wharton, D. (2018) '"Peace Village", a fake city just outside the DMZ, serves as metaphor for North Korean athletes at the Olympics', *Los Angeles Times*, [online] 17 February, Available from: https://www.latimes.com/sports/olympics/la-sp-olympics-north-korea-mystery-20180217-story.html

Wheatley, M. (2012) *The Wheatley Review of LIBOR: Final Report*, London: HM Treasury.

Wheen, F. (2004) *How Mumbo-Jumbo Conquered the World: A Short History of Modern Delusions*, Glasgow: HarperCollins.

'Which senators have benefited the most from NRA money?' (ND) *Brady Campaign to End Gun Violence*, [online], Available from: https://elections.bradyunited.org/take-action/nra-donations-116th-congress-senators

White, R. (2008) 'Depleted uranium, state crime and the politics of knowing', *Theoretical Criminology*, 12(1): 31–54.

White, R. (2013) *Environmental Harm: An Eco-Justice Perspective*, Bristol: Policy Press.

White, R. (2018) *Climate Change Criminology*, Bristol: Policy Press.

White, T. (2018) 'What did Hannah Arendt really mean by the banality of evil?', *aeon*, [online] 23 April, Available from: https://aeon.co/ideas/what-did-hannah-arendt-really-mean-by-the-banality-of-evil

Whitehouse, S. (2017) *Captured: The Corporate Infiltration of American Democracy*, London: The New Press.

'WHO Coronavirus (COVID-19) Dashboard' (2023) *World Health Organisation*, [online], Available from: https://covid19.who.int/?mapFilter=deaths

'Who is Elizabeth Holmes? Theranos founder begins 11-year prison sentence', [online] *The Economic Times*, 1 June, Available from: https://economictimes.indiatimes.com/news/international/uk/who-is-elizabeth-holmes-theranos-founder-begins-11-year-prison-sentence-today-details-here/articleshow/100629352.cms?from=mdr

Wienberg, C. (2022) 'Danske Bank's ex-CEO Borgen acquitted in $325 Million civil case', *Bloomberg*, [online] 8 November, Available from: https://www.bloomberg.com/news/articles/2022-11-08/danske-s-ex-ceo-borgen-acquitted-in-325-million-civil-case?leadSource=uverify%20wall

Will, S., Handelman, S. and Brotherton, D. (2013) *How They Got Away with It: White Collar Criminals and the Financial Meltdown*, New York: Columbia University Press.

Williams, K., Papadopoulou, V. and Booth, N. (2012) *Prisoners' Childhood and Family Backgrounds: Results from the Surveying Prisoner Crime Reduction (SPCR) Longitudinal Cohort Study of Prisoners*, London: Ministry of Justice.

Williams, M. (2015) 'A peek inside North Korea's intranet', *38 North*, [online] 6 July, Available from: https://www.northkoreatech.org/2015/07/06/a-peek-inside-north-koreas-intranet/

Wilson, D., Yardley, E. and Pemberton, S. (2016) 'The "Dunblane massacre" as a "photosensitive plate"', *Crime, Media, Culture: An International Journal*, 13(1): 55–68.

Winlow, S. (2014) 'Some thoughts on Steve Hall's *Theorising Crime and Deviance: A New Perspective*', *Journal of Theoretical and Philosophical Criminology*, 6(2): 168–93.

Winlow, S. (2022) 'Beyond measure: on the marketization of British universities, and the domestication of academic criminology', *Critical Criminology*, 30: 479–94.

Winlow, S. and Hall, S. (2019) 'Shock and awe: on progressive minimalism and retreatism, and the new ultra-realism', *Critical Criminology*, 27(1): 21–36.

Winlow, S. and Hall, S. (2022) *The Death of the Left: Why We Must Begin from the Beginning Again*, Bristol: Policy Press.

Winlow, S., Hall, S. and Treadwell, J. (2017) *The Rise of the Right: English Nationalism and the Transformation of Working-Class Politics*, Bristol: Policy Press.

Wolf, N. (2012) 'Revealed: how the FBI coordinated the crackdown on Occupy', *The Guardian*, [online] 29 December, Available from: https://www.theguardian.com/commentisfree/2012/dec/29/fbi-coordinated-crackdown-occupy

Wolfsfeld, G., Segev, E., and Sheafer, T. (2013) 'Social media and the Arab Spring: politics comes first', *The International Journal of Press/Politics*, 18(2): 115–37.

Wong, J. and Levin, S. (2018) 'Standing Rock protesters hold out against extraordinary police violence', *The Guardian*, [online] 29 December, Available from: https://www.theguardian.com/us-news/2016/nov/29/standing-rock-protest-north-dakota-shutdown-evacuation

Wong, K.L.X. and Dobson, A.S. (2019) 'We're just data: exploring China's social credit system in relation to digital platform ratings cultures in Westernised democracies', *Global Media and China*, 4(2): 220–32.

Wood, L.J. (2015) *Crisis and Control: The Militarization of Protest Policing*, London: Pluto Press.

'World's billionaires 2011: a record year in numbers, money and impact' (2011) *Forbes*, [online] 9 March, Available from: https://www.forbes.com/2011/03/08/world-billionaires-2011-intro.html?sh=62fabb162acc

Wrathall, M. (2005) *How to Read Heidegger*, London: Granta Books.

Yar, M. (2012) 'Critical criminology, critical theory and social harm', in S. Hall and S. Winlow (eds) *New Directions in Criminological Theory*, London: Routledge, pp 52–65.

'Yemen: events of 2019' (2019) *Human Rights Watch*, [online], Available from: https://www.hrw.org/world-report/2020/country-chapters/yemen

Yeung, J. and Bae, G. (2023) 'They eat ice cream and read "Harry Potter", but these North Korean YouTubers aren't what they seem', *CNN*, [online] 5 February, Available from: https://edition.cnn.com/2023/02/04/asia/north-korea-youtuber-yumi-intl-hnk-dst/index.html

Yilek, C. (2022) 'Who is Viktor Bout? Russian arms dealer known as the "Merchant of Death" swapped for Brittney Griner', *CBS News*, [online] 8 December, Available from: https://www.cbsnews.com/news/viktor-bout-russia-arms-dealer-merchant-of-death-brittney-griner/

Zakaria, F. (1998) *From Wealth to Power: The Unusual Origins of America's World Role*, Princeton: Princeton University Press.

Zarya, V. (2017) 'The 2017 Fortune 500 includes a record number of women CEOs', *Fortune*, [online] 7 June, Available from: https://fortune.com/2017/06/07/fortune-women-ceos/

Zedner, L. (2011) 'Putting crime back on the criminological agenda', in M. Bosworth and C. Hoyle (eds) *What Is Criminology?,* Oxford: Oxford University Press.

Zerjal, T., Xue, Y., Bertorelle, G., Wells, R.S., Bao, W., Zhu, S. et al (2003) 'The genetic legacy of the Mongols', *American Journal of Human Genetics*, 72: 717–21.

Zhang, P. (2022) 'China to step up internet censorship with stricter rules for social media and streaming sites', *South China Morning Post*, [online] 18 November, Available from: https://www.scmp.com/news/china/politics/article/3199997/china-step-internet-censorship-stricter-rules-social-media-and-streaming-sites

Zhou, V. (2023) '"iPhones are made in hell": 3 months inside China's iPhone city', *rest of world*, [online] 31 January, Available from: https://restofworld.org/2023/foxconn-iphone-factory-china/

Zimmerling, R. (2005) *Influence and Power: Variations on a Messy Theme*, Netherlands: Springer Science & Business Media.

Žižek, S. (2008) *Violence*, Surrey: Profile Books.

Žižek, S. (2010) *Living in the End Times*, London: Verso.

Zuboff, S. (2020) *The Age of Surveillance Capitalism: The Fight for a Human Future at the New Frontier of Power*, New York: PublicAffairs.

Zysman-Quirós, D. (2019) 'White-collar crime in South and Central America: corporate-state crime, governance, and the high impact of the Odebrecht corruption case', in M.L. Rorie (ed) *The Handbook of White-Collar Crime*, Oxford: Wiley-Blackwell, pp 363–80.

Index

A

academic integrity 168–9, 182
academic peer reviews 171
academics 163, 167, 179–82
  see also universities
accountancy firms 93
accumulating wealth vii
acquired immune deficiency syndrome
  (AIDS) 55
activist-based scholarship 171
Adbusters 58
'Afghan War Logs' 140
Afrewatch 124
African National Congress (ANC) 112
Afzal, Ahmad 53
agrochemicals 128
Air Cess 101
air pollution 40
Alejandro, J. 142
Alphabet Inc. 130
Altbach, Philip 179
Al Yamamah arms sales 112
Alzola, M. 66
Amazon.com, Inc. 65, 130–1, 159–60
Amazon delivery drivers 119–20
Amazon Prime 130
Amazon rainforest 88
American-dominated order 6
  see also United States (US)
American Petroleum Institute 87
Amnesty International 110, 111, 124
Anderson, Sean 114
Andrews, Tom 111
Anglo Arms 100
Angola and 'Angolagate' trial 111
animal populations 87–8
Anthropocene 9, 86
Anti-Money Laundering (AML) 92, 181
Apple Inc. 65, 122–4, 130
APPLE technique 123
Arab Spring 90
Arcadia Group Ltd 5
Arendt, Hannah 18–19, 107–8, 111
arms dealers 100–2, 104

arms industry 100–7
Arms-to-Iraq scandal 106
arms trade 97, 106–7, 109–10
Arms Trade Treaty (ATT) 102–3, 109
artificial heart valves 56
artificial scarcity 41
Asbjørnsen, Peter Christen 160
Assange, Julian 139–40
asset management 77–8
'asset manager society' (Christophers) 77
Associate Press 72
Assyrian Empire 5
Atkinson, R. 11
Atlantic Council 138
attainment gaps 167
austerity 40, 47
Australia
  GDP 65
  Strategic Policy Institute 148
autonomy harm 40

B

Bacon, T. R. 17, 23
Bad Pharma (Goldacre) 54
BAE Systems 112, 113
Bakan, J. 163
Baltimore 70
banality of evil 107–12
Bangladesh 128
Bangladesh Accord on Fire and Building
  Safety 127
Bankhaus Herstatt 90
bank liquidity 79
Bank of England 81
Barclay, Steve 72
Barton Moss anti-fracking camp, UK 61
Basel Committee 92
BBC 151–3, 175–6
BBC News 119
BBC Radio 4 96
being watched 156
Belfort, Jordon 118
Bellingcat 141
Bell-Metereau, R. 156

INDEX

Ben Ali, Zine El Abidine 90
Bentham, J. 20
Bernays, Edward 85–6
Beyond Criminology (Hillyard) 8
Bezos, Jeff 130, 142, 159
Bhopal disaster, India 122
Bhopal, K. 163
BHS 5
Biden, Hunter 84
Biden, Joe 90–1, 101, 178
Big Brother 156–7
big tech 133–4
billionaires vii–viii, 65
bills of exchange 81
BioNTech 56
biopower 144
Bird, Derrick 98
black and minority ethnic citizens 61
Black Lives Matter 27
Black Mirror (TV series) 143–4, 146
Blackstone Inc. 77–8
Blair, Tony 164–5
Blavatnik School of Government 174
'blue hydrogen' 71
Boggan, S. 109–10
Boghossian, Peter 171
bogus students 175–6
Bolton, P. 177
Bonds, E 34
Boohoo 160
Borgen, Thomas 80–1
Bouazizi, Mohamed 90
Bout, Victor ('Merchant of Death') 101–2
BP 114
Brazil 65
Brexit 90
bribes 113
British Raj 7
Brooker, Charlie 146
Brookfield Asset Management 77–8
Brown W. 66
Buchanan, Graham 114
Bufacchi, V. 32
Burns, Terence, Lord Burns 73
business ethics 79
Byzantine Empire 173

C

Cambodia 128
Cambridge Analytica 86
Cameron, David 88, 165
Campaign Against Arms Trade 104
campus crime 172
cancel culture 168–71
Canning, V. 42
capitalism 33, 61, 78, 132–3, 154–60, 183
capitalist realism 132–3
Capitol Hill, Washington 138–9, 141
Captured (Whitehouse) 66–7

carbon emissions 88
Cardiff University Study 152
Carlyle Group 59
Carson, W. G. (Kit) 114
Castillo, C. 142
celebrities 157
censorship 146–7, 149, 168
The Center for Public Integrity 72
Central Intelligence Agency (CIA) 84, 140
centralise forms of power 25–6
Chambliss, William 78
Chantix (smoking cessation drug) 56
Chapman, D.W. 179
Chiang Kai Shek 4
child labour 124–5
China vi, 110–11
    global purchasing power 184
    malign influence 12
    media control and censorship 146–7
    official schools 173
    propaganda 147–9
    social credit system 144–6, 155
    social media influencers 148
    students paying cash 181
    Supreme People's Court 145
    Uyghurs 4–5, 148
China Central Television 147
China Labour Bulletin 126–7
Chomsky, Noam 25
Christchurch shooting, New Zealand 141
Christophers, B. 77–8
chumocracy vii
cigarettes 86
Cissel, M. 59, 60
*Citizens United vs. Federal Election
    Commission* 67
City of London 81, 91, 93
civilising processes 45, 46
'civility' of Western culture 51
civil unrest vi
Clean Clothes Campaign 128
Clegg, Nick 165
climate change 33–4, 70
clinical trials 54
Clinton, Hillary 67
clothing and fast fashion 127, 128
CO_2 emissions 87
Coates, Denise vii
cobalt 124–5
Cobalt Red (Kara) 124–5
Coca-Cola 129–30
coercive power and policing 14, 61
coffee 128
Cole-Hamilton, David 125
Collins, Victoria 102
colonial policing 60–1, 62
Columbine Mine Massacre 59
commodity fetishism 123–4
community values 48

231

competitive individualism 46–7, 48
competitive interpersonal relations 133
Comprehensive schools 165
conflicts of interest 73
Congo Free State 7
Conservation Law Foundation 129
conspiracy theories 83–4
constitutive criminology 37
constructionism 21
construction of crime 38
consumer and household debt 11
'consumer capitalist utopia' 130
consumer ideology 50, 134
consumerism v, 51, 85, 127, 132–4, 172
contaminated blood scandal 54–5
contemporary social theory 9–10
Cook, J. 160
Cook, Jeffrey 106, 112
Cooper, V. 32
Coordinator of the Alliance Against
    Genocide 108–9
Copson, L. 39, 41–2
Corbyn, Jeremy 153
corporate crime 74, 115–16, 118, 120–2
corporate elites vi, 27–8, 185
corporate giants 65–74, 66–7
corporate harms 114, 115–16, 122
corporate homicide 122
Corporate Observatory Europe 73–4
corporate surveillance model 157
corporate wrongdoing 118–19
The Corporation (Bakan) 163
corporations
  capturing personal details 158
  climate crises 70
  free speech rights 67
  and the gig economy 119
  partnerships with universities 164
  perpetuating 'normality' 117
  political activities 66–7, 74
corruption 10, 80, 84, 90–1, 95
corruption perception index 6
Costa, Antonio Maria 79
Cotton Pledge 127
'The Courage of the Truth' (Foucault) 22
COVID-19 pandemic vii, 56–7, 65, 99,
    126–7, 172
COVID-19 vaccines 56, 72
COVID Corporate Financing Facility 88
Creditanstalt bank bankruptcy 89
Credit Suisse 93
crime 7–8, 13–14, 23, 38–9, 43, 46
'crimes of everyone' 50
crimes of the powerful viii–ix, 4, 6–8, 10–11,
    44, 114–15, 120
criminality and harm 14, 37–8, 52
criminal justice system 31, 37
criminal markets 11, 14
criminal violence 97–8

criminogenic moral culture 10
'criminogenic' organisations 91
criminology 7–9, 11, 163
  cancel culture 169
  and crime 43
  'crimes of the powerful' 4, 44
  criminal violence 97–8
  economic imperatives of policing 62
  environmental destruction 86
  and 'harm' 36–7
  myth of 'crime' 38
  and zemiology 15, 36, 42
critical criminology 15, 44
critical thought and employability 165
cronyism 152, 185
Crouch, C. 65
Crozier, Adam 63
cultural hardening 48
cultural irrelevance 133
cultural violence 35
Cumbria, UK 98
cyberspace 160

D

Dahl, R.A. 16, 23–4
Dalai Lama 84
Danske Bank 80–1
Darfur, Western Sudan 110
Davies, Howard 174
Davies, Jon 129
Davies, P. 8
Davison, Jake 98
'day zero' water scarcity 130
deaptative ideological order of symbols 132
death of optimism v
Debord, G. 154
debt bondage 128
decline of democracy 12
Deepwater Horizon oil spill 117, 121, 122
deforestation 128
degrees 165, 172, 175
delivery drivers 119–20
Deloitte 93
democratic governments 164
Democratic Republic of Capitalism 161
Democratic Republic of Congo 111, 124, 125
De Montfort University 180
'deniable fiddles' (Evans and Pegg) 112
denials 116–17
deregulated and neoliberal capitalist
    realism 48
deviant leisure perspectives 134
dictatorships 25
Digital Forensic Research Lab (Atlantic
    Council) 138
digital servitude 158
direct violence 32
'The Dirty Dozen' (COSH) 131
dirty money 90–5

INDEX

'disavowal' (Žižek) 116–17
'disciplinary points' (Amazon) 131
'disciplinary power' (Foucault) 20, 21, 144
dishonest education agents 175–6
Distillers Company 54
dividend payments 68
dividing and conquering societies 44
Doyal, L. 40
drug profits 79
Duggan, M. 56
Dunblane massacre 98, 99
Dye, T. R. 28

E

East India Company 4, 7
e-cigarettes 73
ecological damage of leisure 41
ecological genocide v
economic avarice 78
economic models of 'crime' 79
Edge Hill University 180
education 164–5, 179
  see also higher education
educational meritocracy 166
Eichmann, Adolf 107–8, 111
Eisenhower, Dwight D. 97
Elias, N. 45, 47
Eliaz, Eddy 100
elites 27–8
elite education 162–3
elite universities 163, 166, 174
Ellis, A. 47
embedded harms 41
Embrick, D.G. 61
emotivism 42–3
empires and slavery 7
employability skills 165
Enders Analysis 142
Enders, Claire 142
England
  Environment Agency 67
  homicide rates 47
  Office for Fair Access 172
  Office for Students 172–3, 180
  Public Health England 40
  student debts 178
  water utilities 67–8
The Enigma of Social Harm (Raymen) 42
Enron 117, 118
entrepreneurial academics 165
environmental crimes 9, 86
environmental harms 41
Ernst & Young 93
Escamilla, Telesfora 119
essential social assets 77–8
Estonia 80–1
ethical capitalism 183
etiquette 46
Europe 6–7

European Banking Authority 81
European Renaissance 173
Evans, R. 112
Everard, Sarah 3
'evil' 111
excessive harm 12
'excessive investors' (Henry and
  Milovanovic) 37

F

Facebook 86, 158, 160
factor concentrate 54–5
Fallon, Katie 104
Fashion Revolution 128
Fashion Transparency Index 128
fast fashion 127–8, 133–4
fast-food industry 129
fear of irrelevance and insignificance 134
Federal Bureau of Investigation (FBI) 59
federal student loan fraud 175
Felson, R.B. 32
Ferrell, J. 156
The Ferret 73
Feuer, A. 138
Final Solution (Nazis) 107–8
financial crash 2008 47, 57–8, 89–90, 120–1
financial crime 80, 81–3, 94–5, 121
financial elites vii–viii
financial liberalisation 91
financial services 78, 94
Fine Cotton Textiles 53
firearms control 98
Flamel Tech 59
Flint Water Crisis 68–9
Flor, Michael 56–7
Floyd, George 138
F Minus 70
Forbes 158
forests and wetlands 88
Forex (foreign exchange) 96
for-profit security and policing 64
Forster, A. 169
fossil fuel industries 70–1, 86–7
Foster-Carter, Aidan 153
Foucault, Michel 19–22, 25–6, 144
Foxconn 125–7
France 111
Franklin National Bank 90
'freedom of reach' (Islam) 157–8
freedom of speech 67, 168–71
free-market ideologists 84–5
Freetown, Sierra Leone 110
Frenkel, S. 138, 158
front companies 91–2
Fujitsu 63

G

Gab and Parler 138
Gabon 34

Gaddafi, Saif al-Islam 174
Gainford, Joseph (Jack) Pease, 1st Baron 152
Galtung, Johan 15, 32, 35, 40
gambling industry 41
gender 2–3
Gender Critical Research Network (OU) 170
gender identity 169
Genghis Khan 4
genocides 108–9, 111
Genocide Watch 108–9
George I, King 82
'gig economy' 119–20
Gilded Age 65–6
Global Financial Crisis 79
global financial groups 87
global neoliberalism 163
Global North 34, 74, 87
global punitive systems 60–1
Global South 34, 74, 77, 87
global warming hoax 84
    see also climate change
Goebbels, Joseph 86
'going postal' shootings 23
Goldacre, Ben 54
good manners 46
Goody, Jade 157
Gordon Gekko (Wall Street) 100
Gordon Riots 62
Gough, I. 40
government by corporations 66
governments 164, 185
GPT 106
graduates paying for assignments 172
Grafton College of Management
    Sciences 176
Gramsci, A. 161
Gray, G.C. 120
Gray, Valdimar 119
'Graze' theory (Kelly) 116, 117
Graz, J.C. 85
Great Depression 89
'Great Resignation' 167
Greenfield, P. 34
Greenpeace UK 70
Green, Phillip 5
Greensill Capital 88
Greensill, Lex 88
Greenwald, Glenn 140
Grenfell Tower fire 32, 117, 122
Grievance Studies Hoax 171
Gross, Edward 91
The Guardian v, 140–1, 142
guilds 173
gun lobby 71
gun violence 71, 103

H

haemophilia 54, 55
Hajjah government airstrike 141

Hall, S. 44, 45, 46, 47–50, 51, 60, 132–3
harm
    consumerism and leisure 133–4
    contested term 183
    and criminality 14, 37–8, 52
    and criminology 8, 36
    defining 39, 42–3
    motivations to inflict 49–50
    and social harm 43
    and violence 15, 30–2
    see also social harms; zemiology
harmful libidinal drives 47
'haves' and 'have-nots' 11
Hayes, Rutherford B. 66, 74
Hayes, Tom 95, 96
Hayward, C.R. 20–1
health and safety laws 121, 128
Heidegger, Martin 48
Henry, S. 37
hepatitis 54–5
Herald of Free Enterprise disaster 121
Hicks, Bill 183
Higgins, Elliot 141
higher education 163–6, 168, 171–3, 181
    see also education; universities
high-ranking jobs 166
high-tech crime 4
Hillary: The Movie 67
Hillman, A. 66
Hillyard, P. 8, 38, 39, 40, 41
historical framing of power 4
historical shaping of the contemporary 5
Hitler 89, 108
H. Kori GmbH 108
Hobbes, Thomas 17–18, 25, 45, 138
Holmes, Elizabeth 117, 118
Holocaust 18, 107–8
homicide rates 40, 44–5, 47, 89, 99–100
Hong Kong 12, 93
Hopgood, S. vi
Horizon accounting system 63
House of Lords 73–4, 166
Houthis, Yemen 105
HSBC 80
Hubble, S. 177
Hudgell Solicitors 64
Huffman, Felicity 175
human blood plasma 54–5
human economic activities and nature 87–8
human immunodeficiency virus (HIV) 54
human need theory (Doyal and Gough) 40
human rights abuses 148
Human Rights Watch 105, 110
Hutu people, Rwanda 35
hyper-liberalism 85

I

identifying harms 31
identity politics 9–10, 171

INDEX

'idle points' (Amazon) 131
illusion of choice 184
'imaginary' stage of infancy 132
Income-Contingent Repayment (ICR)
  rate 177
Income Contingent Student Loans
  (2002–2006) Plc 177
independent thought 157
individual and the state 47
individualism 46–7, 50–1, 134
industrial capitalism 78
Industrial Revolution 164
inequalities of wealth 13–14, 58
infancy 132
Infected Blood Inquiry (UK) 55
influence 23–5
Instagram 154
interconnectedness 26–7
interest rates 95–6
International Monetary Fund 87
international students 173
internet 11, 150–1
interpersonal violence 45, 48
investigative journalism 139–43
'invisible crimes' (Davies) 8
IP addresses 150
iPhones (Apple) 122–4, 125–7
Iran 22
Iraq 106
'Iraq War Logs' 140
Isaacson, W 123
Islamic Caliphates 4
Islam, R. 157–8
Isle of Man 110
Italy 65

J

January 6 Capitol attack 138–9, 141
Jensen, Wendi Jade 155
Jewish deaths 107
Jobs, Steve 123, 159
Johnson, Boris v
joint-stock companies 83
Jones, L. 167
journalism 139–43

K

Kang, C. 158
Kara, Siddharth 124–5
Kauzlarich, D. 26–7
Keim, G. 66
Kelly, C. 116, 117
Kennedy, Anthony 67
Kijong-dong village, North Korea 150
knife crime 99–100
Korean Central News Agency 149
KPMG 93
Kuldova, T.Ø. 10, 45–6, 47, 90–1
Kwangmyong intranet system 150

L

Lacan, Jacques 34, 132
Lacey, N. 36
Lacie Pound (*Black Mirror*) 143–4
The Lancet 55
Langstaff, Brian 55
Lanier, Jaron 155
Lasn, Kalle 58
late capitalism 10, 51, 74–5, 117
'late modern' era 2
Lattimer massacre 59
law enforcement 59, 60–1
Lay, Kenneth 118
lead poisoning 69
lead shot 98–9
leaks 139–40
legal profession 93–4
Legionnaires' disease 69
legitimate and illegitimate business 91
legitimate forms of power 25–6
Lehman Brothers 120
leisure 41, 134
Leopold II, King 7
'leviathan' (Hobbes) 138
Leviathan (Hobbes) 18
Levi, M. 93–4, 118
liberal individualism 48
Liberia 110
Lindner, S. 179
Lindsay, James 171
Lineker, Gary 152–3
'line leaders' (*xianzhang*) 126
lobbyists and lobbying 66–7, 70–4, 185
London 11, 93
The London Economic 151–2
London Interbank Offered Rate (LIBOR) 95–6
London School of Economics 174
Lord of War (film) 100–1
The Lowball Tapes (BBC Radio 4) 96
Luxembourg 94
Lynes, A. 35, 160

M

Machin, D. 118–19
Macquarie Group Limited 77–8
Malaysia Airlines Flight 17, 141
malpractice 79
Mandela, Nelson 112
manipulating voting decisions 86
Marchant, Paul 128
Marine Police, London 62
market economies 46
marketisation
  and academic integrity 168–9, 181–2
  corporate dominance vi
  higher education 172, 173
  loan agreements and fraud 175–6
  mental manipulation 85–6
  university system 165

235

Marxism 22
Mason, John 106, 112
mass murders 111
 see also genocides
material wealth 132–3
Matrix Churchill 106
Mattei, U. 80
Mayr, A. 118–19
May, Theresa 55
Mazur, Paul 85
McConnell, Mitch 71
McDonald's Corporation 129
media viii, 136–61
 authoritarian regimes 151
 China 146–7
 corporate crime 118, 122
 Eastern and Western practice 153–4
 'leviathan' 137–8
 ownership 142–3
 reporting working conditions 119–20
 and violence 116, 117
medieval Western Europe 173
Meek, J. 57
megacities 9
Megacorp investigative podcast 131
mental manipulation 85–6
Merck Schering-Plough Corporation 59
meritocracy 166
Meta (formerly Facebook, Inc.) 130
Mexico 129–30
Microsoft 65, 130
middle-class media 157
middle-class parents 168
Military Circle 27–8
'military-industrial complex' (Eisenhower) 97
Mills, C. Wright 27–8, 97, 100, 184
Mills, T. 151
Milovanovic, D. 37
Mil-Tec 109–10
mining 125
minority voices 168
Mirror 131
'mirror stage' of development 132
Misra, Seema 64
Moane, Michelle, Baroness Mone vii
Moderna, Inc. 56
modern capitalism 6–7
Modise, Joe 113
Molina, B. 123
money laundering 11, 79–81, 92–5
monopolies and public interest 5–6
Mont Pelerin Society 84
Moore, Michael 69
moral powers (*potestas*) 17
Morris, Stanley 92
mortality rates 57, 90
mortgage-style student loans 177
Movement for the Survival of the Ogoni
 People 86–7

MTV 156–7
multi-billionaires vii–viii
multinational corporations 87
Muncie, J. 36
murders *see* homicide rates
Murdoch, Rupert 142
Murray, Susan 156
Musk, Elon 142, 159, 160
Muslim schools 173
Myanmar 110–11, 128
Myers, M. 163

N

Nader, L. 80
National Crime Agency (UK) 92, 95
national debt 81, 82
National Health Service (NHS) 57
National Rifle Association (NRA) 71, 100
national security 90–1
National Security Agency (NSA) 140
National Union for the Total Independence
 of Angola 111
National Union of Students 167
natural gas 70–1
Nazi Germany 107
Nazi party 89, 108
negative beliefs 132
Neo-Aristotelian ethics 42
neocolonial capitalist exploitation 64
neoliberal agenda 157, 184–5
neoliberal capitalism 47–8, 132, 185
neoliberal economic policies 184
neoliberalism 26, 50, 84–5
neoliberal model of higher
 education 164, 173
neoliberal political economy 49
nepotism 185
Nestlé S.A. 130
Newburn, T. 38
news media 115–16, 137, 155
New World prisons and penal colonies 60–1
The New York Times 56, 59–60, 73, 158
Noakes, Sheila, Baroness Noakes 73
Noelle-Neumann, E. 168
non-disclosure agreements 168
'normality' (Žižek) 134
Norris, Pippa 168
North Korea 149–51, 153
North Sea oil industry 114
'Nosedive' (*Black Mirror*) 143–4, 146

O

Obama, Barack 71
'objective violence' (Žižek) 33, 57, 116
'objects in the relationship of power' 24
Occupy Wall Street movement 57–60, 65
O'Connor, S. 131
Ogoni Nine 86–7
oligarchs 9, 76, 184–5

236

INDEX

Onikoyi, Olajide 175
online economy and surveillance 156–7
On the Take (Chambliss) 78
ontologically insecurity 51
On Violence (Arendt) 18
OpenSecrets 71–2
Open University (OU) 170–1, 176
'Operation Triggerlock' (US Department of Justice) 100
opioid crisis 56, 72
Opium Wars 4
Organisation for Economic Co-operation and Development (OECD) 88, 94
organised crime 79
ornamental consumerism 123
Orwellian gaze 156
Ouellette, Laurie 156
outsourcing harm 128
Owen, David 55
Oxbridge 166
Oxfam 105
OxyContin painkiller 56

P

pacification processes 48–9
packaging waste 129
Paddington rail crash 118–19, 120, 122
panopticon 20
Panorama (BBC) 175–6
'parasitic' free-market ideology vi
Park Seong-Cheol 151
Parsons, Talcott 19
Pearce, Frank viii, 61
Pease, Joseph, 1st Baron Gainford (Jack) 152
Pegg, D. 112
Pemberton, S.A. 39, 40–1, 42
People's Bank of China 145
People's Daily 147
People's Movement for the Liberation of Angola 111
Perkel, C. 58
Peterloo Massacre 62
Pfizer 56, 72
pharmaceutical companies 53–4, 56, 71–2
PhD students 167, 174
phishing scams 173–4
Phoenix, Jo 169–71
physical harms 40
physical power (*potentia*) 17
physical violence 43, 47, 115–17
physics 16–17
Pieth, Mark 92
Pinker, S. 47
Plasmodium falciparum 165–6
plastic bottles 129
plastic pollution 129
Plastic Soup Foundation 129
Plato 17
playful contestation 21

plunder 13, 76–7
Plymouth, UK 98
Pole, Andrew 158
police brutality 61–2, 138
police powers 3–4
political instability 90
Political Instability Task Force 108
Political Leadership 27–8
political protests 138
political science 24
politicians' share dealings 73–4
politics and money 88
pollution 125, 129
polytechnics 164
  see also universities
Ponzi systems 83
the poor and powerless 44
poor wages and working conditions 129
positive beliefs and value systems 132, 133
'post-democracy' (Crouch) 65
post-Enlightenment power 22
Post Office Horizon scandal 62–4
poverty 40
power 1–3, 12–17
  corrupting 10
  defining 16–17, 27
  as diffuse 19–20
  and domination 2, 14, 44
  gender 2–3
  influencing change 27, 28
  influencing social groups 25, 138
  as malleable 16, 29
  oppressing the weak 21
  pervasive force 144
  philosophies 17–29
  physics 16–17
  political context 24
  and privilege 183–4
  as relative 18
  right and wrong 22–3
  state sovereignty 25
  and US global order 5
  and violence 18–19, 23
The Power Elite (Mills) 97
power elites 27–8, 121
powerlessness 23, 29
power relations 3, 39
precariat vi, vii, 183, 185
predatory corporate advertising 86
Prempro drug 56
'preventable harm' 41
PricewaterhouseCoopers 68, 93
Primark 127–8
prisons 53, 60–1
privacy 158
private education 162, 166
private equity business model 68
private policing 62–3
private prisons 53

privatisations 53, 57, 67–8
privilege 10, 183–4
problematic voices 168
proceeds of organised crime 79
profit margins 121
Progressive Era 66
pro-gun lobby 98
proliferation of harm 48
propaganda 86, 147–51
Propaganda (Bernays) 85–6
property crimes 47
prosumer media 138, 142
'pseudo-pacification' (Hall) 46–9
public relations (PR) 56
public shaming 145–6
Puckrose, Helen 171
Pujol, Melissa 102
Purdue Pharma 55–6, 72
Putin, Vladimir 5

Q

QAnon conspiracy 83–4

R

racial and sexual abuse 129
Radio Free Asia 153
Rambo knives 100
Ray, L. 36
Raymen, T. 41, 42, 45–6, 47, 183
Raytheon 71, 141
Reagan, Ronald 85
reality TV 156–7
'real' selves 132
The Real World (MTV) 156–7
recessions 90
recidivism rates 38–9
Recuero, R. 34
recycling and repurposing information 141–2
regulatory elite compliance industries 10
Reiman, J. 61
Reindorf, Akua 170
Reindorf Review 170
relational harms 40
repetitive motion injuries 126
research funding 164
Restorick, Paul 110
Revolutionary Armed Forces of
   Colombia 102
'revolving door' phenomenon 115
reward cards 158
Rich Crime Poor Crime (Webster) 76
Rockefeller, John D. 139
Roman Empire 5
'Roosevelt Recession' 89
Roosevelt, Theodore 66
Rothe, D. 26–7
Royal Mail Group 63
Rugeley, UK 131
rule of law 4, 13

ruling classes 61, 154
Russell Group of universities 180
Russia vi, 110–11
Russian invasion of Ukraine 6, 76, 109
Rwanda genocide 35, 109–10
Ryan, F. 148

S

Saab 113
Sabido, Pascoe 74
Sackler family 55–6
Saleh, Ali Abdullah 105
Sandy Hook mass shooting 71
Santos, Eduardo dos 111
Saudi Arabia 104–6, 112
Savimbi, Jonas 111
Savini, D. 119–20
Schlosberg, Justin 153
Schuler, D. 66
Schwendinger, H. 37
Schwendinger, J. 37
secrecy jurisdictions 88–9, 94–5
self-expression 133
self-perpetuating cycles 82
self-pitying well-offs 10
   see also social elites
Seltzer, Mark 116
Serbia 110–11
serial murders media representations 116
sewage discharges 68
'shadow economy' (Hall and Winlow) 49
shaming 145–6
Sharp, Richard 151–2
Shein 160
Shellard, Dominic 180
'shell' companies 94–5
Shell plc 86
shooting as a sport 98–9
Sicknick, Brian 138–9
Sierra Leone 110
Sinclair, Upton 139
Singer, William ('Rick') 175
Skilling, Jeffrey 118
Skripal, Sergei 141
Slapper, G. 118
slavery 7, 81–2
smartphone supply chains 122–5
Smedley, Robert 180
Smith, O. 41
smuggling weapons 97
Snowden, Edward ('Cincinnatus') 140–1
Snyder, Rick 69
'social activism' model 59
social advancement 162
'social' component of harm 41
social elites 7, 10, 28, 163
social groups 25
social harms 36–40, 41–3
   see also harm; zemiology

INDEX

social media
  academics and universities 167, 168
  China censoring information 148
  deleting 155
  ill-thought opinions 155–6
  influencers 148, 154–5
  and news media 155
  political protests 138–9
  predatory corporate advertising 86
  reusing content 142
  Western credit system 155–6
social media ratings 143–4
social mobility 166
Social Mobility Commission 166
social order 62
social science 14, 24, 29
social voyeurism 156
sociological theory 27–8
socio-symbolic violence 11
South Africa 112–13
South Sea Company ('South Sea Bubble') 81–3
Spain 82
special liberty 48–9
spending habits 158
spiral of silence thesis (Noelle-Neumann) 168
Sporting Wholesale 100
stagflation crises 85
Standing Rock, US 61
Stanford Research Institute 87
Stanford University 175
Stanko, E.A. 32
Starmer, Keir 153
state-corporate nexus 6
'state of nature' (Hobbes) 45
'structural oppression' 14
'structural violence' (Johan Galtung) 32–3
student loans and debts 175–80
Student Loans Company (SLC) 175, 176–7
subjective violence 34, 116
Süddeutsche Zeitung 93
sugary drinks 129–30
Sunak, Rishi 179
'superficial' objects (Debord) 154
super injunctions 167
super-rich 11
surveillance capitalism 156–8
Surveying Prisoner Crime Reduction (SPCR) 38
Sutherland, Edwin 26, 36–7
Sutton Trust 166
Swansea University 172
Swiss banking 93
symbiotic relations 26–7
symbolic orders 46, 132, 133, 134
symbolic violence 34–5
Syracuse University 70

T

Taliban 12
Tarbell, Ida 139

Target Brands, Inc (Target) 158
target-driven league tables 169
tax havens 94–5
Taylor, Charles 110
Taylor, Ian 98
teaching as value-for-money exchange 167
technocrats 158–61
television 156–8
'TERF' 169, 170
Thailand 101–2
thalidomide 54
Thames River Police 62
Thames Water 67
Thatcher, Margaret vii, 85, 164
Theranos Inc. 117–18
Thomas, Noel 64
Tiananmen Square massacre 147
Tifft, L. 37–8
TikTok 154, 160
Tilbury, Essex 131
Times Higher Education league tables 165
Titanic, RMS 137
Tombs, S. 38, 39, 40, 42, 118
Topf and Söhne 108
'top-up' tuition fees 164
total power 25
'toxic sovereignty' (Tudor) 50
Trafigura 121
transatlantic slave trade 4, 7, 61
transcendental materialism 45
transgender critical views 169
Transparency International 6, 92, 179
transparent financial flows 88–9
Trans-Saharan slave trade 4
Travelour (UK) Ltd, 109
Treaty of Utrecht 82
'trickle-down' economics 58
Tricontinental: Institute for Social
    Research 124
'triggers' 86
Trovan drug trial 56
Trump, Donald v, 84, 86, 90, 138, 160
truth as construct of power 21
'truths' (Foucault) 20
Tudor, K. 50–1
tuition fees 164–5
Tutsi people 35
Twitter (X) 160

U

Uber Technologies, Inc. (Uber) 159
Ukraine 6, 109
ultimate life goals 154
ultra-realism 43–52
unions 67
United Arab Emirates 105
United Kingdom (UK)
  All-Party Parliamentary Group on
    Hydrogen 70–1

arms exports 106–7
Bubble Act 1720 83
chumocracy vii
contaminated blood scandal 54–5
Corporate Manslaughter and Corporate
  Homicide Act 2007 121
Criminal Finances Act 2017 92
defence exports 104, 105
Department for International Trade 105
financial liberalisation 91
financial services sector 88–9, 94
firearms control 98
food industry 129
GDP 65
Health and Care Act 2012 57
House of Lords 166
House of Lords Industry and Regulators
  Committee 73–4
immigration policy 152–3
Infected Blood Inquiry 55
knife crime 99–100
ministers, lobbyists and political
  advisers 72–3
money laundering 95
National Crime Agency 91
Office for National Statistics 40
'open licence' system 104–5
Orders in Council 110
privatised prisons 53
Proceeds of Crime Act orders 64
Saudi Armed Forces Projects 112
Serious Fraud Office (SFO) 96
standard individual export licences
  (SIELs) 104
Student Loans Company (SLC) 175
UK Defence and Security Exports 104
Unexplained Wealth Orders 92
United Nations (UN)
  Charter 6
  General Assembly 102–3
  High Commissioner for Refugees 108
  Human Rights Council 111
  Human Rights Office of the High
    Commissioner 148
  Office for Disarmament Affairs 109
  Office on Drugs and Crime 94
  sanctions 110
  Security Council 110
United States (US) vi
  American self-interest 184
  Bipartisan Campaign Reform Act 2002 67
  Capitol attack January 2021 138–9, 141
  CIA 84, 140
  corrosive impact of corporations 74
  corruption as national security issue 90–1
  Department of Homeland Security 59
  FBI 59
  Federal Election Commission 67
  federal student loan fraud 175

Food and Drug Administration 56
Gilded Age 65–6
global hegemony 25, 184
government by corporations 66
gun control 100
gun deaths 23, 103
income and wealth disparities 58
Inflation Reduction Act 2022 72
munitions used in Yemen 105
National Council for Occupational Safety
  and Health (COSH) 131
police brutality and shootings 61
private prisons 53
privatised healthcare 56–7
student loan forgiveness 178
university admissions scandal 175
World War II 25
Universal Declaration of Human Rights 108
universities
  academic mission 179
  'accessible' courses 165–6
  AML regulations 181
  cash payments to 180–1
  consumerist education 172
  as corporate entities 164, 165
  corruption 163, 179
  course fees 174–5
  degrees 165, 172, 175
  elite status and branding 166
  exploiting workforce 167
  generating financial resources 179
  and guilds 173
  'low-quality' courses 179
  marketisation 165
  and polytechnics 164
  rates of pay 167, 180
  remote teaching and assessments 172
  research funding 164
  rich and the elite 163, 164
  social mobility 166
  state-corporate nexus 164
  statutory responsibilities 169
  students and middle-class parents 168
  widened participation 181
  see also academics; higher education
University College London 40
University of Cambridge 173
University of Essex 169–70, 181
The University of Manchester 181
University of Oxford 173, 174–5
unregulated marketplaces 85
unscrupulous executives 121
Uyghurs 4–5, 148

V

Vatican Bank 90
'Vault 7' (CIA documents) 140
vehicular homicides 119
Vidyarthi, Anoop 110

INDEX

violence
  conceptualisations 31–2
  decline 46
  defining 31–6
  financial turmoil 89–90
  and harm 15, 31
  ontic/physical violence 48, 115–16
  and power 18–19, 23
Violence (Žižek) 57
violent libidinal drives 48
virtue signalling 10
visceral violence 117
Viswanatha, A. 138–9
von Blomberg, M. 145

W

Wall Street (film) 100
Wang, Y. 147
warehouse tours 159–60
War of the Spanish Succession 82
war on terror 25
waste 129
watchmen 62
water resources 130
water utilities 67–9
wealth transfers 65
wealthy power elites 60
Weber, Max 18, 24
Webster, B. 76
Weedon, C. 3
Wheatcroft, Patience, Baroness
  Wheatcroft 151–2
Wheen, F. 22
white-collar criminality 26, 36–7
Whitehouse, Sheldon 66–7
White, Micah 58
Whyte, D. 32
WikiLeaks 139–40
Wilkinson stores (Wilko) 5
Wilson, D. 47, 48, 99
Winlow, Simon 44, 46, 48–50, 51, 60,
  132–3, 173, 181
The Wolf of Wall Street (film) 118
Wolfsberg AML Principles for Private
  Banking 92–3
women
  as CEOs 28
  financial elites vii
  marketing cigarettes to 86
  repressive regimes 12

thalidomide 54
trans-inclusive 169
Wood, Brian 110
working-class students 165, 167
working-class villainy 157
working conditions
  Amazon 119–20, 130–1
  fast-fashion industry 127–8
  iPhones 125–7
World Bank 87
World Conference against Racism, Racial
  Discrimination, Xenophobia and
  Related Intolerance 7
World Economic Forum 85
World Health Organization 55
world orders 6
World Trade Organization 87
World War II 25
worldwide academic corruption index 179
World Wildlife Fund 87
'wound culture' (Seltzer) 116
Wragg, E. 160

X

Xinjiang, China 148–9
XKeyscore 140–1

Y

Yale University 175
Yar, M. 39
Yemen 104–6, 141
Yemen Data Project 105
Young, Josh 139–40
Yu, H. 145
Yuri Orlov (*Lord of War*) 100–1

Z

Zedner, L. 36
zemiology 8, 15, 36, 39, 41–2
  see also harm; social harms
zero-hour contracts 119
Zetter, Lionel 72–3
Zhengzhou, China 125
Žižek, Slavoj 15, 33, 34, 57, 116–17, 133, 135
Zondo Commission 113
Zscaler, Inc. 173–4
Zuboff, S. 156, 158
Zuccotti Park, New York 58–9
Zuckerberg, Mark 142, 159
Zuma, Jacob 112, 113

Printed in the USA
CPSIA information can be obtained
at www.ICGtesting.com
JSHW011955140624
64842JS00005B/49